AIMEDIA 2025

The First International Conference on AI-based Media Innovation

July 6th – 10th, 2025

Venice, Italy

AIMEDIA 2025 Editors

Stephan Böhm, RheinMain University of Applied Sciences< Germany

Printed from e-media with permission by:

Curran Associates, Inc.
57 Morehouse Lane
Red Hook, NY 12571

Some format issues inherent in the e-media version may also appear in this print version.

International Academy, Research, and Industry Association (IARIA)
412 Derby Way
Wilmington, DE 19810

Phone: (408) 893-6407
Fax: (408) 527-6351

petre@iaria.org

Additional copies of this publication are available from:

Curran Associates, Inc.
57 Morehouse Lane
Red Hook, NY 12571 USA
Phone: 845-758-0400
Fax: 845-758-2633
Email: curran@proceedings.com
Web: www.proceedings.com

AIMEDIA 2025

Forward

The First International Conference on AI-based Media Innovation (AIMEDIA 2025), held between July 6th – 10th, 2025 was an inaugural conference series on AI in Media designed to explore the impact of AI technologies on news production, content creation, media distribution, and audience engagement.

The media landscape is seeing significant transformation thanks to AI capabilities in natural language processing, image recognition, and content generation and consumption. Technological influence is ubiquitous and growing, from automated journalism to personalized content delivery and deepfake detection.

This conference delved into cutting-edge research, ethical considerations, and future trends in AI that are driving changes in the media industry and academia curricula. These include film, music, interactive media, immersive environments, and distribution models.

AIMEDIA served as an innovative stage for networking, collaboration, and exchange of ideas that will pave the way for the next wave of media innovations in terms of creating and distributing media and also challenging our perceptions on creativity, privacy, and trust in the digital age.

By bringing together scientists, innovators, and education leaders, this event aimed to reveal the challenges and opportunities presented by the integration of AI across different media sectors.

We take here the opportunity to warmly thank all the members of the AIMEDIA 2025 technical program committee, as well as all the reviewers. The creation of such a high-quality conference program would not have been possible without their involvement. We also kindly thank all the authors who dedicated much of their time and effort to contribute to AIMEDIA 2025 We truly believe that, thanks to all these efforts, the final conference program consisted of top-quality contributions. We also thank the members of the AIMEDIA 2025 organizing committee for their help in handling the logistics of this event.

We hope that AIMEDIA 2025 was a successful international forum for the exchange of ideas and results between academia and industry and for the promotion of progress in the field of AI-based media. We also hope that Venice provided a pleasant environment during the conference and everyone saved some time to enjoy the historic charm of the city.

AIMEDIA 2025 Chairs

AIMEDIA 2025 General Chair
Stephan Böhm, RheinMain University of Applied Sciences – Wiesbaden, Germany

AIMEDIA 2025 Steering Committee

Júlio Monteiro Teixeira, Universidade Federal de Santa Catarina, Brazil
Anna Jupowicz-Ginalska, University of Warsaw, Poland
Barbara Brandstetter, Hochschule Neu-Ulm, Germany
Clement Leung, The Chinese University of Hong Kong Shenzhen, China
Atreyee Sinha, Edgewood College Madison, USA

Joni Salminen, University of Vaasa, Finland
Konstantinos (Constantine) Kotropoulos, Aristotle University of Thessalonik, Greece

AIMEDIA 2025 Publicity Chairs

Matthias Harter, RheinMain University of Applied Sciences, Germany

AIMEDIA 2025

Committee

AIMEDIA 2025 General Chair

Stephan Böhm, RheinMain University of Applied Sciences – Wiesbaden, Germany

AIMEDIA 2025 Steering Committee

Júlio Monteiro Teixeira, Universidade Federal de Santa Catarina, Brazil
Anna Jupowicz-Ginalska, University of Warsaw, Poland
Barbara Brandstetter, Hochschule Neu-Ulm, Germany
Clement Leung, The Chinese University of Hong Kong Shenzhen, China
Atreyee Sinha, Edgewood College Madison, USA
Joni Salminen, University of Vaasa, Finland
Konstantinos (Constantine) Kotropoulos, Aristotle University of Thessalonik, Greece

AIMEDIA 2025 Publicity Chairs

Matthias Harter, RheinMain University of Applied Sciences, Germany

AIMEDIA 2025 Technical Program Committee

Rahul Agarwal, Columbia University, USA
Mohammed Fadhl Albdadwi, Computer Engineering, Aden University, Yemen
Ilaria Amaro, University of Salerno, Italy
Kaddar Bachir, Université d'Ibn Khaldoun Tiaret, Algeria
Israel Braglia, Universidade Federal de Santa Catarina, Brazil
Barbara Brandstetter, Hochschule Neu-Ulm, Germany
Julio Cesar Duarte, Military Institute of Engineering, Brazil
Steve Chan, Decision Engineering Analysis Laboratory, USA
Alice Cheng, North Carolina State University, USA
Stephen Collins, Macquarie University, Sydney, Australia
Alex Connock, Saïd Business School, University of Oxford & (b) Exeter, UK
Vincenzo De Masi, Beijing Normal University - Hong Kong Baptist University | United International College, Hong Kong
Rafael del Vado, Universidad Complutense de Madrid, Spain
Attilio Della Greca, University of Salerno, Italy
Maximilian Eder, Ludwig-Maximilians-Universität München, Munich, Germany
Omri Gillath, University of Kansas, USA
Michael Graßl, Hochschule Magdeburg-Stendal, Germany
Binbin Gu, University of California, Irvine, USA
Matthias Harter, RheinMain University of Applied Sciences, Germany

Copyright Information

Table of Contents

Deepfake Music and Listener Sentiments: A Large-Scale Analysis of YouTube Comments.

Francisco Tigre Moura
Marketing and Communication
IU International University of Applied Sciences
Bonn, Germany
Email: francisco.tigre-moura@iu.org

Visieu Lac
Business Management
IU International University of Applied Sciences
Bad Honnef, Germany
Email: visieu.lac@iu.org

***Abstract*—This study investigates emotional responses to deepfake music by analyzing 31,363 YouTube comments using 'twitter-roberta-base-sentiment-latest' model. The research addresses an important gap in the literature by focusing on user sentiments towards Artificial Intelligence (AI)-generated deepfake songs that mimic human voices, contrasting them with non-deepfake AI music (instrumental or relaxation genres). Findings reveal a surprising predominance of positive and neutral sentiments towards deepfake music, particularly in genres like Rock/Pop and Cartoon, though negative reactions are more pronounced when renowned human voices are mimicked. The study also identifies genre-specific patterns and a longitudinal decline in novelty-driven engagement, especially within Rap/Hip-Hop. Compared to non-deepfake AI music, which consistently triggers positive sentiments, deepfake music evokes more mixed responses, suggesting that voice mimicry remains a critical aspect. The findings contribute to the understanding of how AI creativity influences listener emotions and perceptions, while raising timely questions regarding authenticity and acceptance of deepfake art.**

Keywords—Artificial Intelligence; Sentiment analysis; Deepfake; Deepfake Music.

I. INTRODUCTION

The creation of novel songs using Artificial Intelligence (AI) "*deepfake*" tools (tools that allowed users to, for example, create unauthorized tracks mimicking voices of renown artists or celebrities) has gained great popularity and is now impacting the music sector. For example, in 2023 a deepfake song cloning the voices of Drake and The Weekend (titled "Heart on My Sleeve") represented the first deepfake track to become a viral hit (over 20 million streams in 2023 on Apple Music [1]). Since then, deepfake songs have become increasingly popular, with an extraordinary number of tracks being released online, resembling the voices of artists such as Frank Sinatra, John Lennon, Freddy Mercury, Taylor Swift, Kanye West, Kurt Cobain and many others. In view of the various technological, ethical and legal challenges of "*deepfaking*" voices [2], including how to legally protect artists, the music industry has reacted. Universal Music and Google, for example, have started negotiations for the development of tools that allow users to produce deepfakes music legitimately and financially reward the copyright holders [3].

Given that AI, and its unauthorized use in deepfakes, drastically alters the fundamental nature of creative processes in music, and the extraordinary impact and threats it poses to various sectors [4], it is crucial to further understand the human response towards deepfake music. However, although the current literature has addressed many aspects regarding human acceptance towards AI generated music [5]-[7][27], to our knowledge, it has yet to investigate human response to deepfake music, thus representing a significant gap. In view of the ever-growing amount of deepfake art, including music, and tools available for their creation, and the relevance of addressing this phenomenon, this study aims to investigate two main research questions:

- **RQ1:** *What sentiments do YouTube users hold towards deepfake music?*
- **RQ2:** *How have the sentiments of YouTube users towards deepfake music changed over time?*

To address both questions, in the next section the paper debates human response towards AI generated or co-created music, followed by section on deepfake and music. Afterwards, Section 4 describes the methodology of the study, while Section 5 reveals the findings. Finally, Section 6 concludes the paper by presenting the conclusions and limitations of the study.

II. HUMAN RESPONSE TOWARDS AI GENERATED OR CO-CREATED MUSIC

The understanding of human response towards innovation and technology generated or co-created outputs is, overall, complex and multifaceted. Several factors such as demographic variables, gender, and educational levels all play a role in acceptance [8][9]. Concerning human response towards AI generated or co-created music, recent literature found also that music professionals often hold different attitudes when compared to listeners in general [5]. Also, despite the rather overall negative perceptions towards AI generated music [10] and perception biases [11], a controlled experiment revealed that effects are weakened if respondents hold a positive perception towards the song they listen to [5]. Moreover, the listener's level of involvement with music and the context of their involvement should also be considered

[7]. Hong et al. also further emphasized that the perception of AI as an independent creative agent affects how its music is received. For instance, those who view AI as a musician tend to appreciate its music more than those who do not [12]. This emphasizes the importance of the creative process in influencing acceptance and response.

Another example of composer bias (preference for human composer in contrast to AI as composer) was revealed through a series of experiments developed by [10]. The studies revealed that due to the "AI-sounding" of electronic music, participants were more accepting of AI as composer and the music it generates, when compared to classical music, as it resembles a more "human-sound". Furthermore, a recent systematic review of 30 studies investigated human emotional responses elicited by AI-composed music (e.g., arousal, enjoyment, interest and liking), with a focus on understanding the emotional authenticity and expressivity of such compositions [13]. The review suggested that, while AI can help explore emotional authenticity in music, there remains significant skepticism and preference for human-composed music among listeners and music professionals. The review also emphasized that factors, such as music genre, cultural context, and age group confound the understanding of emotional responses, and suggests the development of advanced analytical methods, for example using machine learning and deep learning (adopted in this paper), to enhance the comprehension and effectiveness of AI in music composition [13]. Finally, all studies mentioned here have focused on human responses towards novel or authentic compositions (non-deepfakes) created independently by or co-created with AI.

III. Deepfakes and Music

Although there is not a consensus regarding the definition of deepfakes, [14] defends that "as its name implies, the term "deepfake" is derived from the combination of "deep" (referring to Deep learning (DL)) and "fake". It is normally used to refer to manipulation of existing media (image, video and/or audio) or generation of new (synthetic) media using DL-based approaches" (p.2). Importantly, as [14] defend, deepfakes enhance the naturalness of artificial agents (regardless of format), improving their ability to generate empathy and emotional connection with humans that are exposed to or interact with them.

The recent developments in machine and deep learning technologies have enabled an extraordinary increase in deepfakes use for authentic purposes, for instance, entertainment [16], but also for various malicious purposes, such as misinformation. In view of the advances in deepfakes, the extreme challenge of identifying it, and its high level of persuasiveness, many authors have raised serious concerns regarding the social impact it already causes and may cause in the future [17][18].

The current literature involving deepfake music is largely focused on voice identification, rather than human response. In this regard, recent studies have suggested that, different to speech voices, identifying deepfake singing voices is particularly more challenging, due to the role of melody, rhythm, and the broader range of timbre in singing [19][20]. Moreover, detecting deepfake singing voices presents a unique challenge due to the interference of background music, which can mask the artifacts used to identify synthesized voices [20]. For example, unlike speech deepfakes, where the vocal track is often isolated, singing voices are typically surrounded by musical arrangements that include instrumental accompaniments and digital effects. This layering of sounds makes it difficult to discern the subtle cues of synthesis, as the instruments and other musical elements can mask or mimic these artifacts. Additionally, the artistic nature of music production, with its wide range of timbres and dynamic variations, adds another layer of complexity to the detection process. Traditional speech countermeasure systems, when applied to these mixed audio tracks, often fail to accurately distinguish between authentic and fake singing, leading to significantly higher error rates.

Next, we discuss the methodology of our study, which aimed to investigate sentiments of listeners towards deepfake music.

IV. Methodology

The methodology section will first describe the sample of YouTube channels used in the study, followed by the process for sentiment analysis.

A. *Sample of YouTube Channels and Type of Songs*

The first step consisted of collecting a large sample of YouTube channels containing deepfake music. Importantly, to ensure that sentiments analyzed were specific to deepfake music, it was necessary to contrast them with AI generated music that did not mimic human-like voices. The inclusion criteria of YouTube channels consisted of: (a) videos explicitly labelled as deepfake music or AI generated music; (b) contained a minimum of 10 videos, and (c) most videos contained large number of comments. The initial selection consisted of 62 channels. After further screening, a final sample of 44 channels was used for the analysis, as displayed in Table I.

TABLE I. OVERVIEW OF CHANNELS, VIDEOS AND COMMENTS OF DEEPFAKE AND NON-DEEPFAKE AI MUSIC.

Type	Voice Mimicking	Genre	No. of Channels	No. of Videos	No. of Comments
Deepfake Music	Renown Human Voices	Rap/Hip-hop	6	190	7,558
		Rock/Pop	23	1,151	13,544
	Fictional Characters	Cartoon	5	249	5,937
Non-Deepfake AI Music	Does Not Apply	Instrumental	2	247	5,396
		Relaxation	8	697	724
		Total	**44**	**2,534**	**33,159**

Next, channels were classified into two broad categories:

(1) "Deepfake Music": Included songs which used AI to mimic voices. This category was split into two sub-categories, according to the type of voice mimicking:

(1a) "Renown Human Voices": Included songs that mimicked voices of famous and recognizable human artists or celebrities (e.g., Kurt Cobain, Kanye West, Taylor Swift, Adele, Frank Sinatra, Donal Trump, Barack Obama and Joe Biden) performing popular songs from other artists, or novel compositions. Examples included Kurt Cobain (former lead singer of the grunge band Nirvana) singing "Wonderwall" (Originally composed and recorded by Oasis), and Freddie Mercury (former lead singer of British rock band "Queen") singing "Hey Jude" (originally composed and recorded by "The Beatles"). This sub-category was composed of two music genres: Rap/Hip-Hop, Rock/Pop.

(1b) "Fictional Characters": Included deepfake songs which did not mimic voices of renown human artists, but instead, of fictitious characters. The main genre derived from this category is "Cartoon". For example, the cartoon character "Bluey" singing "Bumble Bee".

(2) "Non-Deepfake AI music": Included instrumental songs, or atmospheric sounds, composed by AI, and that did not include voices. Two genres comprise this category: Instrumental and Relaxation (not songs, but AI generated soundscapes for relaxation and focus, for example).

By using the YouTube Application Programming Interface (API), comments were extracted from the videos published by the channels.

B. *Sentiment Analysis*

Prior to the sentiment analysis, comments underwent pre-processing consisting of: (1) elimination of punctuation marks and stop-words, and (2) normalization through lemmatization. This preprocessing filtered out records lacking meaningful textual content, resulting in a higher-quality dataset with reduced noise. The cleaned dataset served as input for sentiment analysis, which classified comments into three categories: positive, negative, or neutral based on the emotions expressed. This step is essential as it reveals the overall emotional tone of the comments, offering valuable insights into user perceptions and opinions [21].

To achieve this, we utilized the Twitter-roBERTa-base model developed by CardiffNLP [22], which has been validated in previous sentiment studies [23][26]. While many sentiment analysis models have been created using various datasets, such as movie reviews [24], we chose a Twitter-based model due to the nature of user comments on YouTube, which are typically brief, written in a social media style, and often include emojis.

This model classifies comments into 'positive', 'neutral', and 'negative' categories. The sentiment analysis was performed to understand the general sentiment of the comments and to identify any prevalent trends or patterns in the audience. Also, one of the key advantages of the CardiffNLP model is its ability to provide a detailed numerical breakdown of sentiments, showing the distribution of positive, neutral, and negative sentiments at the corpus level as well as the individual comment level. The CardiffNLP Twitter-roBERTa-base model (specifically, cardiffnlp/twitter-roberta-base-sentiment-latest) was trained on approximately 124 million tweets from January 2018 to December 2021 and fine-tuned for sentiment analysis, effectively incorporating emojis [25]. Furthermore, to validate the effectiveness of the Cardiff model, we benchmarked it against several sentiment analysis models, including OpenAI's GPT-3.5-turbo. Our independent tests using the dataset [29] showed that the Cardiff model achieved the best performance, with an accuracy score of 0.72, outperforming OpenAI's GPT-3.5-turbo, which had an accuracy score of 0.66. Thus, the higher accuracy score of the Cardiff model indicated its greater reliability in accurately classifying the sentiments of the comments in our dataset and therefore was adopted.

V. RESULTS

Prior to the analysis, comments were pre-processed as described in section IV.B of this paper. This text processing reduced the initial dataset by roughly 6.8% on average. Table II, shown below, depicts the reduction in the number of comments per genre, after the text processing, which resulted in a final sample of 31,363 comments used for the study.

TABLE II. OVERVIEW OF CHANNELS, VIDEOS AND COMMENTS OF DEEPFAKE AND NON-DEEPFAKE AI MUSIC.

Type	Voice Mimicking	Genre	No. Comments Before Text Processing	No. Comments After Text Processing
Deepfake Music	Renown Human Voices	Rap/Hip-hop	7,558	7,178
		Rock/Pop	13,544	13,003
	Fictional Characters	Cartoon	5,937	5,604
Non-Deepfake AI Music	Does Not Apply	Instrumental	5,396	4,931
		Relaxation	724	647
		Total	**33,159**	**31,363**

Next, the results of the sentiment analysis are provided through two perspectives: overall sentiment and a longitudinal analysis.

A. *Overall Sentiment Analysis*

The CardiffNLP model results are illustrated in Figure 1, which presents the sentiment distribution across different genres.

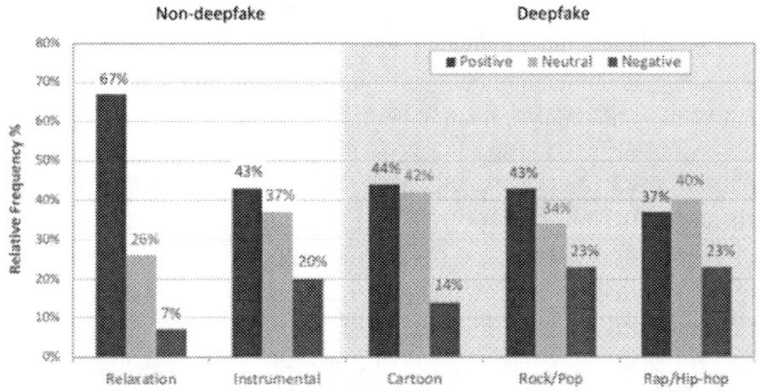

Figure 1. Overall display of sentiments by genre.

Figure 1 illustrates that, overall, sentiments towards non-deepfake AI music (*Relaxation* and *Instrumental*) are predominantly positive, with 67% and 43% of positive sentiments respectively. *Relaxation* also indicated the lowest negative sentiment among all genres (7%), reinforcing the potential for AI use in such music applications. Regarding deepfake music, *Cartoon* and *Rock/Pop* revealed most positive sentiments (44% and 43% respectively). *Rap/Hip-Hop* represented the main exception, where neutral sentiment exceeds positive sentiment (40%). The predominance of positive sentiments represents a surprising finding, as it conflicts with findings from Shank et al. (2023), who noted that listeners tend to be biased against music they believe was created by an AI, especially if music does not meet their expectations of what an AI could produce. Concerning negative sentiments, the deepfake music genres *Rock/Pop* and *Rap/Hip-hop* exhibited the highest proportion of negative sentiment (23% each) of all genres. This represents an important finding, as these genres normally involve renown human voices, suggesting the sensitivity of listeners towards the use of deepfake technology towards people they recognize. This issue is discussed later in this paper for future research agenda.

B. *Longitudinal Analysis of Sentiments*

Furthermore, we analyzed the data as a function of time, thus allowing the visualization of listeners' sentiment trend. Results are reported per week of each year within the dataset, as seen in Figure 2, which shows a distribution on a 100% scale.

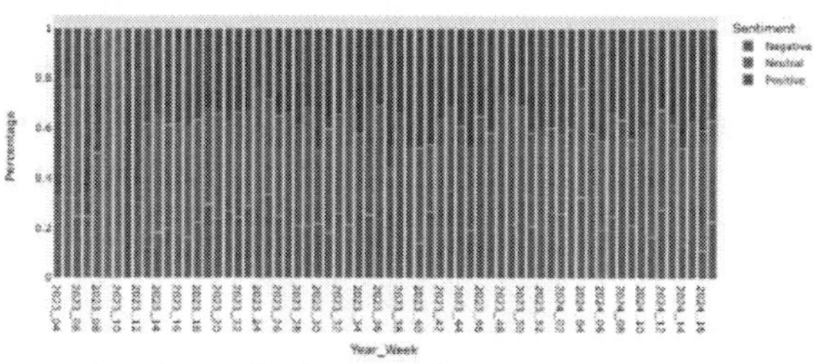

Figure 2. Distribution of sentiments for Rap/Hip-Hop on a 100% frequency scale

Results regarding *Rap/Hip-Hop* indicate two important findings. First, although not displayed in the graph, we identified in the data a high incidence of comments at the start of 2023, followed by steady decline. This may suggest an indication that, for this genre, the novelty effect quickly diminished, an aspect that requires further investigation in future studies. Secondly, and importantly, that the distribution of sentiments towards deepfake *Rap/Hip-Hop* music remains stable over time, with a greater predominance of neutral and positive sentiments (Figure 2).

Regarding the genre of *Rock/Pop*, results indicate that (differently to *Rap/Hip-Hop*), the volume of deepfakes comments has been increasing considerably over time, which may indicate a greater implementation of deepfake technology within this genre. Nevertheless, the general sentiment shown on Figure 3 reveals a growing negative sentiment trend, a finding that requires further future investigation.

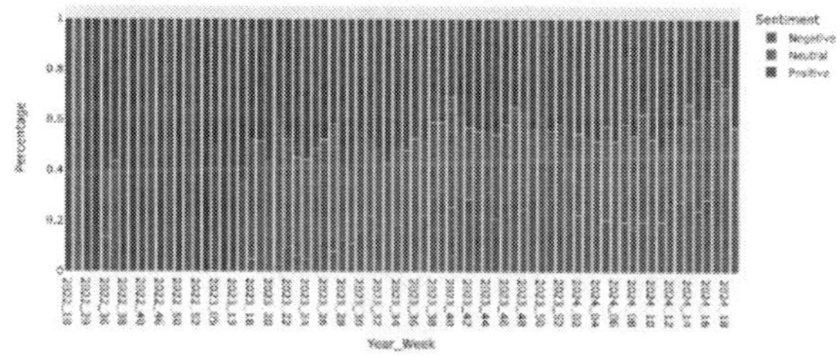

Figure 3. Distribution of sentiments for Rock/Pop within a 100% frequency scale.

Furthermore, the temporal analysis for the genre of *cartoon* indicated a stable trend regarding the overall sentiment of comments, displaying a predominance for positive and neutral sentiments, and very low negative sentiment (Figure 4), in comparison to other genres.

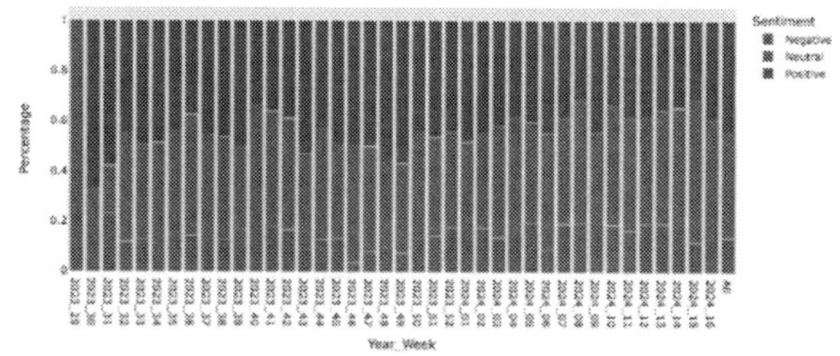

Figure 4. Distribution of sentiments for Cartoon within a 100% frequency scale.

Further results reveal that the range of comments for AI music (non-deepfakes) is considerably broader (when compared to deepfake music categories), potentially because the technology was earlier accessible for independent creators. Overall, the results for the *Instrumental* genre suggest a stable trend regarding volume of comments and sentiments, which indicate largely positive and neutral responses (Figure 5).

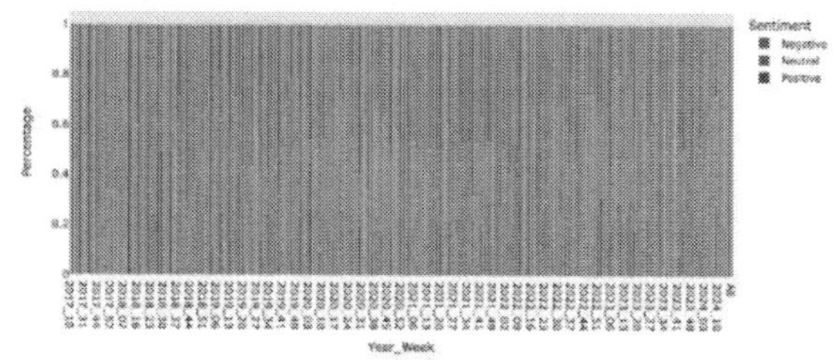

Figure 5. Distribution of sentiments for Instrumental within a 100% frequency scale.

Finally, the analysis for the genre of *Relaxation* also indicated largely displays positive sentiments towards this type of AI generated music (Figure 6).

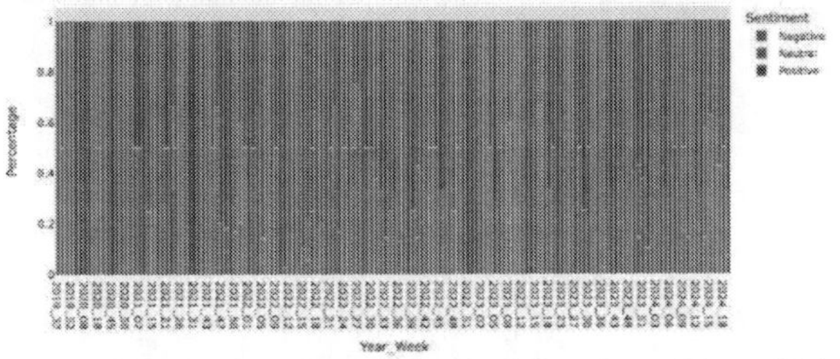

Figure 6. Distribution of sentiments for Relaxation within a 100% frequency scale.

The next sections will address the limitations of the study and provide a critical reflection on the results.

VI. LIMITATIONS

Results from the study should be interpreted in light of a few limitations. First, the analysis is based on a sample of YouTube comments, which may not be representative of the broader population and potential biases related to the cultural and geographic distribution of comments must be considered. Also, channels used for the analysis displayed varying levels of quality, based on the artistic and technological skill of the developer. For example, knowing what key and pitch the artist normally sings can be a factor when creating deepfake music. Such variation of deepfake quality certainly impacted the sentiment of comments. Thus, this issue should be addressed in future studies. Secondly, some music genres might be more accepting than others towards the use of AI, as rap-hip-hop, for example, often uses Autotune [24], which resembles robotic voices often found in AI in deepfake songs. Furthermore, the sentiment analysis models (Twitter-roBERTa-base model developed by CardiffNLP) used may contain limitations in accurately capturing the nuances of human emotions, particularly in mixed or ambiguous comments. Finally, focusing only on channels that self-label as "deepfake" may exclude secret or non-discrete deepfakes, and potentially over represent novelty seeking audiences.

VII. CONCLUSION AND FUTURE WORK

The analysis revealed that while the general sentiment towards *deepfake music* is rather positive, a comparison with *non-deepfake AI music* provides more revealing insights. Overall, listeners tend to be more negative towards *deepfake music*, in contrast to non-deepfake. One interpretation, which requires further investigation, is that it may be due to concerns regarding AI's ability to replicate human emotional depth and authenticity. However, based on observations of comments during the analysis, positive sentiment prevails when the genre or focus of the song involves entertainment factors (e.g., humor or satire) and emotional connection. Despite these concerns, the broader acceptance of AI-generated music, particularly *deepfake music*, is evident, with neutral and positive comments making up a significant portion of user feedback. Specifically, 37% of comments were neutral, indicating curiosity or ambivalence as the audience adapts to AI as a creative agent. Moreover, positive sentiments accounted for nearly 40% of the comments in deepfake genres like Rap, Hip-hop, Rock, and Pop, suggesting a promising level of acceptance. Overall, the combined neutral and positive sentiments (77%) outweigh the negative sentiments (23%), indicating a potential shift in public perception towards AI-composed or co-created music.

Regarding sentiments towards *non-deepfake AI music*, results revealed a largely positive sentiment. This contradicts previous studies which have shown a rather negative attitude towards AI music [5]. This finding may suggest that this issue is genre dependent. Listeners may be generally positive about non-deepfake AI music as it does not mimic human voice, thus being skeptical about deepfake AI-generated music using renown human voices. Reference [24] further elaborates on this skepticism, highlighting that emotional engagement with AI-composed music is a complex issue influenced by factors such as music genre, cultural perspective, and age group. Their research highlights the ongoing doubt and preference for human-made music, despite AI's potential to explore emotional authenticity. Thus, our findings align with these insights, emphasizing that the genre of music significantly influences listeners' attitudes towards AI-generated compositions.

Moreover, the longitudinal analysis also revealed relevant insights. First, regarding deepfake music, the genres of *Rap-Hip-Hop* and *Cartoon* indicated stable sentiment trends, with generally low negative sentiments, and predominance of positive and neutral ones. Both genres have also revealed a steady decrease in the total volume of comments, potentially suggesting that the novelty effect may be vanishing. On the other hand, the analysis indicated a different trend for *Rock/Pop*. In this genre, the increasing volume of comments and growing negative sentiment reinforces the need for further investigation towards deepfake music contrasting further genres. Lastly, the non-deepfake genres (*Instrumental* and *Relaxation*) indicated very stable trends, of low negative sentiments, and number of comments. This strengthens the notion that the mimicking of human voices through AI is the main factor to trigger sentimental responses towards AI music.

Finally, the limitations and the conclusions of the study indicate future directions for this investigation. First, future studies should extend the genre analysis, contrasting further genres (e.g., electronic, blues, jazz, country) to gain a more holistic understanding of the acceptance of deepfake music. Second, regarding results, no inferential statistics were reported due to formatting restrictions. Thus, not allowing the reporting of whether the differences found across sentiments are statistically significant, which represents a limitation of the paper. This will be addressed in the future. Third, future research should explore and further compare models using larger and more diverse datasets, including comments from different platforms and cultural contexts.

REFERENCES

[1] M. Mendez II, "The Drake AI song is just the tip of the iceberg," *Time Magazine*, 2023. [Online]. Available: https://time.com/6273529/drake-the-weeknd-ai-song/. [Accessed: May 20, 2025].

[2] H. H. S. Josan, "AI and Deepfake Voice Cloning: Innovation, Copyright and Artists' Rights," *Artificial Intelligence*, 2024.

[3] A. N. Nicolaou and M. Murgia, "Google and Universal Music negotiate deal over AI 'deepfakes'," *Financial Times*, 2023. [Online]. Available: https://www.ft.com/content/6f022306-2f83-4da7-8066-51386e8fe63b. [Accessed: May 20, 2025].

[4] M. Sareen, "Threats and challenges by DeepFake technology," in *DeepFakes*, Boca Raton, FL: CRC Press, 2022, pp. 99–113.

[5] F. Tigre Moura and C. Maw, "Artificial intelligence became Beethoven: how do listeners and music professionals perceive artificially composed music?," *Journal of Consumer Marketing*, vol. 38, no. 2, pp. 137–146, 2021, doi: 10.1108/JCM-02-2020-3671.

[6] H. Chu, et al., "An empirical study on how people perceive AI-generated music," in *Proc. 31st ACM Int. Conf. on Information & Knowledge Management (CIKM)*, 2022, pp. 304–314.

[7] F. Tigre Moura, C. Castrucci, and C. Hindley, "Artificial Intelligence Creates Art? An Experimental Investigation of Value and Creativity Perceptions," *Journal of Creative Behavior*, vol. 57, pp. 534–549, 2023, doi: 10.1002/jocb.600.

[8] G. Tellis, E. Yin, and S. Bell, "Global consumer innovativeness: cross-country differences and demographic commonalities," *Journal of International Marketing*, vol. 17, no. 2, pp. 1–22, 2009, doi: 10.1509/jimk.17.2.1.

[9] I. Tussyadiah and G. Miller, "Perceived impacts of artificial intelligence and responses to positive behaviour change intervention," in *Information and Communication Technologies in Tourism 2019*, Cham: Springer Verlag, 2018, pp. 359–370. [Online]. Available: www.tussyadiah.com/ENTER2019_TussyadiahMiller.pdf.

[10] D. B. Shank, C. Stefanik, C. Stuhlsatz, K. Kacirek, and A. M. Belfi, "AI composer bias: Listeners like music less when they think it was composed by an AI," *Journal of Experimental Psychology: Applied*, vol. 29, no. 3, p. 676, 2023.

[11] R. Zenieris, *Perception and Bias towards AI-Music*, Bachelor's thesis, University of Twente, 2023..

[12] J. W. Hong, Q. Peng, and D. Williams, "Are you ready for artificial Mozart and Skrillex? An experiment testing expectancy violation theory and AI music," *New Media & Society*, vol. 23, no. 7, pp. 1920–1935, 2021.

[13] P. Fernando, T. V. Mahanama, and M. Wickramasinghe, "Assessment of human emotional responses to AI–composed music: A systematic literature review," in *Proc. 2024 Int. Res. Conf. on Smart Computing and Systems Engineering (SCSE)*, vol. 7, pp. 1–6, Apr. 2024

[14] E. Altuncu, V. Franqueira, and S. Li, "Deepfake: Definitions, performance metrics and standards, datasets and benchmarks, and a meta-review," *arXiv preprint arXiv:2206.07788*, 2022.

[15] W. D. Weisman and J. F. Pena, "Face the uncanny: The effects of doppelganger talking head avatars on affect-based trust toward artificial intelligence technology are mediated by uncanny valley perceptions," *Cyberpsychology, Behavior, and Social Networking*, vol. 24, pp. 182–187, 2021, doi: 10.1089/cyber.2020.0175.

[16] B. Usukhbayar and S. Homer, "Deepfake videos: The future of entertainment," *ResearchGate*, Berlin, Germany, 2020.

[17] J. T. Hancock and J. N. Bailenson, "The social impact of deepfakes," *Cyberpsychology, Behavior, and Social Networking*, vol. 24, no. 3, pp. 149–152, 2021.

[18] M. Sareen, "Threats and challenges by DeepFake technology," in *DeepFakes*, Boca Raton, FL: CRC Press, 2022, pp. 99–113.

[19] D. Afchar, G. M. Brocal, and R. Hennequin, "Detecting music deepfakes is easy but actually hard," *arXiv preprint arXiv:2405.04181*, 2024.

[20] Y. Zang, Y. Zhang, M. Heydari, and Z. Duan, "Singfake: Singing voice deepfake detection," in *Proc. ICASSP 2024 IEEE Int. Conf. on Acoustics, Speech and Signal Processing (ICASSP)*, Apr. 2024, pp. 12156–12160

[21] S. Yang and H. Zhang, "Text mining of Twitter data using a latent Dirichlet allocation topic model and sentiment analysis," *International Journal of Computer and Information Engineering*, vol. 12, no. 7, pp. 525–529, 2018.

[22] CardiffNLP, "Cardiff Natural Language Processing," 2024. [Online]. Available: https://cardiffnlp.github.io/

[23] M. A. Jahin, M. S. H. Shovon, and M. F. Mridha, "TRABSA: Interpretable sentiment analysis of tweets using attention-based BiLSTM and Twitter-RoBERTa," *arXiv preprint arXiv:2404.00297*, 2024.

[24] H. Guo, "Comparison of neural network and traditional classifiers for Twitter sentiment analysis," *Highlights in Science Engineering and Technology*, vol. 38, pp. 1062–1070, 2023, doi: 10.54097/hset.v38i.5996

[25] J. Camacho-Collados et al., "TweetNLP: Cutting-edge natural language processing for social media," in *Proc. Conf. on Empirical Methods in Natural Language Processing (EMNLP)*, 2022.

[26] M. A. Jahin, M. S. H. Shovon, and M. F. Mridha, "TRABSA: Interpretable sentiment analysis of tweets using attention-based BiLSTM and Twitter-RoBERTa," *arXiv preprint arXiv:2404.00297*, 2024.

[27] V. Lac and F. T. Moura, "Sentiment analysis of AI generated music using latent Dirichlet allocation (LDA)," in *Proc. AIMC 2024*, Sep. 9–11, 2024.

[28] C. Provenzano, "Making voices: The gendering of pitch correction and the auto-tune effect in contemporary pop music," *Journal of Popular Music Studies*, vol. 31, no. 2, pp. 63–84, 2019.

[29] M. Yasser, "Twitter Tweets Sentiment Dataset," *Kaggle*, 2021. [Online]. Available: https://www.kaggle.com/datasets/yasserh/twitter-tweets-sentiment-dataset. [Accessed: May 22, 2025].

CNNs in Musical Performance and Arrangement: Recognizing and Managing Bowed Instrument Techniques Across Cultures

Xinyuan Zhu
School of Science and Engineering
The Chinese University of Hong Kong, Shenzhen
Shenzhen, China
email: xinyuanzhu@link.cuhk.edu.cn

Clement Leung
School of Science and Engineering
The Chinese University of Hong Kong, Shenzhen
Shenzhen, China
email: clementleung@cuhk.edu.cn

***Abstract*—This study explores the application of AI-assisted techniques in analyzing and classifying bowed string instruments from Chinese and Western traditions, focusing on the comparison between the erhu and the violin. Using a combination of spectrogram analysis, Mel-Frequency Cepstral Coefficients (MFCCs), and Convolutional Neural Networks (CNNs), the study captures the distinct timbral and articulation differences between the two instruments. Particular attention is given to bowing techniques such as vibrato, portamento, pizzicato, which manifest differently due to structural and acoustic variations. Beyond recognition, this research contributes to AI-assisted music arrangement and composition, providing tools to analyze and synthesize playing techniques across different musical traditions. By bridging Eastern and Western bowed instrument performance styles, this approach supports both cultural heritage preservation and innovation in contemporary music production.**

***Keywords-AI-assisted music creation*; *Audio fingerprinting*; *Spectrogram matching*; *Convolutional neural networks*; *Audio signal processing*.**

I. Introduction

Music creation and arrangement rely heavily on accurate music recognition technologies, which facilitate the identification and integration of musical elements in various production contexts. Numerous techniques have emerged in the field of music recognition, significantly improving music retrieval, automated generation, and media management [1]. Central to these developments is audio fingerprinting, which segments an audio signal into small time windows and transforms them into frequency domain representations via Fourier analysis [2]–[4] . This method allows for the extraction of distinctive "fingerprints" based on unique spectral characteristics, which are used to match audio tracks across platforms like Shazam and Echoprint [5]. Complementing this, spectrogram matching uses visual representations of sound and relies on CNNs to detect patterns in these spectrograms, making it possible to classify music even in noisy environments [6] [7]. Additionally, rhythm and chord matching further enriches the recognition process by analyzing temporal features and harmonic progressions within a track, helping identify musical patterns and styles [8]. Lastly, lyrics matching extends the scope of music recognition by using Natural Language Processing (NLP) to transform sung vocals into text [9]. This text is then matched against a lyrics database to identify songs, making it particularly useful for recognizing cover versions or different renditions of the same song, where the melody might differ but the lyrics remain consistent.

These methodologies, each using unique aspects of audio processing and analysis, highlight the complexity and dynamic nature of music recognition technology. They not only improve the accuracy and efficiency of music identification but also enrich the user experience across various digital platforms, paving the way for innovative applications in the music and media industries.

Although these techniques have greatly enhanced our ability to identify and categorize music, current research predominantly focuses on the design and technological recognition of a certain musical instrument [10] [11], exploring innovative computational methods and digital fabrication that enable musical instrument identification and song matching. However, there remains a notable gap in the research specifically targeting the detailed identification of playing techniques on single instruments, especially within the domain of traditional Chinese music. This is a critical area for music learning and cataloging, as understanding and preserving the unique playing techniques of traditional music not only plays a crucial role in cultural heritage and education but also greatly enhances music creation and arrangement by providing deeper insights into the expressive potential of these instruments [12]. Furthermore, there's a need for developing technologies that can assist in the nuanced detection of specific musical styles and techniques, which are often overlooked in broader music recognition systems [13]. Thus, this paper presents a novel deep-learning model designed to recognize various playing techniques of two bowed string instruments from different musical traditions—the Western Violin and the Chinese Erhu. Section 2 details the theoretical foundations of audio processing and CNNs. Section 3 describes the system architecture and implementation. Section 4 presents experimental results for Violin and Erhu techniques. Section 5 compares the bowing techniques between the two instruments. Section 6 discusses implications and future work.

II. Theory

This section introduces the theoretical principles underlying the signal processing and deep learning operations implemented in the system. For different playing techniques, such as focusing on pitch and playing frequency, we employ various approaches to handle pitch and playing frequency to ensure the most suitable solution for a specific technique. These techniques are described below.

1) Audio Signal Processing:

a) Pitch Shifting: Pitch shifting alters the frequency content of the audio without changing the tempo. Here, the Short-Time Fourier Transform is expressed as STFT. It can be expressed using the phase vocoder approach in the frequency domain:

$$\text{pitch\_shifted\_data} = \text{STFT}^{-1}(\text{STFT}(\text{data}) \cdot e^{j\omega\delta})$$

where δ denotes the pitch shift in radians, and ω is the angular frequency vector.

b) Audio Stretching: Time-stretching changes the duration of the audio signal. Using the phase vocoder method, the operation is defined as:

$$\text{stretched\_data} = \text{STFT}^{-1}(\text{STFT}(\text{data}) \cdot e^{j\phi})$$

where ϕ is a phase adjustment applied to maintain continuity in the time-stretched signal.

2) Feature Extraction:

a) Mel-Spectrogram: The Mel-spectrogram is computed from the Short-Time Fourier Transform (STFT) of the signal, mapped onto the Mel scale:

$$\text{Mel}(f) = 2595 \log_{10}\left(1 + \frac{f}{700}\right)$$

$$\text{mel\_spec} = |\text{STFT}(\text{data})|^2$$

where f is the frequency in Hz.

b) MFCCs: Mel Frequency Cepstral Coefficients (MFCCs) are derived from the logarithm of the Mel-spectrogram, followed by a Discrete Cosine Transform (DCT):

$$\text{MFCCs} = \text{DCT}(\log(\text{mel\_spec}))$$

3) Convolutional Neural Networks:

a) Convolutional Layer: A convolutional layer in a CNN can be mathematically modeled as:

$$\text{output} = \sigma(\mathbf{W} * \mathbf{X} + \mathbf{b})$$

where $\mathbf{W}$ represents the kernel weights, $\mathbf{X}$ is the input, $\mathbf{b}$ is the bias, and σ is a nonlinear activation function, such as ReLU defined by $\sigma(x) = \max(0, x)$.

b) Pooling Layer: Pooling layers reduce the spatial dimensions of the input feature maps:

$$\text{pooled} = \max_{k,l}(\text{input}[i + k, j + l])$$

for max pooling over the window defined by indices k and l.

This detailed theoretical foundation ensures the robustness and comprehensiveness of the specifications, guiding the practical implementation of the proposed audio processing and CNN methodologies.

III. Architecture and Details

This section elaborates on the system architecture and implementation specifics designed for the project, including algorithm selection, software development practices, and Python programming techniques utilized. Each component's functionality and its integration within the system are clarified for thorough understanding.

A. System Architecture

The system is structured around several key functionalities which include:

- **Data Preprocessing:** Initial steps such as normalization, noise reduction, and data augmentation are applied to the audio data to enhance model performance and robustness. In addition, we cut training pieces to be 3 seconds long each, labling them with 1 if they have certain feature and 0 if they don't have. Each playing technique is associated with a separate dataset comprising approximately 500 audio segments, with 70% allocated for training, 15% for validation, and 15% for testing.
- **Feature Extraction:** Utilizing the `librosa` library, features such as MFCCs, spectral contrast, and tonnetz are extracted, which are crucial for the audio signal analysis.
- **Convolutional Neural Network (CNN):** The model employs CNN architectures, implemented using TensorFlow and Keras, to process and classify audio data effectively.

B. Implementation Details

1) Algorithm Selection: The project employs CNNs due to their effectiveness in audio and image processing tasks. CNNs are chosen for their ability to identify hierarchical patterns in data, which is essential for the analysis of complex audio signals.

2) Software Development: Python is selected as the main programming language, supported by its extensive libraries and frameworks that facilitate the implementation of data science and machine learning algorithms efficiently.

3) Frameworks and Libraries: Key frameworks and libraries used in the project include:

- **TensorFlow and Keras:** For designing, training, and validating deep learning models. These frameworks offer comprehensive tools that aid in the rapid development and deployment of ML models.
- **Librosa:** A library for music and audio analysis, providing the necessary functionalities to implement music information retrieval systems.

4) Model Development: The model takes features from Mel-spectrograms and MFCCs as input, represented as 2D time–frequency matrices. It consists of three convolutional layers with 3x3 kernels, each followed by max-pooling. The model was trained for 100 epochs with a batch size of 32. A final dense layer with softmax activation handles classification. Training uses categorical cross-entropy loss and the Adam optimizer.

C. Instrument Introduction

This study explores two bowed string instruments from different musical traditions: the Violin, a cornerstone of Western classical musicand the Erhu, a representative Chinese traditional instrument. While both instruments share similarities in their bowed playing technique, they exhibit distinct structural, tonal, and expressive differences.

1) Violin: The Violin is a Western bowed string instrument that has been a central part of orchestral, chamber, and solo music for centuries as shown in Figure 1(a). It typically has four strings tuned in perfect fifths (G-D-A-E) and is played with a horsehair bow. Unlike the Erhu, the Violin has a fingerboard, allowing for precise pitch control and a broader range of fingering techniques. It is known for its brilliant and resonant tone, capable of a wide range of expressive dynamics, from delicate pianissimo to powerful fortissimo.

2) Erhu: The Erhu, as shown in Figure 1(b), is a traditional bowed instrument with a distinctive timbre that is often described as mimicking the human voice. Unlike the Violin, the Erhu has only two strings, tuned a perfect fifth apart, and lacks a fingerboard, which allows for continuous gliding motions, producing characteristic portamento effects. The bow is positioned between the two strings, requiring a unique bowing technique where the player alternates between inner and outer strings. The Erhu's sound is softer and more nasal compared to the Violin, and it is widely used in Chinese folk, traditional, and contemporary music.

By comparing these two bowed string instruments, this study aims to highlight the unique playing techniques, timbral qualities, and expressive characteristics that differentiate Chinese traditional and Western classical music traditions.

(a) Violin (b) Erhu

Figure 1: The Violin and Erhu

IV. RESULTS

This section focuses on the detection and analysis of four essential playing techniques for the violin: portamento, pizzicato, vibrato, and chords, as well as three techniques for the erhu: pizzicato, portamento, and horse neighing. Detailed explanations and visual representations of each technique are provided in the following subsections.

For the full code, training pieces, and testing cases, please refer to the following GitHub and Google Drive repositories: GitHub Repository, Google Drive Repository.

A. Violin pizzicato

The violin's pizzicato showcases its versatility and dynamic articulation. By plucking the strings instead of bowing, it produces crisp, percussive tones that range from delicate to forceful. This technique adds rhythmic clarity and timbral variety, enriching both classical and contemporary compositions. Beyond its technical role, pizzicato enhances expressive depth, allowing performers to craft playful, agile, or dramatic effects, highlighting the violin's adaptability across musical genres.

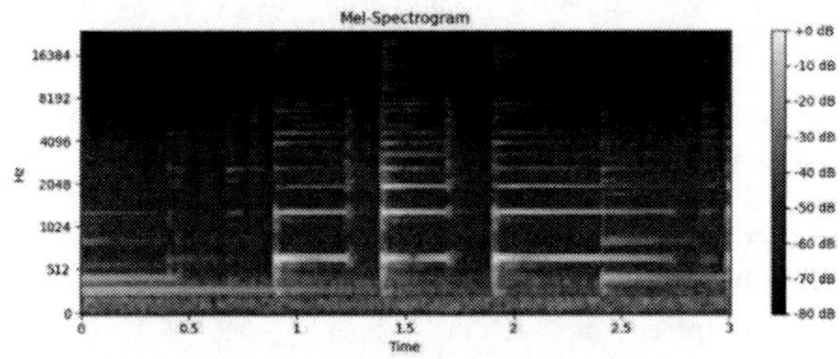

(a) Pizzicato spectrogram

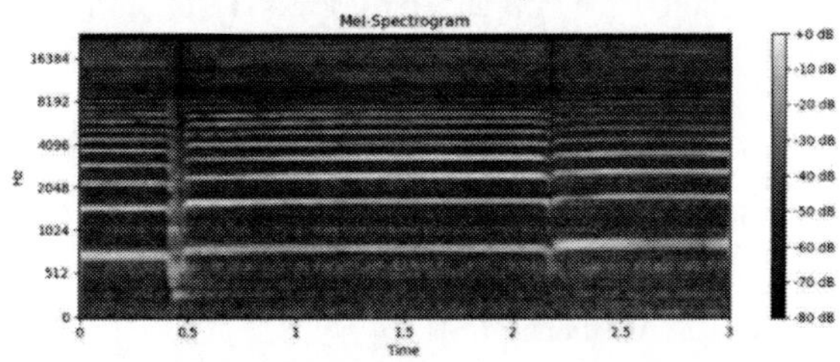

(b) Spectrogram without pizzicato

Figure 2: Comparison of violin pizzicato audio spectrograms

Figure 2(a) showcases pizzicato, the core distinguishing feature is the discrete, rapidly decaying frequency components, evident in the short, isolated horizontal bands. Each note exhibits a sharp attack followed by a quick fade. The gaps between notes indicate the lack of sustained bow pressure, reinforcing the percussive and transient nature of pizzicato articulation. In contrast, Figure 2(b) shows a violin performance without pizzicato, characterized by continuous and sustained horizontal bands that indicate prolonged bowing. The accuracy under 20 test cases is 100% with a threshold of 0.38.

B. Violin Vibrato

Violin vibrato is an essential and nearly omnipresent technique, appearing in almost every performance. It is created by oscillating the fingertip on the string, producing continuous pitch variations. This enriches the tone, adding warmth, depth, and expressiveness. Vibrato is so frequently used that a note without it often feels unusual in classical violin playing.

This detailed spectrogram Figure 3 vividly illustrates a violin performance incorporating vibrato, which is clearly discernible through the distinct, wavering patterns of the

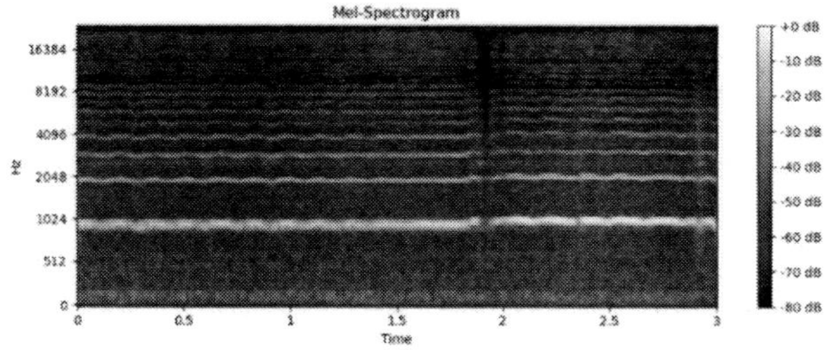

Figure 3: Vibrato spectrogram

frequency bands. These oscillating bands represent the subtle pitch variations characteristic of vibrato. The analysis demonstrates exceptional precision, achieving an accuracy of 100% at a threshold value of 0.18, underscoring the reliability and effectiveness of the method used to detect and quantify this acoustic feature.

C. Violin Portamento

Violin portamento is a smooth sliding technique that connects two notes seamlessly. It is produced by gliding the finger along the string while maintaining contact, creating a continuous pitch transition. This effect adds expressive fluidity. Portamento is frequently used in both classical and contemporary music to enhance emotional depth, making melodic passages sound more lyrical and connected. Its subtle or exaggerated application depends on stylistic interpretation, shaping the expressiveness of a performance.

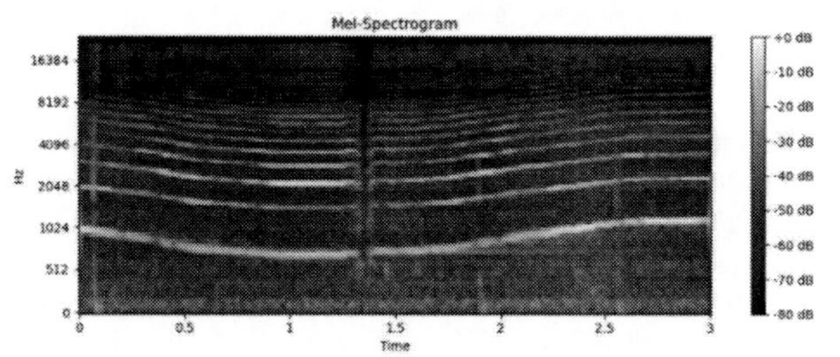

Figure 4: Portamento spectrogram

Figure 4 represents violin with portamento, characterized by smooth, diagonal transitions between frequencies. These sloping lines indicate a continuous pitch glide, as the player's finger slides between notes without discrete separation. The accuracy is 100 % at the threshold of 0.07.

D. Violin Chords

Violin chords involve playing multiple strings simultaneously, creating a rich harmonic texture. They can be performed as double stops, where two notes are played together, or as triple/quadruple stops, where three or four strings are struck in succession. This technique adds depth, power, and resonance, commonly found in orchestral, solo, and folk music for dramatic or harmonic emphasis.

Figure 5(a) represents a series of chords, as clearly evidenced by the densely packed horizontal bands that span

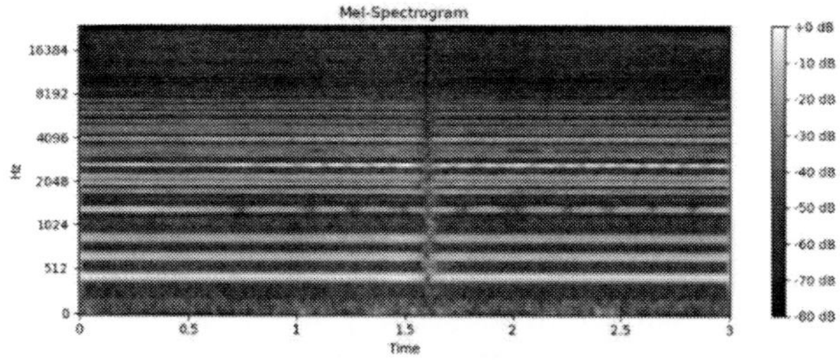

(a) Chords spectrogram

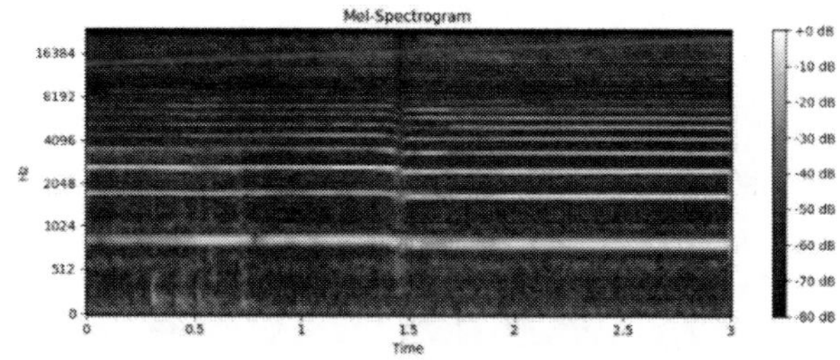

(b) Spectrogram without chords

Figure 5: Comparison of chord audio spectrograms

across multiple frequency ranges. These bands indicate the simultaneous vibration of multiple strings, each contributing to the overall harmonic structure. This dense clustering of frequencies is a hallmark of polyphonic music, where multiple pitches are sounded together to form harmonies. In contrast, Figure 5(b), which represents a violin playing without chords, displays a markedly different pattern. Here, the horizontal bands are fewer in number and more evenly spaced, reflecting the individual notes being played in a monophonic manner. Each band corresponds to a single pitch, with the spacing between them indicating the intervals of the melody. Figure 6 below shows the model accuracy for detecting chords on violin.

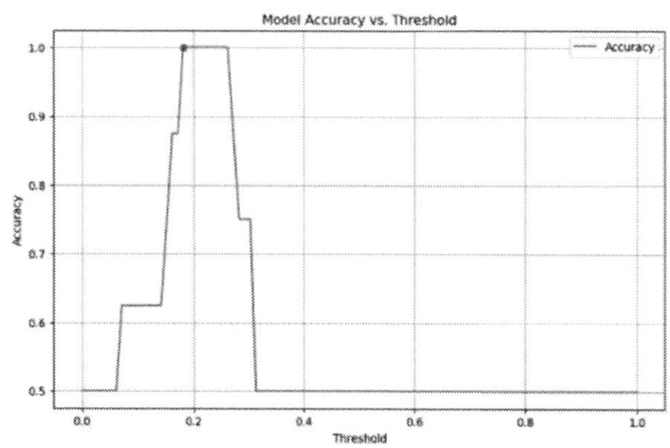

Figure 6: Model effectiveness in detecting chords on violin.

E. Erhu Pizzicato

The pizzicato technique on the erhu exemplifies the instrument's versatility and expressive range. This technique involves plucking the strings with the fingers, rather than using the bow, producing a sharp, percussive sound that contrasts with the typical bowed tones of the instrument. The pizzicato's unique timbre and rhythmic precision make it an effective tool for creating lively, staccato passages that add dynamic contrast to musical phrases. This technique's ability to produce clear, articulated notes with a distinct percussive quality allows performers to inject a new layer of expression into their music, enhancing the emotional depth and rhythmic complexity of a piece.

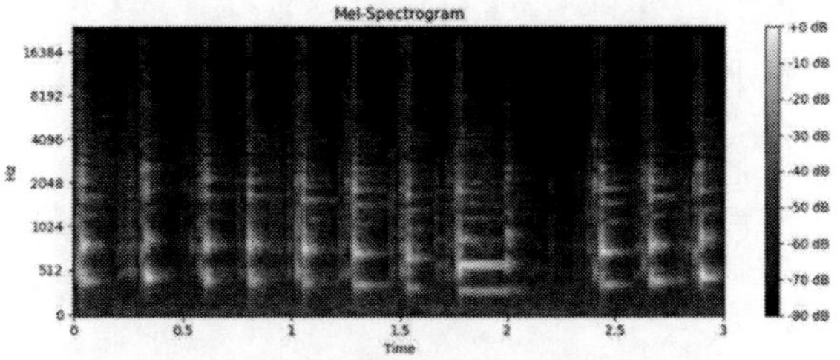

(a) Pizzicato spectrogram

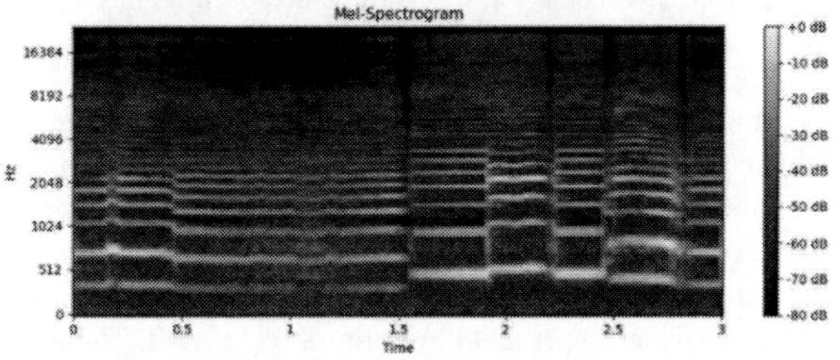

(b) Spectrogram without pizzicato

Figure 7: Comparison of erhu pizzicato audio spectrograms

In Figure 7(a), the characteristics of a pizzicato played on the erhu are visually evident. The defining feature is the presence of sharp, distinct vertical lines that appear at regular intervals. These lines represent the short, percussive nature of the pizzicato notes, which decay quickly and lack sustained resonance. In contrast, Figure 7(b) lacks these pizzicato features. Instead, it displays smoother, more continuous horizontal bands, indicative of sustained, bowed notes typical of traditional erhu playing. Here, we employ 200 test pieces to evaluate the model. The highest accuracy achieved is 98.02%, with the best threshold set at 0.578. Here, we demonstrate the ROC curve as shown in Figure 8. For this model, the precision is 0.9756, the recall is 0.9877, the F1-score is 0.9816, and the AUC score is 0.9850.

F. Erhu Portamento

The portamento technique on the erhu showcases the instrument's ability to convey emotional depth and seamless movement between notes. This technique involves sliding the pitch between two notes, creating a smooth, continuous transition rather than a distinct jump. The erhu's rich, fluid sound is often used to mimic the human voice, allowing the performer to evoke a sense of intimacy and vulnerability. Portamento is frequently employed in both traditional and

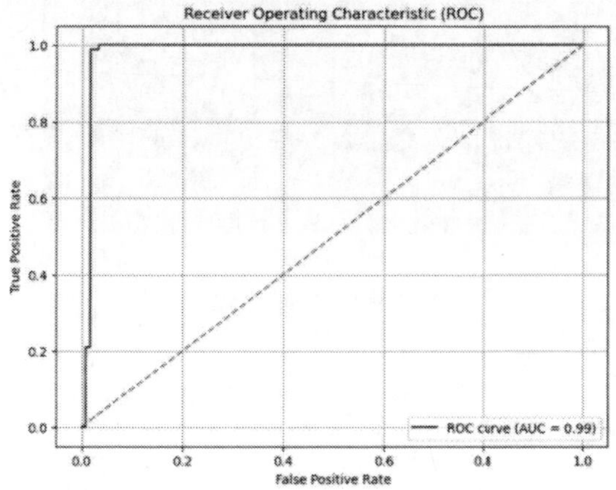

Figure 8: ROC curve for detecting pizzicato on erhu.

contemporary erhu music to enhance the lyrical quality of melodies, providing a sense of narrative flow and emotional continuity.

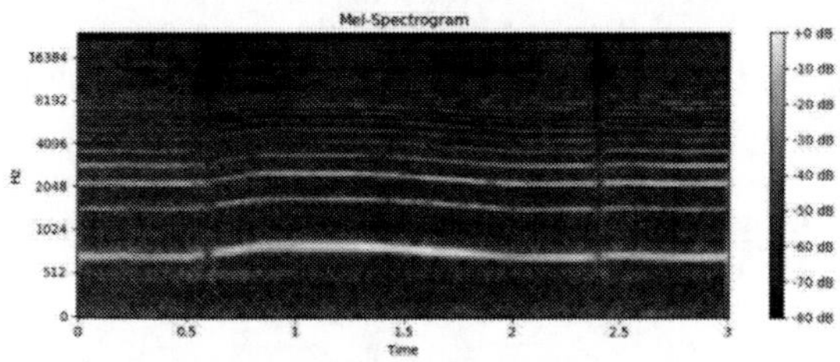

Figure 9: Portamento spectrogram

In Figure 9, the defining characteristics of portamento on the erhu can be observed. The smooth, continuous transitions between frequencies are evident, marked by sloped, connected lines that represent the sliding motion of the player's fingers along the string. This creates a fluid, expressive sound with gradual pitch changes.

As the portamento effect on the Erhu is not always distinct, and normal bowing can sometimes produce portamento-like characteristics, the accuracy is 62.8% at a threshold of 0.25.

G. Erhu Horse Neighing

The horse neighing technique on the erhu is a distinctive and evocative expression of the instrument's ability to mimic natural sounds. This technique involves a combination of fast bowing, specific finger pressure, and sliding motions that produce a sound resembling the neighing of a horse. The erhu's two strings and the player's control over bowing speed and intensity allow for the creation of sharp, high-pitched sounds that imitate the rhythm and tone of a horse's whinny.

In Figure 10, the characteristics of the "horse neighing" sound on the erhu are evident. The texture is dense and irregular, with rapid, fluctuating frequency patterns that create a chaotic and dynamic visual representation. These features correspond to the high-pitched, vibrating sound that mimics

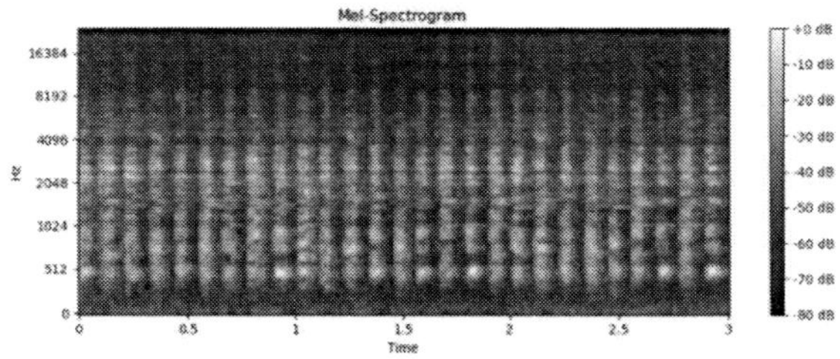

Figure 10: Horse neighing spectrogram

the neighing of a horse, achieved by rapid bowing and finger movements.

Here, we employ 180 test pieces to evaluate the model. The accuracy and the optimal identification threshold are presented below. The highest accuracy comes to 100%, with the best threshold set at 0.03.

V. Comparison of Bowing Techniques

The erhu and violin, as representatives of Chinese and Western bowed string instruments, exhibit distinct differences in playing techniques, articulation, and spectral characteristics. These differences arise from their structural design, musical traditions, and expressive focus, which are clearly reflected in their Mel-spectrograms.

The violin, with its four-string setup and fingerboard, allows for precise articulation, harmonic richness, and diverse bowing techniques. The spectrograms of violin performances show dense harmonic overtones, sustained resonance, and well-defined pitch transitions. In contrast, the erhu's two-string, fretless design enables continuous pitch glides, broader vibrato, and unique timbral effects, as reflected in its spectrogram. The absence of a fingerboard results in smoother portamento, appearing as gradual frequency slopes. Erhu vibrato is broader and more fluid, leading to a more expressive but less structured modulation compared to the violin.

While both instruments share core bowing techniques, such as vibrato, portamento, and pizzicato, their execution differs significantly. The violin excels in precision, harmonic layering, and articulation control, while the erhu prioritizes expressive fluidity, dynamic phrasing, and microtonal variation. By combining deep learning with spectral analysis, this study effectively distinguishes Chinese and Western bowed instrument performance styles, demonstrating the potential of AI in capturing nuanced musical expression.

VI. Conclusion and Future Work

This study applied AI-assisted techniques to analyze and classify bowing techniques of two culturally distinct bowed string instruments—the erhu and the violin. The experiments focused on detecting and analyzing four essential violin techniques—portamento, pizzicato, vibrato, and chords—as well as three primary erhu techniques—portamento, pizzicato, and horse neighing. The spectrogram analysis revealed distinct spectral patterns for each technique, demonstrating how structural differences between the instruments affect their articulation and sound production. These classification results could support AI-assisted music arrangement by automatically annotating performance techniques, enabling intelligent audio mixing and digital orchestration.

Beyond technical classification, this study provides valuable insights into the contrasts between Chinese and Western bowed instruments, bridging traditional musicology with computational analysis. The findings contribute to both cultural heritage preservation and modern AI-assisted music composition, offering potential applications in automated music arrangement, interactive music synthesis, and digital instrument modeling. In addition, while this study focuses on violin and erhu, the approach can be extended to other bowed instruments, subject to retraining on appropriately labeled datasets.

Future work will focus on expanding the dataset to include additional bowing techniques and other western and chinese instruments, refining model accuracy through advanced neural network architectures, and exploring real-time performance analysis. In addition, future work will compare CNNs with RNNs and transformer-based architectures to explore their effectiveness on time-series classification. By integrating AI with musicology, this research paves the way for a deeper understanding of global musical traditions and their computational representations.

References

[1] C. H. Chen, Ed., "Handbook of pattern recognition and computer vision," World Scientific, 2015.

[2] D. P. W. Ellis, B. Whitman, T. Jehan, and P. Lamere, "The Echo Nest musical fingerprint," in Proc. 2010 Int. Symp. Music Information Retrieval, 2010.

[3] J. Haitsma and T. Kalker, "A highly robust audio fingerprinting system with an efficient search strategy," Journal of New Music Research, vol. 32, no. 2, pp. 211-221, 2003.

[4] A. Wang, "An industrial strength audio search algorithm," in Int. Conf. Music Information Retrieval (ISMIR), 2003.

[5] D. P. Ellis, B. Whitman, and A. Porter, "Echoprint: An open music identification service," 2011.

[6] M. Young, "The Technical Writer's Handbook," Mill Valley, CA: University Science, 1989.

[7] D. Williams, A. Pooransingh, and J. Saitoo, "Efficient music identification using ORB descriptors of the spectrogram image," EURASIP Journal on Audio, Speech, and Music Processing, pp. 1-17, 2017.

[8] A. Shenoy and Y. Wang, "Key, chord, and rhythm tracking of popular music recordings," Computer Music Journal, vol. 29, no. 3, pp. 75-86, 2005.

[9] Z. Guo, Q. Wang, G. Liu, J. Guo, and Y. Lu, "A music retrieval system using melody and lyric," in Proc. 2012 IEEE Int. Conf. Multimedia and Expo Workshops, pp. 343-348, 2012.

[10] R. C. Rujia, A. Ghobakhlou, and A. Narayanan, "Musical instrument recognition in polyphonic audio through convolutional neural networks and spectrograms," 2024.

[11] G. A. V. M. Giri and M. L. Radhitya, "Musical instrument classification using audio features and convolutional neural network," Journal of Applied Informatics and Computing, vol. 8, no. 1, pp. 226-234, 2024.

[12] R. Michon, O. S. Julius, M. Wright, C. Chafe, J. Granzow, and G. Wang, "Mobile music, sensors, physical modeling, and digital fabrication: Articulating the augmented mobile instrument," Appl. Sci., vol. 7, no. 12, pp. 1311, 2017.

[13] A. Acquilino and G. Scavone, "Current state and future directions of technologies for music instrument pedagogy," Frontiers in Psychology, vol. 13, 2022, https://doi.org/10.3389/fpsyg.2022.835609.

LLM-based Few-shot Action System for NPCs in Virtual Reality Games

Fan Wang
Meta Platforms, Inc.
Burlingame, CA, USA
e-mail: fanwang@meta.com

Wen Zhou
Meta Platforms, Inc.
Burlingame, CA, USA
e-mail: zhouwen@meta.com

Rongze Gui
Meta Platforms, Inc.
Burlingame, CA, USA
e-mail: danielgui@meta.com

Jinqiao Li
Meta Platforms, Inc.
Columbus, OH, USA
e-mail: jqli@meta.com

Radoslaw Malicki
Meta Platforms, Inc.
Vancouver, BC, Canada
e-mail: radmalicki@meta.com

Andrey Staroseltsev
Meta Platforms, Inc.
Burlingame, CA, USA
e-mail: staroseltsev@meta.com

***Abstract*—Current trends in the game industry include making games more immersive and realistic through developing games in Virtual Reality (VR) and integrating Generative Artificial intelligence (AI) in Non-Player Characters (NPCs). As Large Language Model (LLM) based conversational NPCs start to emerge and show success in traditional video game medium, we seek to answer the question of "can we leverage LLMs to build believable NPCs that can make logical actions and interact with players naturally in VR?" In this paper, we introduce a design of an LLM-based action system with few-shot learning for NPCs in VR worlds. The use of few-shot learning would allow for rapid adaptation to new games without massive data requirement or expensive model training. We also include an evaluation plan to assess our designed system's performance.**

Keywords-Action Agent; Large Language Model; NPC in Virtual Reality; Agentic Workflow; Retrieval-Augmented Generation.

I. INTRODUCTION

In game worlds, Non-Player Characters (NPCs) are software agents whose actions are not directly controlled by a human player. Player-NPC interaction serves as an important role in enhancing players' experience, by providing companionship and motivating social engagement, giving guidance or helping to advance the game plots, or just adding to the world's ambiance to make the world more dynamic and lifelike [1][2].

In recent years, the rapid advances in Large Language Models (LLM), such as GPT4 [3] and LLama 3 [4] have been impacting the video game field [1]. There is increasing interest from game developers in experimenting and integrating LLM-based AI NPCs in video games [5]. In industry, companies including Inworld AI (partnered with Microsoft Xbox) [6] and ConvAI (partnered with NVidia) [7] are building products that enable developers to build conversation-based AI NPCs that can listen to players and output natural language along with facial expressions. In academics, there is also quite a few previous research proposing design for intelligent NPCs [8][9]. However, most of this work was done on games from a traditional medium (a 2D screen) and the primary function of the LLM-based NPCs is to have conversations. Little has been done with a focus on action planning for NPCs in a Virtual Reality (VR) environment.

VR unveiled a new degree of immersion by enabling the feeling of "presence" for players, 3D environment inputs, and physical character embodiment, which makes VR an ideal medium for realistic player-NPC interaction. Most recently, Meta introduced generative AI NPCs in Meta Horizon Worlds such as Bobber Bay Fishing [10], but those NPCs are primarily conversational. Previous studies have shown that players value the interactivity of physical motion uniquely offered by VR - it would be favored to have NPCs that can provide continuous human-like agency or physical actions, which are triggered by natural interactions (dialogues or gestures) instead of controller buttons or story plots [2][11][12]. We hope to leverage the immersive advantages of VR, examine the potential of LLMs in VR gameplay, and lay the groundwork for future development of believable VR NPCs that:

- Can be invoked by natural player-NPC interaction and understand players' intention;
- Can perceive and understand the 3D VR world environment, plan and execute physical actions intelligently;
- Can be easily extended to different games with a few-shot learning schema.

There are five sections in this paper. In Section 2, we discuss previous work that is related to our research topic. In Section 3, we introduce a design for a scalable LLM-based NPC action system. In Section 4, we present the basic prototyping experiment settings and its preliminary results, as well as a plan for a full, comprehensive evaluation. In Section 5, we briefly summarize the conclusion and future work.

II. RELATED WORK

Most NPCs in conventional computer games make actions based on a pre-defined action system heuristics. Traditional AI planning algorithms are generally used to power such action systems. One of the most prominent approach is Goal-Oriented Action Planning (GOAP), where NPC / Agents are driven with specific goal and heuristics. Earlier researches had been focusing on these algorithms, including some examples of application and optimization in hide-and-seek games [13][14]. Researches also focused on improve the naturalness and believably for NPCs, through techniques like dynamic reputation system and Observer-Orient-Decide-Act (OODA) theories [15][16]. Recent researches also explored machine-Learning techniques to enable more intelligent NPC actions, including behavior tree design, and cognitive and emotional models (FatiMA and PSI) [17][18].

After the LLM surge in 2022, researches also discussed enriching NPC through Generative-AI technologies. Some of the LLM-based AI Agents explore VR game settings to enrich conversational and behavioral experiences in NPC-human interaction [2][9][19]. Few researches have touched on LLM-based action system. The State-of-the-Art (SOTA) gameplay agent with action is VOYAGER, which created a single Generative-AI powered agent player in a Mincraft game [8]. The work used a Retrieval-Augmented Generation (RAG) powered iterative prompting method to prompt a GPT-4 model and execute actions in gameplay. However, generative action-system for interactive NPCs in VR are not widely researched.

III. Proposed Design

The proposed design introduces a novel action system for LLM-based NPCs in VR games. This framework leverages dynamic world perception and game knowledge injection to enable intelligent, context-aware interactions between NPCs and players. The system is designed to extend across multiple types of games using few-shot learning, supporting interactions through natural inputs from player actions or in-game events. As illustrated in Figure 1, the system has the following key components:

1. Dynamic World Perception Injection:

- The system continuously gathers real-time data from the game world, including:
  - **Objects:** Items available in the environment.
  - **Events:** Ongoing activities or situations.
  - **State:** Current game or player status (e.g., health, location).
  - **Location:** Spatial data of game elements or characters.
- This perception data is filtered and ranked to ensure only the most relevant information influences NPC behavior.

2. Game Knowledge Injection:

- Game-specific rules, available functions, and object interaction logic are injected into the framework.
- An *available action list* is dynamically updated to ensure NPC behavior aligns with the current game context and mechanics.

3. NPC Memory Injection:

- Based on the world perception and game rules, the relevant information from following memories are also retrieved for NPCs to plan the next actions:
  - NPC's knowledge about itself: identity, personality, backstory.
  - NPC's short-term memory within the same session.
  - NPC's long-term memory.
- These memories are also accumulated and summarized for developing reflections.

4. Prompt Construction:

- The core of the action system is prompt engineering, which combines:
  - **World Perception Data:** Extracted objects, events, and states.
  - **Game Rules and Knowledge:** Embedded functions and interactions.
  - **NPC Data:** NPC's persona, short-term and long-term memory.
  - **Few-shot Learning Examples:** Pre-selected or dynamically chosen examples.
  - **User Commands:** Inputs from the player or game system.
- Multiple formats, such as JSON, YAML, and XML, are used to structure these prompts.
- An *embedding-based example selector* helps identify the most relevant few-shot learning examples to tailor NPC behavior.
- The prompt is also augmented with *chain-of-thought* [20] for improving NPC's planning logic.

5. Model Zoo Utilization:

- The system leverages a collection of LLMs, such as LLaMA-3 models (8B and 70B) [4], to generate structured outputs.
- These models are queried to predict an appropriate action plan or natural language responses for NPCs.

6. Structured Output:

- The framework provides actionable outputs in a structured format to ensure consistency across various game scenarios. Key outputs include:
  - **Action or No Action Decision:** Determining if an NPC should respond to a given scenario.
  - **Function Call List:** A sequence of game functions to be executed.
  - **Function Chaining:** Enabling complex actions to unfold over time.
  - **Natural Language Response:** Generating appropriate conversational dialogue between NPCs and players.
- NPC will execute actions based on this structured output, and the outcome resulted from these actions are fed back to NPC's memory as a reflection.

This design framework creates a cohesive system where NPCs can perform dynamic actions and engage in meaningful dialogues based on real-time game events. The use of few-shot learning ensures adaptability to various game types with minimal retraining, offering a scalable solution for enriching player-NPC interactions across VR worlds.

IV. Experiments & Evaluation Plan

To validate the effectiveness of our proposed LLM-based NPC action system, we conducted a basic prototyping experiment, and also planned a comprehensive set of enriched experiments across several domains. These experiments focus

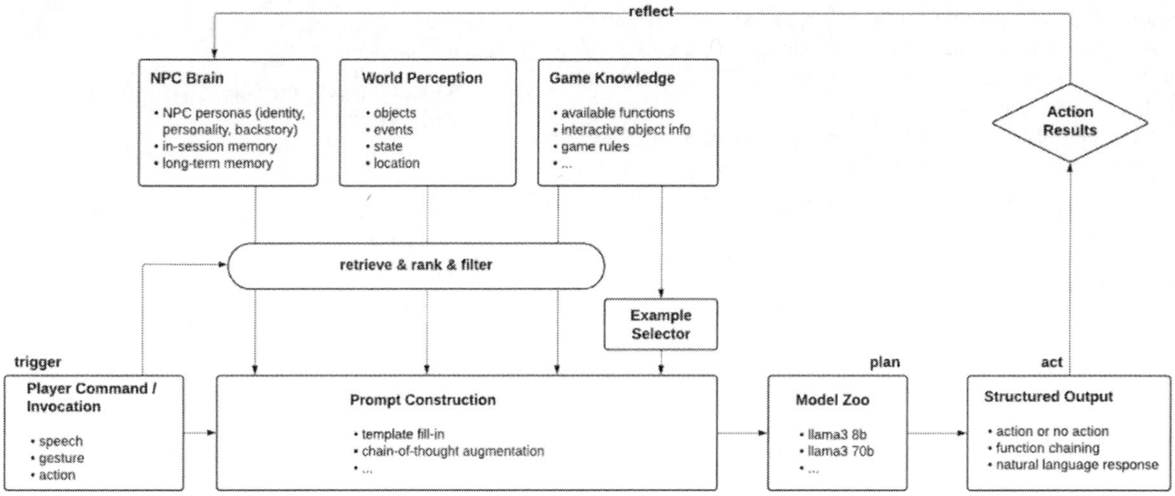

Figure 1. Overview of few-shot LLM-based NPC action system design.

Figure 2. Example test setup for the basic prototyping experiment. The end-to-end playtest is done in Meta Horizon World with a Meta Quest headset [21].

on assessing the model's adaptability, natural invocation, and ability to generate accurate responses in real-time dynamic VR environments.

A. Basic Prototyping Experiment Setup

We implemented the basic skeleton in the system design and did a prototyping experiment to prove the feasibility of this design, using Llama models with H100.

1. Data Generation and Scenario Design:

- We generated around 120 game scenarios with varying environment settings and user commands to test the prototype action system.
- An example scenario is (as shown in Figure 2):
  - **Environment:**
    - You **SEE** green target, red target, tree, green room, red room, and player.
    - You **HAVE** a gun.
    - You are **NEAR** a table.
  - **User Command:** Put the gun on the table, then go to the red room and pick up the apple.

2. Prototype Evaluation and Prompt Iteration:

- We iteratively tested the prototype system with multiple prompt designs to improve the performance.
- We explored different formats such as **JSON**, **YAML**, and **XML** to evaluate their impact on response generation and structured outputs.

3. Few-shot Learning Evaluation:

- To improve response quality, we tested different numbers of few-shot examples that cover different in-game scenarios, such as invalid but semantically correct command.
- Preliminary results showed that more relevant examples improve system performance, validating the importance of example selection.

B. Enriched Experiments Plan

In addition to basic prototyping interaction scenarios, we planned more complex experiments aligned with the paper's goal of achieving natural, multi-game adaptive interactions:

- **Cross-Game Adaptability:** The system is planned to be tested on scenarios from different types of games (e.g., puzzle games, adventure games, and role-playing games) to evaluate how well the LLM-based NPCs adapt without retraining.
- **Multi-Step Tasks:** Evaluations included sequences requiring NPCs to perform chained actions (e.g., collect, carry, and deliver items) to measure function chaining effectiveness.
- **Real-Time Inputs and Dynamic Changes:** NPCs will be exposed to changing environments mid-action (e.g., new objects appearing or targets moving) to test real-time adaptability.

- **Voice Input Integration:** In alignment with VR settings, we will test voice-based user inputs, assessing how accurately the system processes and acts on these commands.

C. Evaluation Metrics

The evaluation plan focuses on key metrics relevant to the system's performance across different environments and interaction scenarios:

- **Accuracy:**
  - Measured by how accurately the NPCs interpret user commands and execute the intended actions.
  - We already have preliminary proof-of-concept results from different prompt formats for the Basic Experiment setting:

TABLE I. MODEL ACCURACY WITH DIFFERENT PROMPT FORMATS.

Format	*Model*	*Accuracy*
JSON	llama3-70B	86.40%
JSON	llama3-8B	70.91%
YAML	llama3-8B	76.40%
XML	llama3-8B	69.10%

- **Response Latency:** Evaluated based on how quickly the NPCs respond to commands, ensuring timely interaction in VR environments.
- **Action Quality:** Assessed by measuring whether multi-step actions were executed correctly and in sequence.
- **Natural Invocation Success:** A measure of how accurately the system responds to natural language inputs without requiring predefined triggers or extensive training.
- **Adaptability Across Games:** Evaluated by measuring how well the system performs in multiple game genres with minimal prompt reconfiguration.
- **User Study Results:** We will engage human subjects participating in multiple playtest sessions with a VR headset and give feedback through a survey. The survey will be focusing on understanding the participants' subjective satisfaction/affection ratings on 1) their interaction with the NPCs (including invocation), and 2) the intelligent level of NPC's action planning.

V. CONCLUSION & FUTURE WORK

This paper presented a design for an LLM-based few-shot action system for NPCs in VR games. We did a proof-of-concept experiment with the very basic implementation, and the results revealed acceptable accuracy as well as an emphasis on the importance of example selection. We have also proposed a comprehensive experiment and evaluation plan to be done after the full implementation, which will allow us to assess the effectiveness of the system in handling the complex, dynamic, and natural interactions across various VR game types.

In the future, we seek to further improve our system, and explore creative solutions for using the latest technology to deliver new level of immersion, interactivity, and engagement for VR game players. Specifically, we will compare our system with other action-generation frameworks such as GOAP to evaluate the strengths and trade-offs of different approaches in game scenarios through user study. Key limitations of the current system include hallucination, and privacy concerns, which we plan to mitigate through introducing response grounding and user identifiable information masking. We also aim to implement a fuzzy memory module to better protect sensitive user data.

REFERENCES

[1] R. Gallotta et al., "Large language models and games: A survey and roadmap," *IEEE Transactions on Games*, 2024.

[2] M. Yin and R. Xiao, "Press a or wave: User expectations for npc interactions and nonverbal behaviour in virtual reality," *Proceedings of the ACM on Human-Computer Interaction*, vol. 8, no. CHI PLAY, pp. 1–25, 2024.

[3] J. Achiam et al., "Gpt-4 technical report," *arXiv preprint arXiv:2303.08774*, 2023.

[4] A. Grattafiori et al., "The llama 3 herd of models," *arXiv preprint arXiv:2407.21783*, 2024.

[5] M. Sas, "Unleashing generative non-player characters in video games: An ai act perspective," in *2024 IEEE Gaming, Entertainment, and Media Conference (GEM)*, IEEE, 2024, pp. 1–4.

[6] "Inworld - Build custom AI applications for gaming," Accessed: May 12, 2025. [Online]. Available: https://inworld.ai/ai-for-gaming.

[7] "ConvAI - Conversational AI Characters," Accessed: May 12, 2025. [Online]. Available: https://convai.com/.

[8] G. Wang et al., "Voyager: An open-ended embodied agent with large language models," *arXiv preprint arXiv:2305.16291*, 2023.

[9] H. Wan et al., "Building llm-based ai agents in social virtual reality," in *Extended Abstracts of the CHI Conference on Human Factors in Computing Systems*, 2024, pp. 1–7.

[10] "Bobber Bay Fishing," Accessed: May 12, 2025. [Online]. Available: https://horizon.meta.com/world/365118142359176/.

[11] Y. Jang and E. Park, "An adoption model for virtual reality games: The roles of presence and enjoyment," *Telematics and Informatics*, vol. 42, p. 101 239, 2019.

[12] M. Ochs, N. Sabouret, and V. Corruble, "Simulation of the dynamics of nonplayer characters' emotions and social relations in games," *IEEE Transactions on Computational Intelligence and AI in Games*, vol. 1, no. 4, pp. 281–297, 2009.

[13] E. Long, "Enhanced npc behaviour using goal oriented action planning," *Master's Thesis, School of Computing and Advanced Technologies, University of Abertay Dundee, Dundee, UK*, 2007.

[14] D. A. Suyikno and A. Setiawan, "Feasible npc hiding behaviour using goal oriented action planning in case of hide-and-seek 3d game simulation," in *2019 Fourth International Conference on Informatics and Computing (ICIC)*, IEEE, 2019, pp. 1–6.

[15] J. Mooney and J. M. Allbeck, "Rethinking npc intelligence: A new reputation system," in *Proceedings of the Seventh International Conference on Motion in Games*, 2014, pp. 55–60.

[16] Z. Lin, Z. Zhang, X. Sun, and H.-T. Zheng, "Make npc more realistic: Design and practice of a hybrid stealth game npc ai framework based on ooda theory," in *International Conference on Human-Computer Interaction*, Springer, 2024, pp. 321–328.

[17] M. Y. Lim, J. Dias, R. Aylett, and A. Paiva, "Creating adaptive affective autonomous npcs," *Autonomous Agents and Multi-Agent Systems*, vol. 24, pp. 287–311, 2012.

[18] X. Zhu, "Behavior tree design of intelligent behavior of non-player character (npc) based on unity3d," *Journal of Intelligent & Fuzzy Systems*, vol. 37, no. 5, pp. 6071–6079, 2019.
[19] H. Wan et al., "Building llm-based ai agents in social virtual reality," in *Extended Abstracts of the CHI Conference on Human Factors in Computing Systems*, 2024, pp. 1–7.
[20] J. Wei et al., "Chain-of-thought prompting elicits reasoning in large language models," *Advances in neural information processing systems*, vol. 35, pp. 24 824–24 837, 2022.
[21] "Meta Horizon," Accessed: May 12, 2025. [Online]. Available: https://horizon.meta.com/.

Empowering Persona Creation in Small Organizations

Evaluating ChatGPT 4o for Clustering and Analysis using PersonaCraft

Jefferson Lewis Velasco
Graphic Expression Department
Federal University of Santa Catarina
Florianópolis, Brazil[1]
e-mail: jeffvelasco.crm@gmail.com

Gustavo Modena
Knowledge Engineering Department
Federal University of Santa Catarina
Florianópolis, Brazil
e-mail: gustavoomodena2@gmail.com

Melise Peruchini
Network and IT department
Federal University of Santa Catarina
Florianópolis, Brazil
e-mail: meliseperuchini@gmail.com

Julio Monteiro Teixeira
Graphic Expression Department
Federal University of Santa Catarina
Florianópolis, Brazil
e-mail: juliomontex@gmail.com

Abstract— **This paper explores the use of ChatGPT 4o to assist small organizations in creating data-driven personas by applying an adapted version of the PersonaCraft methodology. Using a retail demographic dataset from Kaggle, the approach demonstrates how the LLM aids in data cleaning, clustering, and statistical testing, culminating in five meaningful customer segments. The k-prototypes algorithm was chosen based on PersonaCraft, and the Kruskal-Wallis test confirmed that numeric variables (especially purchase frequency and age) most effectively differentiate clusters. By producing insights with minimal user effort, ChatGPT 4o underscores the viability of employing LLM-based tools for persona creation and other advanced analytical tasks in resource-constrained contexts.**

Keywords—Generative AI, Artificial Intelligence, Personas, Customer Segmentation.

I. INTRODUCTION

Small organizations often face challenges in creating personas due to the complexity of clustering and other advanced statistical methods needed for accurate segmentation [1]. While data-driven persona generation has traditionally required specialized expertise [2], the rising capabilities of Large Language Models (LLMs) offer a promising alternative [3].

This paper evaluates how Chat Generative Pre-trained Transformer (ChatGPT) 4o can operationalize the PersonaCraft methodology for persona creation by automating key steps—such as clustering and statistical testing—through a natural language interface. This adaptation shows how prompt engineering enables non-experts to segment customers effectively, enabling users without data science expertise to produce robust, data-driven personas. This bridges a key accessibility gap in small organizations.

We apply the PersonaCraft [4] methodology to build personas using a demographic dataset from a bike and bike accessories retail business in Australia, publicly available on Kaggle [5]. GPT executes the Stages and Steps defined by the method, enabling users with minimal background in statistics or coding to engage in persona creation, specifically segmentation tasks.

By systematically incorporating prompts aligned with the PersonaCraft framework, we assess GPT's capability in assisting small organizations in clustering tasks and broadening access to advanced analytical techniques. It is important to note that this work does not aim to evaluate the PersonaCraft methodology itself. Rather, the goal is to examine GPT's capabilities as a data analysis assistant.

This paper is structured as follows: Section II presents the theoretical background. Section III details the employed methodology, including adaptations made to PersonaCraft. Section IV provides results and analysis. Section V offers conclusions and future work. This study addresses the following research question: **How effectively can ChatGPT 4o assist non-expert users in executing the core stages of PersonaCraft for the creation of data-driven personas?**

II. THEORY

Data-driven personas, derived from statistical analyses of real data, ensure credibility by reflecting actual behavioral and demographic patterns rather than assumptions [6]. Their development through clustering algorithms has shown promising applications in the literature, helping identify patterns and create representative audience segments [7].

Recent studies suggest that LLMs can enable non-experts to perform data analysis and code generation using natural language prompts [3], including clustering and concept identification [8]. Some initiatives use LLMs to build

[1] Although all authors are affiliated with Brazilian institutions, the dataset used was chosen for its accessibility, completeness, and relevance to segmentation tasks—not due to a connection with the Australian retail market.

personas—either fully automatically or in combination with human refinement. Combining human input with LLMs often improves results [9].

Despite these advances, challenges remain regarding representativeness, bias, and stereotypes in AI-generated personas [10]. LLMs may reinforce existing patterns or overlook outliers that don't align with dominant clusters. These risks underscore the need for bias mitigation strategies—such as diverse datasets, interpretability checks, or human review. In this study, bias was partially addressed by retaining numeric granularity and reporting statistical significance, though more safeguards are needed for socially sensitive contexts.

III. Methodology

A publicly available dataset was sourced from Kaggle, containing 3,908 rows of simulated customer demographic data modeled after an Australian retail business [5]. Originally intended for educational use, it was selected for its simplicity and similarity to datasets typically available in small organizations. While suitable for this initial application, future studies should explore datasets with richer behavioral or psychographic features to further test GPT's adaptability.

To fit the PersonaCraft framework, minor adjustments were made to accommodate the dataset's simplicity, without altering the methodology itself. For example, "questions" in the original method were mapped to "variables" in our data.

Prompt adaptations were also necessary to better align with GPT's functionality. Compared to the original PersonaCraft prompts, the revised versions included clearer instructions about formatting and handling variables. Numericac columns were kept in continuous form and described using centrality measures (mean, median, and mode).

The study was conducted using the ChatGPT 4o interface via OpenAI's web platform (chat.openai.com). Prompts were submitted iteratively by a non-expert user simulating the role of a typical small-organization user. Prompt structure followed PersonaCraft stages and typically included: (1) context and general objective, (2) task description (e.g., "cluster this dataset using k-prototypes"), and (3) output expectations (e.g., "summarize each cluster using centrality metrics").

Basic understanding of PersonaCraft and statistical concepts—such as clustering techniques and descriptive statistics—was required to guide prompt refinement effectively.

Given the study's focus on cluster generation and LLM support, certain PersonaCraft components were excluded. Specifically, Step 4 of Stage 4 was omitted for scope reasons, while all earlier stages related to segmentation were executed in full. Also, this study did not involve human participants and relied exclusively on anonymized, synthetic data. Therefore, no IRB approval was necessary. Care was taken to comply with privacy standards and research ethics.

IV. Results

In applying the PersonaCraft methodology to the chosen dataset, four major stages were conducted with GPT acting as an assistant. Throughout the process, the LLM guided the user in performing clustering, statistical analysis, and persona generation.

Stage 1: Preparing the Dataset involved removing irrelevant variables (e.g., names, addresses, and other identifying attributes). The retained variables included: gender, age, number of bike-related purchases in the past 3 years, job industry category, wealth segment, car ownership, customer tenure, and state of residence. This streamlined view highlighted the demographic and behavioral patterns relevant to persona creation.

Stage 2: Mapping Variable Types classified each variable according to PersonaCraft categories (e.g., Demographic, Purchasing Behavior, Assets & Ownership). Numeric data—including age, tenure, and purchase frequency—was kept in its original scale to allow accurate calculation of centrality measures (mean, median, mode) during analysis.

TABLE I. Relevant Variable Classification

Variable	*Description*	*Classification*	*PersonaCraft Type*
customer_id	Customer ID index	Numeric	Not applicable
gender	Customer gender (female or male)	Categoric	Demographic
age	Customer age in years	Numeric	Demographic
past_3_years_bike_related_purchases	Number of bike related purchases in the last 3 years	Numeric	Other
job_industry_category	Job Industry the customer is in	Categoric	Demographic
wealth_segment	Wealth segment to which the customer belongs	Categoric	Demographic
tenure	Tenure of the customer in months	Numeric	Other
Owns_Car	If customer owns a car	Categoric	Demographic
State	State of residence	Categoric	Demographic

Stage 3: Data Pre-Processing, involved refining prompt inputs for GPT, classifying the variables into coherent "groups", and creating updated headings.

TABLE II. Variable Groups and Headings

Variable Group	*Description*	*Variables*	*Headings*
Personal Identification	Used to uniquely identify or describe a person.	customer_id	Customer ID
Demographics	Attributes related to socioeconomic status, age,	AGE	Age

	and personal traits.	gender	Gender
		job_industry_category	Job Industry Category
		wealth_segment	Wealth Segment
Purchasing Behavior	Data on purchases or transaction-related behavior.	past_3_years_bike_related_purchases	Bike Purchases Last 3 Years
Customer Tenure	Duration of the customer's relationship.	tenure	Customer Tenure
Assets & Ownership	Indicators of asset ownership	Owns_Car	Car Ownership
Location Information	Geographic location of the customer.	State	State

Stage 4: Persona Generation involves four steps. In Step 1: Clustering, GPT was prompted to select the most suitable clustering method from PersonaCraft for our dataset. Given the mix of numeric and categorical variables, it recommended k-prototypes, a method well-suited for handling both types. Since the algorithm requires a predefined number of clusters [5], GPT applied the Elbow Method to determine the optimal value. As shown in Figure 1, the analysis indicated that k=5 provided best balance between cohesion and interpretability.

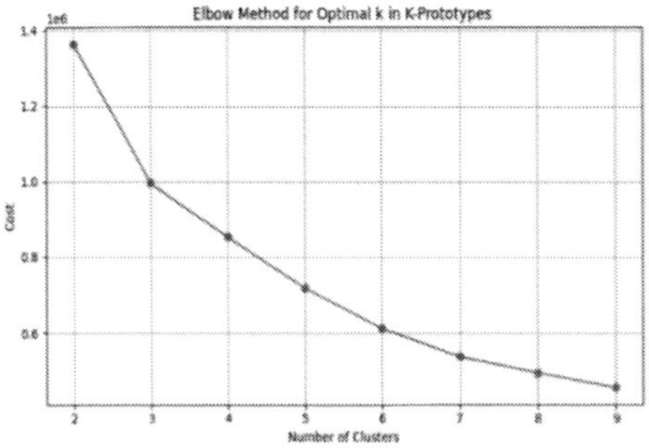

Figure 1. Elbow Method Results

The model proceeded with clustering using this parameter, generating an Excel file with cluster assignments for each record and a visualization of the resulting segments, as shown in Figure 2.

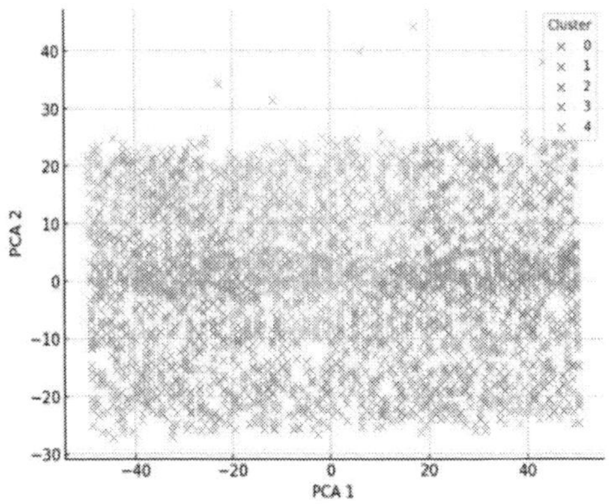

Figure 2. K-Prototypes Clustering PCA Projection

On Step 2: Statistical Analysis, GPT was prompted to calculate the Kruskal-Wallis test across the clusters to identify the variables most effective for differentiating personas. The test revealed that numeric variables (Bike Purchases in the Last 3 Years, Age, and Customer Tenure) had statistically significant variation, while Gender, State, Wealth Segment, Car Ownership, and Job Industry Category showed no significant differences across clusters.

TABLE III. KRUSKAL-WALLIS RESULTS

Variable	*H-statistic*	*p-value*	*Significant*
Bike Purchases Last 3 Years	34.767.060.696.875.200	0.0	Yes
Age	19.713.746.810.310.800	0.0	Yes
Customer Tenure	7.365.761.161.085.200	4,19E-143	Yes
Gender	56.158.533.280.999	22.973.201.404.749.700	No
State	5.162.671.440.601.860	27.100.991.196.740.200	No
Wealth Segment	33.190.520.564.661.200	5.059.193.012.085.890	No
Car Ownership	24.488.311.071.079.600	653.821.209.414.484	No
Job Industry Category	25.407.845.117.565.400	9.925.824.609.188.990	No

By not transforming numeric variables into discrete categories, GPT was able to generate and interpret measures of centrality within each cluster, providing insights into how age, purchase frequency, and tenure shape each persona. Cluster summaries are available in Table IV.

TABLE IV. CLUSTER DESCRIPTIONS

Variable	*Values*	*C1*	*C2*	*C3*	*C4*	*C5*
Gender	Female	468	328	484	295	462
	Male	373	317	471	281	429
Job Industry Category	Manufacturing	173	144	185	107	187
	Financial Services	162	131	179	122	172
	n/a	142	102	165	96	150
	Health	122	86	161	83	144
	Retail	86	66	85	52	69
	Property	46	35	66	46	73
	Entertainment	35	21	30	21	29
	IT	29	26	39	27	29
	Agriculture	25	25	29	10	24
	Telecommunications	21	9	16	12	14
Wealth Segment	Mass Customer	401	328	498	275	449
	High Net Worth	229	162	227	157	220

	Affluent Customer	211	155	230	144	222
Car Ownership	Yes	432	338	472	280	449
	No	409	307	483	296	442
State	New South Wales	456	330	530	316	457
	Victoria	214	155	229	147	253
	Queensland	171	160	196	113	181
Age	Mean	52,11	32,95	47,86	31,25	52,55
	Median	51	32	47	30	51
	Mode	45	27	44	28	44
Bike Purchases Last 3 Years	Mean	14,06	65,38	85,90	23,45	47,22
	Median	14	66	87	25	47
	Mode	2	68	98	27	53
Customer Tenure	Mean	12,34	7,45	11,41	6,82	13,05
	Median	12	6	12	5	13
	Mode	11	1	12	2	18

All underlying data and resultant analyses from this research are available for review upon request.

V. Conclusions and Future Work

Overall, the results demonstrate that ChatGPT 4o can be of significant help in data exploration and clustering tasks, even for users with limited analytic expertise. By adapting PersonaCraft to a simpler retail demographic dataset and employing the model's prompt-driven guidance, viable segments emerged that underline the importance of numeric variables (particularly purchase frequency and age) when distinguishing among diverse customer groups.

These findings suggest that the LLM can be a reliant assistant for small organizations lacking deep data analysis expertise. By guiding the user through data preparation, variable mapping, and clustering steps, the model demonstrated its capacity to bridge knowledge gaps.

Although this research was limited by the simplicity of the dataset and by the absence of direct human validation, the results demonstrate the method's feasibility. Future studies should validate this approach using larger and more complex datasets, as well as through participatory evaluation—where human experts and stakeholders assess the relevance, coherence, and representativeness of the generated personas.

Adopting PersonaCraft's prompt-driven approach as a framework to segment data through LLM allowed for a more accessible and intuitive workflow, enabling persona creation without extensive statistical background or programming experience. These findings point toward broader opportunities for LLM-based tools to support diverse, data-centric tasks within smaller organizations, enabling tailored marketing insights.

References

[1] E. L. Melnic, "How to strengthen Customer Loyalty, using Customer Segmentation?", Bulletin of the Transilvania University of Brasov. Series V: Economic Sciences, pp. 51–60, dez. 2016. [retrieved: March, 2025].

[2] J. Brickey, S. Walczak, and T. Burgess, "Comparing Semi-Automated Clustering Methods for Persona Development", IEEE Transactions on Software Engineering, vol. 38, nº 3, pp. 537–546, May 2012, doi: 10.1109/TSE.2011.60. [retrieved: March, 2025].

[3] J. A. Jansen, A. Manukyan, N. A. Khoury, and A. Akalin, "Leveraging large language models for data analysis automation," PLOS ONE, vol. 20, no. 2, p. e0317084, Feb. 2025, doi: 10.1371/journal.pone.0317084. [retrieved: March, 2025].

[4] S.-G. Jung, J. Salminen, K. K. Aldous, and B. J. Jansen, "PersonaCraft: Leveraging language models for data-driven persona development", International Journal of Human-Computer Studies, vol. 197, p. 103445, mar. 2025, doi: 10.1016/j.ijhcs.2025.103445. [retrieved: March, 2025].

[5] E. Harish, "KPMG Customer Demography Cleaned Dataset", Kaggle. Accessed on: March 19, 2025. [Online]. Available at: https://www.kaggle.com/datasets/harishedison/kpmg-customer-demography-cleaned-dataset. [retrieved: March, 2025].

[6] J. (Jen) McGinn and N. Kotamraju, "Data-driven persona development," in Proceedings of the twenty-sixth annual CHI conference on Human factors in computing systems - CHI '08, Florence, Italy: ACM Press, 2008, pp. 1521–1524. doi: 10.1145/1357054.1357292. [retrieved: March, 2025].

[7] E. Ditton, A. Swinbourne, and T. Myers, "Selecting a clustering algorithm: A semi-automated hyperparameter tuning framework for effective persona development," Array, vol. 14, p. 100186, Jul. 2022, doi: 10.1016/j.array.2022.100186. [retrieved: March, 2025].

[8] F. Lanfermann, T. Rios, and S. Menzel, "Large Language Model-assisted Clustering and Concept Identification of Engineering Design Data," in 2024 IEEE Conference on Artificial Intelligence (CAI), Singapore, Singapore: IEEE, Jun. 2024, pp. 788–795. doi: 10.1109/CAI59869.2024.00150. [retrieved: March, 2025].

[9] N. Arora, I. Chakraborty, and Y. Nishimura, "AI–Human Hybrids for Marketing Research: Leveraging Large Language Models (LLMs) as Collaborators," Journal of Marketing, vol. 89, no. 2, pp. 43–70, Mar. 2025, doi: 10.1177/00222429241276529. [retrieved: March, 2025].

[10] T. Goel, O. Shaer, C. Delcourt, Q. Gu, and A. Cooper, "Preparing Future Designers for Human-AI Collaboration in Persona Creation," in Proceedings of the 2nd Annual Meeting of the Symposium on Human-Computer Interaction for Work, Oldenburg Germany: ACM, Jun. 2023, pp. 1–14. doi: 10.1145/3596671.3598574. [retrieved: March, 2025].

Measuring Usability and User Experience with Eye-Tracking: Predicting Pragmatic and Hedonic Quality using Machine Learning

Fabian Engl, Timur Ezer, Jürgen Mottok
Software Engineering Laboratory for Safe and Secure Systems
OTH Regensburg
Regensburg, Germany
email: {fabian.engl | timur.ezer | juergen.mottok}@oth-regensburg.de

***Abstract*—This paper compares six different Machine Learning (ML) algorithms — the k-nearest neighbor algorithm, a Support Vector Machine, a Multi-Layer Perceptron, a Random Forest, Gradient Boosting, and Adaptive Boosting — in their ability to classify users based on their usability and user experience (UX) ratings, using only eye-tracking data. A study was designed using three different websites from German drinking water providers, with the corresponding usability and UX ratings based on the User Experience Questionnaire (UEQ) and the AttrakDiff questionnaire. In total, 104 participants, contributing over 18 hours of eye-tracking data, took part in the study. The results indicate that Machine Learning models trained on smaller datasets, such as those in the field of eye-tracking, often achieve reasonable F1-scores without the need for extensive hyperparameter tuning. A comparison of random and Bayesian optimization approaches reveals that especially tree-based models benefit from Bayesian optimization. Among all models, the Support Vector Machine and Multi-Layer Perceptron perform the best, averaging F1-scores in the 90 % range, and demonstrating that usability and UX can be predicted using similar approaches across different websites within the same domain. Additionally, no significant difference was found between the usability and UX definitions of the UEQ and the AttrakDiff, suggesting that both are equally suitable for UUX predictions based on Machine Learning and eye-tracking.**

Keywords*-*Machine Learning; Eye-Tracking; Usability; User Experience; UX.

I. Introduction

With the advancing digitization, everyday tasks are progressively shifting towards the digital realm. Relevant information can often only be found in digital form, and users are required to fulfill more tasks by themselves online, ranging from financial transactions to travel arrangements. Websites are among the most typical and widely used digital products in today's society, making it essential to design them with the users needs in mind. Usability and User Experience (UX) play a significant role in digital product design [1], making their assessment during development an important consideration. UUX — the combination of usability and user experience — is typically assessed in more traditional ways, relying on questionnaires or qualitative methods, such as think-aloud protocols [2].

Despite advancements in technologies like Electroencephalogram (EEG) and eye-tracking, which have become more accessible and affordable in recent years [3], they are rarely employed to assess UUX. The vast amount of output data, with sensors producing hundreds of measurements per second, and the required expertise can discourage their use [4]. With the rapidly growing trend of Machine Learning, a new question arises: Can both technologies be combined to address UUX in a more data-driven manner?

This paper addresses the generalizability of UUX measurability when combining Machine Learning models with eye-tracking, training them solely on eye movements. To investigate this, an eye-tracking study was designed, comparing three websites from German drinking water providers. A total of 104 participants took part in the study, resulting in over 18 hours of eye-tracking data and UUX ratings based on the User Experience Questionnaire (UEQ) and AttrakDiff questionnaires. Six commonly used Machine Learning models — k-nearest Neighbors (KNN), Support Vector Machine (SVM), Multi-Layer Perceptron (MLP), Random Forest (RF), Gradient Boosting (GB) and Adaptive Boosting (ADA) Models — were trained to separately classify the users into those who rated the usability and UX of the websites as low and those that rated them high.

This paper is structured as follows: First, Section II addresses related work in the field of eye-movement- and machine-learning-based UUX predictions, with shortcomings, research questions, and hypotheses elaborated in Section III. Following this, Section IV provides a brief introduction to the study design, used questionnaires, demographic information about the participants, and the technical setup. Sections V, Section VI and VII introduce common eye movement metrics, data preperation steps and Machine Learning model evaluation methods, respectively. Section VIII presents the classification results and answers the previously formulated research questions. Finally, Sections IX, X, and XI summarize the results, address the limitations of the current study, and offer an outlook for future research while discussing the implications of the findings.

II. Related Work

Usability and UX have been studied using eye-tracking before, even Machine Learning approaches are nothing new. Here, websites play a significant role. However, when looking at previous publications most of the time only one of the two UUX dimensions is analyzed.

Koonsanit *et al.* [5] for example study the effect of strong and weak signifies in URLs, which consist of differently highlighted links, with and emphasize on usability. They analyze how the level of highlighting helps participants to identify linked sites [5]. Instead of developing features from different types of eye movements, they train their model purely based on heatmaps, which they aggregate using a principal component analysis. They train different Machine Learning models to detect which users were looking at websites with strong and which were looking at those with weak signifies. They compare data from eleven participants and report accuracy results peaking at 90 % for the best model [5].

Cao *et al.* [6] take a similar approach and compare different website prototypes using eye-tracking data. 30 users had to find specific products on four versions of an e-commerce platform. Cao *et al.* train Machine Learning models to predict usage intention, splitting the participants based on their interest in using the website again [6]. They report accuracy, recall and precision metrics ranging from 71.7 % to 85.0 %; 57.5 % to 93.0 % and 62.5 % to 87.0 % respectively, with the deep neural network performing the best [6].

Wang *et al.* [7] studied search engines in particular, measuring how certain eye movement could be used to predict satisfaction levels. In total, eye-tracking data was collected from 48 participants, which were asked to find four different publications in the *Web of Science* database. Satisfaction was measured using a seven-point Likert scale and the predicted using both regression and a classification, which differentiated between the two groups rating the satisfaction low-to-medium of high. Their models achieved accuracies roughly between 64% and 68% in classification and R^2 scores between 0.02 and 0.75 for regression [7].

Pappas *et al.* [8] study whether visual appeal can be predicted based on eye-tracking, further more focusing on how much eye-tracking data is actually required to make valid predictions. They use a questionnaire from [9], which differentiates four different aspects of visual appeal including simplicity, diversity, colorfulness and craftsmanship [9]. Based on data from 23 participants they show that using a random forest regression, 15 to 20 seconds of recording data were enough not make predictions with a Normalized Root Mean Squared Error (NRMSE) of 0.1 to 0.14 across all four different categories. 25 seconds of available eye-tracking data only improved the data marginally, while 10 seconds lead to a noticeable decline in prediction error up to a NRMSE of 0.17 [8].

In addition to aesthetic, Öder *et al.* [10] demonstrate that it is possible to classify and differentiate between users which have previously visited a website and new visitors. While not directly linked to usability or UX their results show that it is possible to distinguish both groups using Machine Learning. As one of few they also report precision, recall and f-scores in addition to the classical accuracy metric. Their F1-Scores range from 0.382 to 0.836 depending on the task, differentiating between simple browsing and searching tasks [10].

Typical eye-tracking metrics used by the different studies consist of fixations, saccades, blinks and even pupil data [6] [8]. Most of the aforementioned papers use features out of multiple categories, with the majority using at least fixations and saccades. The Machine Learning models also varied from simple k-nearest Neighbors algorithms to random forests, support vector machines and even deep learning approaches [6] [8] [10].

III. Research Questions

The screened literature analyzes websites in many different ways, often focusing on specific partial aspects, such as usage intention, visual appeal, differentiating user groups or even usability as a whole. However, they show two severe shortcomings:

First of all, almost none of the papers use their own un-validated questionnaires, readily breaking down the concepts usability and UX. This both makes it difficult to compare individual studies and often fails to depict scientifically accepted UUX models in a broader sense.

Second of all, none of the studies analyze multiple different websites, but rather use eye-tracking as a technology for UUX evaluation with Machine Learning models being used as a tool to analyze the vast and often huge eye-tracking datasets. It remains unclear whether the results reported by the researchers are one-time observations or whether usability and UX can be measured using the same features and Machine Learning models across multiple different websites. For this reason, this paper tries to predict both dimensions using three different websites within the same domain. Further details about the study design and the used labels can be found in Section IV.

Having addressed this current research gap this papers aims at filling the gap regarding these gaps in the research area of machine-learning-based UUX predictions using eye-tracking data. To do so, the following three Research Questions (RQ) and corresponding Hypotheses (H) are presented:

RQ1 How much hyperparameter tuning do ML models require to optimize classification performance based on eye-tracking data?
RQ2 Which Machine Learning models are most suited for predicting UUX using only eye-tracking metrics?
RQ3 How do the Machine Learning predictions differ for usability and UX?
H1 ML models trained on comparatively small datasets, require fewer hyperparameter adjustments to reach near-optimal classification performance.
H2 More complex models, such as neural networks are better in detecting patterns in the eye-tracking data compared to more simpler models, such as decision-tree-based approaches.
H3 The ML models can classify usability more accurately compared to UX.

The selection of the Machine Learning models used in this study - consisting of a k-nearest Neighbors (KNN) algorithm, a Support Vector Machine (SVM), a Multi-Layer Perceptron (MLP), a Random Forest (RF), Gradient Boosting (GB) and Adaptive Boosting (ADA) — was guided by existing literature, with these models being commonly employed in similar studies. It is worth mentioning that there are many other types of ML algorithms available, which are out of scope for this study.

IV. Study Design

This eye-tracking study examines three websites from German drinking water and non-alcoholic beverage manufacturers, selected to represent varying design quality and UX levels. Similar to a study conducted by Hassenzahl *et al.* who uses websites from liquor brands [11], water producers were chosen as a more neutral topic, avoiding biases and influences by factors, such as religious views. All sites were fully interactive and pre-downloaded to ensure consistent content during the recording session.

During the study participants completed tasks of varying difficulty, including finding company founding dates or drink ingredients, with the intent of ensuring varying usability ratings. Each participant had 30 seconds to explore the site freely, followed by a three-minute task. If completed early, they continued browsing to ensure sufficient eye-tracking data. Tasks and questionnaires were mouse-only to keep participants focused on the screen.

A. Usability and UX Questionnaires

As previously mentioned, this paper aims to address usability and UX from a general perspective. These two dimensions are typically measured using questionnaires, with the User Experience Questionnaire (UEQ) and AttrakDiff being the most commonly used in the research field [2]. Both are based on Hassenzahl *et al.*'s model of Pragmatic (also referred to as Ergonomic) and Hedonic Quality. According to this model, a software's appeal is determined by its Pragmatic Quality (PQ), which represents usability, and its Hedonic Quality (HQ), which reflects user experience.

Both the UEQ and AttrakDiff assess usability and UX using bipolar word pairs, such as "boring" and "exciting" on a seven-point Likert scale. As the full versions with 26 and 28 pairs would have made the study too long, their validated short versions with 8 pairs each were used to keep the eye-tracking session manageable.

B. Participants

In total, 104 participant took part in the study, with 43.3% identifying as female ($n = 45$) and 56.7% as male ($n = 59$). Among them, 35.6% ($n = 37$) wore glasses or contact lenses during the study. The average age at the time of the study was 29.4 years ($min = 18$, $max = 67$, $sd = 11.18$).

Regarding education, 57 participants were students, 38 were employees or self-employed, two were retired, and one selected *other*. Among the students, five were also working at least part-time and were therefore counted in both the student and employed categories. Further looking at work experience, 31 participants had less than one year of full-time work experience, 19 had one to two years, 25 had two to five years, 10 had five to ten years, and 19 had more than ten years of experience.

C. Eye-Tracking Setup and Data Collection

The study was conducted using Tobii Pro Lab software (Version 1.232.52758) with up to nine mobile Tobii Pro Fusion eye-trackers operating simultaneously. The eye-trackers recorded at 250 Hz (Firmware Version D3417769DB, Driver Version: 2.10.7.0) and were attached to a 21-inch Full-HD (1920×1080) monitor with a 60 Hz refresh rate. Participants were positioned approximately 65 cm from the screen and instructed to remain still during the study. Whenever possible, direct light was minimized by turning off the ceiling lights and closing the blinds. These methodological choices align with the recommendations of Ezer *et al.* [12] [13].

All participants were briefed and signed a consent form approved by the Joint Ethics Committee of the Bavarian Universities (GEHBa). Participation was voluntary, and anonymous identifiers were used to ensure data privacy. To further maintain data quality, two quality thresholds were specified: a calibration threshold of 0.75, based on prior Tobii Pro Fusion studies [14], with participants excluded if unmet, and a missing data threshold excluding stimuli with over 5 % missing data.

V. Eye Movement Metrics

This section provides an overview of common eye movement metrics and explains how they can be utilized as Machine Learning features for data-driven UUX predictions.

Fixation duration: A fixation is defined as an eye movement where the eye is relatively still for a period of time. The fixation duration describes the time in milliseconds for how long the fixation lasts [15, pp. 526-527].

K-Nearest Fixations: Some UUX studies also explore more complex fixation metrics, such as k-nearest fixations [16]. This concept is typically used for calculating saliency maps and determining the probability that a random fixation falls within a specific area [17], [18]. In this study, k-nearest fixations are not calculated in relation to predefined areas but rather to other fixations, with the goal of identifying spatially more closely viewed areas, as suggested by Yin *et al.*

Fixation Grid: This metric calculates the distribution of total fixations on a stimulus across 50 uniform areas of the screen. These areas are created by placing a 10x5 grid - roughly based on the screen ratio - over the stimulus. Each area on the stimulus can then be assigned a percentage of the fixations it contains, both in relation to the total fixation count as well as fixation duration [19].

Saccade Length: Saccade length is the distance of a saccade from its start to end point [15, p. 448]. The distances between fixations are a coarse approximation of saccade lengths. As done in this study, they are typically calculated as the Euclidean distance between fixation points [15, p. 448]. However, it is worth mentioning that also other implementations, such as the length of the saccade polyline, exist [15, pp. 447-448].

Saccade Velocity: This metric describes the average velocity of a saccade. It can be seen as an approximation of the first derivative of gaze position data with respect to time. [15, p. 463] In this paper, it is calculated by dividing the saccade length by the duration of the corresponding saccade.

Saccade Direction: The saccade direction describes the angle between a saccade and the horizontal axis in the coordinate system of the stimulus. Hereby, the saccade direction represents an idealistic straight line from the start to the end point of a saccade. It does not account for the curvatures of saccades [15, pp. 440-441].

NGRAMs: Similar to k-nearest fixations, NGRAMs represent a more complex saccade metric that quantifies saccade sequences by encoding their direction and length as upper- and lowercase character sequences. To achieve this, all possible saccade directions are divided into eight sections (see Figure 1), with the lowercase letter threshold set to the $Q_{0.25}$ for saccade length based on all saccades of the respective participant on that stimulus. The resulting strings are then transformed into Machine Learning features by extracting all recurring sequences using a sliding window approach, which counts the occurrences of each sequence. This procedure is illustrated in Figure 2. For this study, the sliding window was set to a size of two characters. However, both the window size and the number of sections can be adjusted arbitrarily, with more sections requiring a higher total number of saccades to ensure adequate sequence distribution.

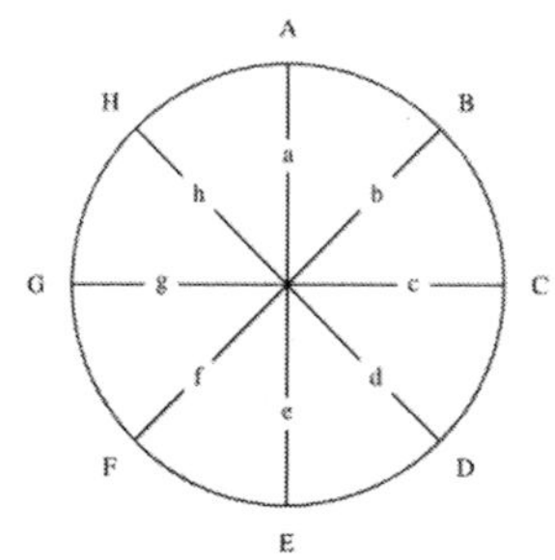

Figure 1. NGRAM Sections; Adaption based on the concept of Bulling *et al.* [20].

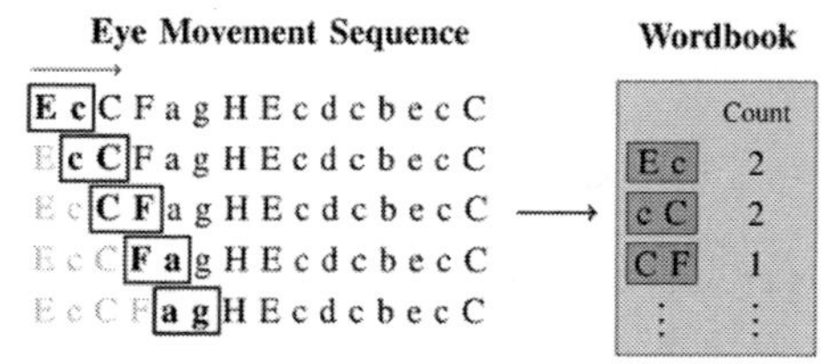

Figure 2. NGRAM to feature conversion; Visulization based on Bulling *et al.* [20].

VI. Data Preparation

Before training the Machine Learning models, the aforementioned eye-tracking metrics were transformed into features. This step, known as feature engineering, is crucial as it aggregates the (semi-)raw data consisting of multiple eye movements into a structured format that Machine Learning models can more easily process to make predictions. Feature engineering typically involves different forms of data representation, such as distributions, vectors, or other aggregation methods [21, pp. 21–25]. Afterwards, correlation-based feature selection was applied to make the dataset more interpretable for ML models, as suggested by Hall [22]:

$$\text{Merit}_s = \frac{k \cdot \overline{r_{cf}}}{\sqrt{k + k(k-1) \cdot \overline{r_{ff}}}}$$

where k is the number of selected features, $\overline{r_{cf}}$ is the average feature-class correlation and $\overline{r_{ff}}$ is the average feature-feature correlation. This merit ensures that only features with a high class- and low inter-feature-correlation remain in the final dataset [22]. Afterwards all features were normalized using a Standard Scaler.

A. Labels

To assess whether Machine Learning can distinguish between low and high UUX ratings, the seven-point Likert scale was split into two classes: < 4 (low) and > 4 (high). Neutral ratings ($= 4$) were excluded to ensure a clear separation between groups. Table VI-A summarizes the final class distributions.

TABLE I. CLASS DISTRIBUTIONS FOR WEBSITES AND LABELS.

Label	Website 1		Website 2		Website 3	
	< 4	> 4	< 4	> 4	< 4	> 4
PQ UEQ	23	65	33	56	14	77
PQ AttrakDiff	22	67	28	58	13	81
HQ UEQ	55	26	50	36	13	91
HQ AttrakDiff	39	47	39	47	7	81

While the first two websites show rather balanced classes, Website 3 deviates notably, especially in Hedonic Quality based on the AttrakDiff Questionnaire. This will be discussed further in Section VIII.

VII. MACHINE LEARNING MODEL EVALUATION

Various metrics can be used to assess the classification performance of Machine Learning algorithms. These metrics allow not only for the comparison of different algorithms but also for the evaluation of the same algorithm under varying hyperparameter settings. In the following subsections, the F1 score is introduced as a key evaluation metric, followed by an exploration of different approaches to hyperparameter tuning.

A. Evaluation Metrics

For two-class problems, multiple metrics can be used to quantify the classification performance of algorithms. Metrics, such as accuracy, precision, F1-score, Cohen's Kappa, and Matthew's Correlation Coefficient, among others, are suitable for this purpose [23] [24]. However, in the present work, we utilize the F1-score as a performance measure, as it is the most commonly used metric [25]. It can be calculated following [26] as:

$$\text{F1-Score} = \frac{2 \cdot TP}{2 \cdot TP + FP + FN}$$

where TP, FP, and FN represent the number of true positive, false positive, and false negative predictions, respectively. The higher the F1-score, the better the classification performance, with F1-score $\in [0; 1]$.

B. Hyperparameter Tuning of the ML Models

Unlike model parameters, which are learned during training, hyperparameters are predefined and remain unchanged throughout the learning process. Thus, it is essential to optimize these hyperparameters in order to improve the classification performance. Several approaches exist for hyperparameter tuning, like random search, grid search, and Bayesian optimization:

Grid Search: Grid search employs a brute-force method for model selection through cross-validation. It systematically explores predefined sets of hyperparameter values, training a model for each combination. The model achieving the highest performance score is chosen as the optimal one. [27, pp. 210-211]

Random Search: An alternative to grid search's exhaustive search is selecting a fixed number of random hyperparameter combinations from user-defined parameter ranges. This method, known as randomized search, samples hyperparameter values randomly and without replacement for the provided distribution. [27, pp. 212-213]

Bayesian Search: Bayesian search works similarly to random search in that it also relies on a fixed number of iterations rather than evaluating all possible parameter combinations. However, instead of selecting parameters completely at random, it considers past classification performance to guide future selections. It chooses hyperparameters based on expected improvement or the upper Gaussian confidence bound, focusing on well performing hyperparameter ranges within the provided search space. By doing so, Bayesian search refines the parameter range iteratively, potentially leading to more efficient optimization requiring fewer iterations. [28] [29]

Since the number of hyperparameters varies between models and no universally applicable set of hyperparameters exists, this paper utilizes only random and Bayesian search to optimize the Machine Learning models. The effectiveness of both approaches is compared in the next section.

VIII. RESULTS

Starting with RQ1, the focus is first set on optimizing the Machine Learning models, specifically analyzing the convergence of F1-scores over time when comparing random search and Bayesian search. It is essential to differentiate between these two approaches, as Bayesian search by default is set to have fewer iterations [29]. To account for this discrepancy, all models were optimized using 100, 500, 1,000, 2,500, and 5,000 iterations for random search, while 10, 50, 100, 150, and 250 iterations were used for Bayesian search. The chosen scaling increases steeply to illustrate F1-score development in relation to computational complexity.

The detailed results of both search methods are presented in Table II and visualized in Figure 3, with iteration as 1 representing a completely untrained model.

Both show that the two optimization approaches generally yield similar final results, with F1-scores increasing sharply at the beginning of the optimization process before gradually plateauing as the number of iterations grows. Examining individual models, Figure 3 reveals a clear trend: models with fewer hyperparameters to tune — such as KNN, SVM, MLP, and ADA — tend to reach an optimization ceiling earlier, with only marginal improvements beyond a certain point. Between 1,000 and 5,000 iterations for random search and 100 and 250 iterations for Bayesian search, these four models show only slight F1-score improvements, ranging from 0.5 % for KNN to 0.9 % for AdaBoost.

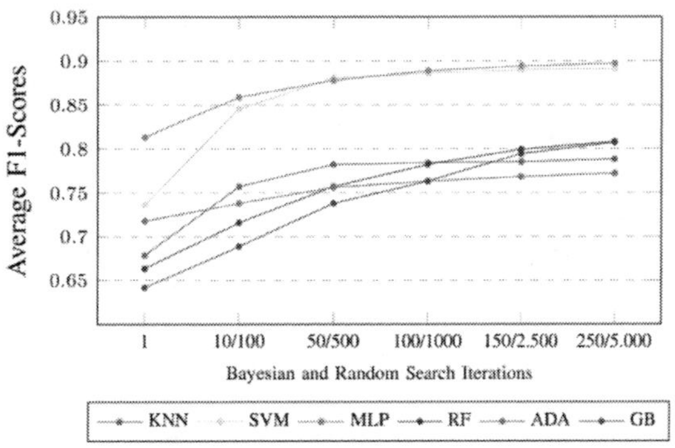

Figure 3. Average F1-Score Development of all Machine Learning Models with increasing Hyperparameter Tuning Iterations based on all websites and labels.

In contrast, algorithms with a larger hyperparameter space, such as Random Forest and Gradient Boosting, continue to show notable improvements even beyond 100/1,000 iterations. The F1-score for Random Forest improved by an average of 2.6 % exceeding these iterations, while Gradient Boosting sees an even greater gain of 4.4 % over the same range. A more detailed view in Figure 4 shows that these gains are particularly pronounced for Bayesian search, which outperforms random search by 2.4 % for the Random Forest and 4.8 % for the Gradient Boosting model. This is likely due to the higher inter-dependencies within the larger hyperparameter space, which are more effectively aligned by Bayesian optimization than by random sampling.

While this effect is primarily evident for Random Forest and Gradient Boosting, Bayesian search also slightly outperforms random search on average across all models (see Figure 5). However, the difference between the two approaches is most pronounced at lower iteration counts, particularly for fewer than 1.000 iterations in random search.

Following up with RQ2, a clear trend emerges when analyzing the performance of different Machine Learning models across all three websites. Figures 6, 7, and 8 present the F1-scores for all models and the four

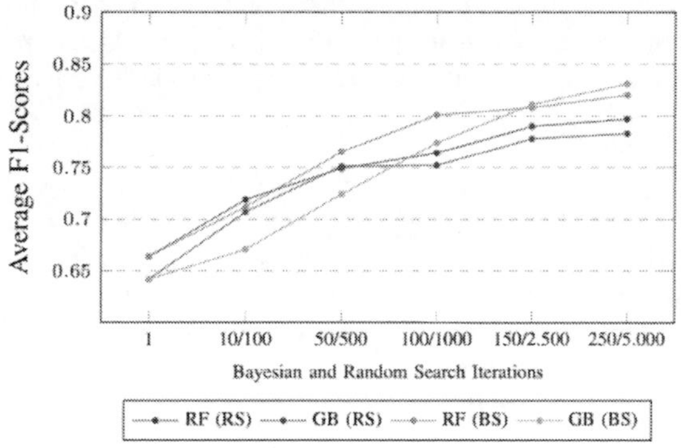

Figure 4. Average F1-Score Development of the Random Forest (RF) and the Gradient Boosting Model (RB) comparing Random Search (RS) and Bayesian Search (BS) based on all websites and labels.

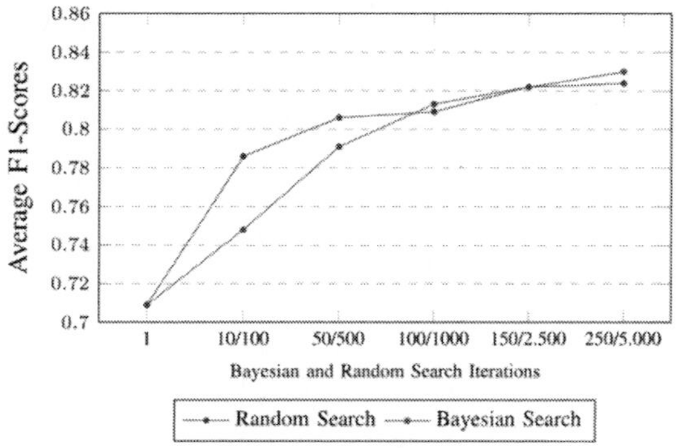

Figure 5. Average F1-Score Development comparing Random and Bayesian Search based on all Machine Learning models, websites and labels.

classification labels across all three websites. Regardless of the website, the SVM and the MLP stand out, as they consistently achieve F1-scores close to or above 90%. On the first two websites, MLP outperforms SVM, though at times only by a negligible lead. However, on the third website, SVM takes the lead, with MLP following closely behind, showing a similar performance trend across all labels.

The three tree-based models — Random Forest, AdaBoost, and Gradient Boosting — demonstrate comparable performance, with Random Forest generally achieving the highest F1-scores out of the three Machine Learning models. Nevertheless, there are exceptions: for the UEQ Pragmatic Quality label on Website 1 and both Pragmatic Quality labels on Website 3, Gradient Boosting outperforms Random Forest by 5.8 % and 5.9 %, respectively. Aside from these cases, Random Forest maintains a slight advantage. Among the tree-based models, AdaBoost consistently underperforms compared to both Random Forest and Gradient Boosting.

Lastly, the k-nearest Neighbor (KNN) algorithm shows inconsistent classification performance across all

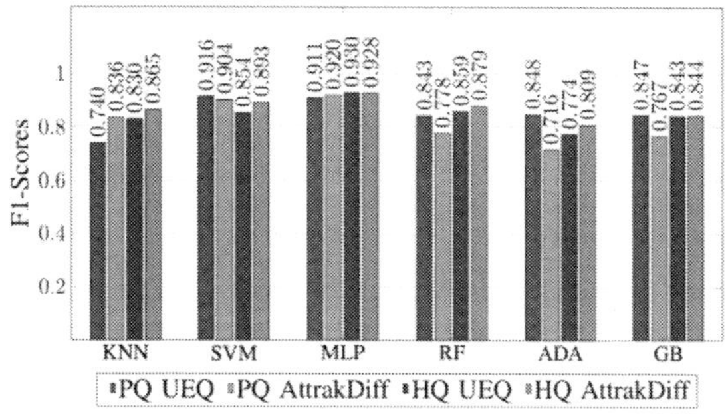

Figure 6. F1-Scores of all Machine Learning Models for the Labels on Website 1.

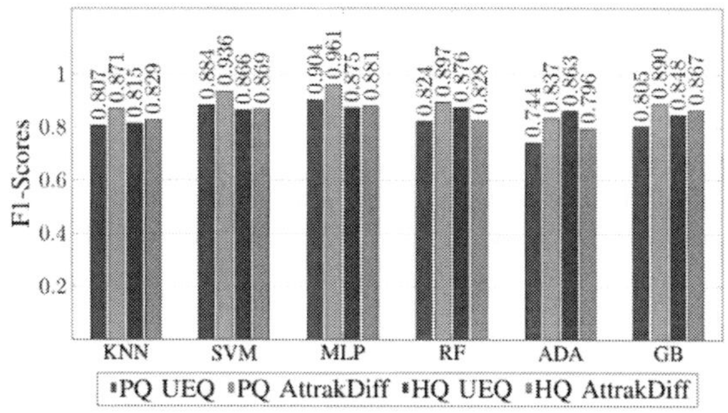

Figure 7. F1-Scores of all Machine Learning Models for the Labels on Website 2.

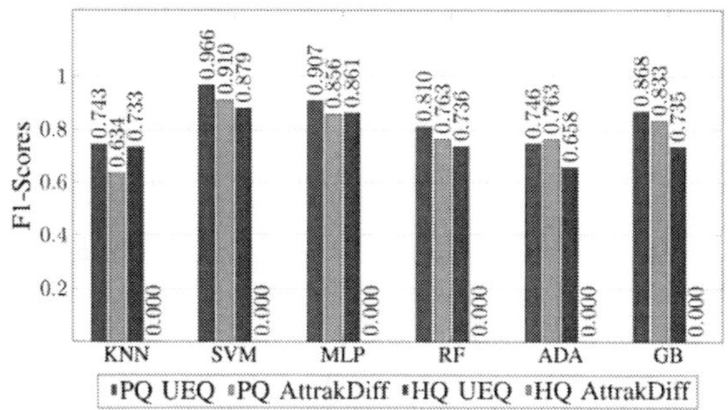

Figure 8. F1-Scores of all Machine Learning Models for the Labels on Website 3.

labels. While it occasionally outperforms the tree-based models, such as for the AttrakDiff Pragmatic Quality label on Website 1, it falls behind in most cases, achieving the lowest F1-scores in four out of eleven labels.

Considering these results, H2 cannot be refuted, as the more complex MLP model frequently outperforms the other models. Yet, in general, both MLP and SVM prove to be adequate choices for classifying participants' UUX ratings based on eye movement data. In contrast, KNN and AdaBoost perform the worst in this study, likely due to their simpler evaluation mechanisms, which rely on spatial distances between data points or single parameter thresholds within individual features (decision stumps). This suggests that while these models can differentiate UUX labels to some degree, more eye movement features are needed at a time to effectively differentiate between the UUX labels.

RQ3 shifts the focus from the performance of the individual models to the broader question of whether usability (Pragmatic Quality) and UX (Hedonic Quality) labels, as defined by the UEQ and AttrakDiff questionnaires, can be reliably predicted. Averaging the F1-scores across all Machine Learning models shows similar results compared to the individual websites including both questionnaires. Thus, proofing their ability to classify the UUX ratings accurately (see Figure 9).

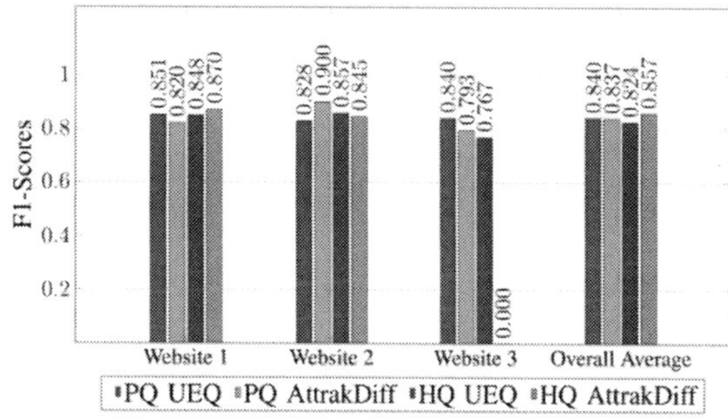

Figure 9. Average F1-Scores of all Machine Learning Models by Websites and Labels.

However, when examining the two questionnaires in detail, some differences emerge across websites. For example, on Website 2, the Pragmatic Quality label from the AttrakDiff questionnaire (89.9 %) was predicted with an average F1-score 7.1 % higher than that of the UEQ (82.8 %). In contrast, on Website 3, this trend reverses, with the UEQ Pragmatic Quality label (83.8 %) outperforming the AttrakDiff (79.3 %) equivalent by 4.7 %. This suggests that the predictability of the two questionnaires may change depending on the underlying stimuli and, therefore, changing eye movement patterns.

However, when averaging results across all websites, these differences become minimal, as shown in Figure 9. For Pragmatic Quality, the difference in classification performance between the questionnaires is only 0.2 %. Although the difference for Hedonic Quality is larger at 3.3 %, it's important to note that AttrakDiff's Hedonic Quality could not be calculated for Website 3 — where all models performed worse overall — due to too few data points. Assuming Website 3 would have followed the same trend as the other sites, Hedonic Quality predictions are likely to even out as well. This is supported by results from Websites 1 and 2, where Hedonic Quality scores between UEQ and AttrakDiff differ by just 0.5 %.

Due to this limitation, H3 can neither be rejected nor supported. Following the aforementioned assumption, both usability (Pragmatic Quality) and UX (Hedonic

Quality) can be classified with nearly identical certainty. Although UX predictions are slightly less accurate than usability predictions, the difference is too small to draw definite conclusions about whether this is a generalizable finding or simply a study-specific artifact. To answer this question, more websites would have to be included in the study.

IX. Summary of results

This study showed that usability (Pragmatic Quality) and UX (Hedonic Quality), as defined by the UEQ and AttrakDiff, can be effectively predicted using Machine Learning models trained solely on eye-movement features. Comparing random and Bayesian hyperparameter tuning, both approaches produced similar results, though tree-based models particularly benefited from Bayesian search, likely due to their complex hyperparameter space. However, performance gains across all models plateaued — around 150 iterations for Bayesian search and 2,500 for random search.

Among all models, the SVM and MLP performed the best, consistently reaching F1-scores in the 90 % range, reaching these scores with even minimal hyperparameter tuning. Out of the tree-based models, Random Forest performs best, followed by Gradient Boosting, while AdaBoost and KNN show the lowest classification performance.

Finally, comparing UEQ and AttrakDiff reveals no differences in predictive performance. Both usability and UX are equally predictable from eye-tracking data, regardless of which questionnaire is used, with average results across all labels and websites showing negligible differences.

X. Limitations

This study has two main limitations. First, it is difficult to determine whether random or Bayesian hyperparameter tuning is superior, as both methods would likely converge to similar results over more iterations. Thus, this comparison should be seen as a general guideline rather than a strict conclusion, particularly for similar eye-tracking datasets. Its applicability to other datasets remains to be tested.

Second, the size of the dataset raises the question of whether the amount of collected data is sufficient. This is a common challenge in eye-tracking research, as data collection is both time-consuming and complex. However, this study includes a relatively large participant pool and diverse stimuli compared to similar studies. Future research could strengthen these findings by incorporating more participants and websites.

Additionally, class imbalances in the dataset may have influenced classification performance. As noted in Section VII, using additional metrics, such as Cohen's Kappa or Matthew's Correlation Coefficient alongside the F1-score would provide a more comprehensive evaluation of model performance in handling imbalanced data.

XI. Conclusion and Future Work

This paper contributes to the growing field of data-driven UUX research based on eye-tracking, demonstrating within a broader context what previous studies have shown in more narrow use cases: both usability and UX, as defined by commonly used UUX questionnaires, such as the UEQ and AttrakDiff, can be predicted by training Machine Learning models on eye movement data. The findings suggest that this predictability is not limited to a single product but extends across a range of similar digital products within the same domain. This supports the assumption that specific eye movement patterns are systematically linked to participants' perception of a product's usability and UX.

Building on these findings, future studies could explore several aspects of UUX. One next step could include a broader range of websites to further test the generalizability of eye-tracking-based UUX predictions. Another key question is whether trained Machine Learning models can identify patterns across multiple websites rather than being limited to one. If so, datasets could be expanded by aggregating data from different websites, improving both hyperparameter tuning and prediction robustness.

Additionally, the labels could be examined in more detail. This study classified only between low and high UUX ratings. Future research should explore whether models can distinguish between low, neutral, and high scores, moving beyond binary classification. Success in this area could enable regression models to predict continuous UUX scores, allowing for more nuanced assessments of usability and UX.

Despite these opportunities for future work, the present results are already highly promising, with the highest F1-scores among existing literature in this research field.

Acknowledgments

This study was conducted as part of the EDIH *Digital Innovation Ostbayern (DInO)*, which is funded by the European Union and the European Funds for Regional Development (EFRE) (References: 101083427 and 20-3092.10-THD-105) as well as by the 'German Federal Ministry of Education and Research' (BMBF) through the granting of the 'Bavarian State Budget' (ZD.B) (FKZ: 16-1541).

The study was approved by the Joint Ethics Committee of the Bavarian Universities (GEHBa) (Reference: GEHBa-202312-V-155-R).

We acknowledge the use of DeepL Write (DeepL SE, https://www.deepl.com/write) and ChatGPT (OpenAI,

TABLE II. OVERVIEW OF F1-SCORES FOR ALL MODELS, WEBSITES, LABELS, AND HYPERPARAMETER OPTIMIZATION METHODS. F1-SCORES THAT NO LONGER SHOW IMPROVEMENT ARE GRAYED OUT. THE BEST RESULTS ARE MARKED BASED ON THE OPTIMIZATION METHOD THAT ACHIEVED THE HIGHEST SCORE: RS = RANDOM SEARCH, BS = BAYESIAN SEARCH, X = IDENTICAL RESULTS.

Website	Label	Algorithm	Untrained Model	Random Search (RS)					Bayesian Search (BS)					Best Result
				100	500	1.000	2.500	5.000	10	50	100	150	250	
Website 1	PQ UEQ	KNN	0.664	0.699	0.723	0.723	0.734	0.740	0.684	0.723	0.723	0.723	0.723	0.740 (RS)
		SVM	0.720	0.905	0.905	0.916	0.916	0.916	0.916	0.916	0.916	0.916	0.916	**0.916 (X)**
		MLP	0.799	0.890	0.897	0.897	0.897	0.897	0.872	0.897	0.911	0.911	0.911	0.9111 (BS)
		RF	0.644	0.736	0.736	0.750	0.792	0.823	0.763	0.769	0.823	0.843	0.843	0.843 (BS)
		ADA	0.742	0.808	0.822	0.822	0.848	0.848	0.799	0.799	0.811	0.811	0.811	0.848 (RS
		GB	0.593	0.755	0.807	0.807	0.807	0.807	0.745	0.757	0.794	0.847	0.847	0.847 (BS)
	PQ AttrakDiff	KNN	0.701	0.831	0.831	0.836	0.836	0.836	0.779	0.831	0.831	0.831	0.831	0.836 (RS)
		SVM	0.737	0.900	0.900	0.900	0.900	0.904	0.855	0.855	0.904	0.904	0.904	0.904 (X)
		MLP	0.853	0.919	0.919	0.919	0.920	0.920	0.851	0.887	0.906	0.906	0.919	**0.920 (RS)**
		RF	0.663	0.666	0.744	0.744	0.762	0.762	0.684	0.723	0.778	0.778	0.778	0.778 (BS)
		ADA	0.713	0.702	0.716	0.716	0.716	0.716	0.698	0.698	0.713	0.713	0.716	0.716 (X)
		GB	0.582	0.702	0.702	0.702	0.716	0.731	0.680	0.680	0.742	0.767	0.767	0.767 (BS)
	HQ UEQ	KNN	0.693	0.778	0.830	0.830	0.830	0.830	0.774	0.830	0.830	0.830	0.830	0.830 (X)
		SVM	0.800	0.837	0.854	0.854	0.854	0.854	0.822	0.837	0.842	0.854	0.854	0.854 (X)
		MLP	0.889	0.907	0.915	0.930	0.930	0.930	0.835	0.838	0.869	0.881	0.895	**0.930 (RS)**
		RF	0.708	0.748	0.764	0.816	0.832	0.832	0.784	0.784	0.849	0.851	0.859	0.859 (BS)
		ADA	0.718	0.745	0.770	0.770	0.772	0.774	0.745	0.759	0.759	0.770	0.770	0.774 (RS)
		GB	0.617	0.764	0.812	0.812	0.826	0.826	0.675	0.811	0.819	0.819	0.843	0.843 (BS)
	HQ AttrakDiff	KNN	0.769	0.865	0.865	0.865	0.865	0.865	0.821	0.865	0.865	0.865	0.865	0.865 (X)
		SVM	0.858	0.892	0.892	0.892	0.893	0.893	0.812	0.881	0.881	0.881	0.881	0.893 (RS)
		MLP	0.893	0.917	0.927	0.928	0.928	0.928	0.880	0.893	0.917	0.917	0.928	**0.928 (X)**
		RF	0.743	0.715	0.775	0.775	0.801	0.814	0.737	0.802	0.868	0.868	0.879	0.879 (BS)
		ADA	0.719	0.773	0.809	0.809	0.809	0.809	0.771	0.784	0.795	0.795	0.798	0.809 (RS)
		GB	0.742	0.729	0.751	0.751	0.805	0.805	0.642	0.739	0.832	0.844	0.844	0.844 (BS)
Website 2	PQ UEQ	KNN	0.690	0.793	0.807	0.807	0.807	0.807	0.755	0.755	0.788	0.788	0.793	0.807 (RS)
		SVM	0.800	0.865	0.884	0.884	0.884	0.884	0.800	0.884	0.884	0.884	0.884	0.884 (X)
		MLP	0.874	0.874	0.888	0.888	0.904	0.904	0.847	0.871	0.874	0.874	0.888	**0.904 (RS)**
		RF	0.711	0.730	0.758	0.769	0.792	0.792	0.708	0.772	0.777	0.794	0.824	0.824 (BS)
		ADA	0.725	0.738	0.741	0.744	0.744	0.744	0.713	0.738	0.738	0.738	0.738	0.744 (RS)
		GB	0.663	0.729	0.738	0.740	0.788	0.795	0.692	0.732	0.732	0.752	0.805	0.805 (BS)
	PQ AttrakDiff	KNN	0.708	0.871	0.871	0.871	0.871	0.871	0.861	0.871	0.871	0.871	0.871	0.871 (X)
		SVM	0.766	0.934	0.934	0.934	0.934	0.936	0.843	0.914	0.914	0.916	0.916	0.936 (RS)
		MLP	0.922	0.961	0.961	0.961	0.961	0.961	0.838	0.917	0.961	0.961	0.961	**0.961 (X)**
		RF	0.755	0.826	0.826	0.826	0.862	0.862	0.749	0.785	0.861	0.882	0.897	0.897 (BS)
		ADA	0.795	0.798	0.798	0.803	0.809	0.835	0.767	0.795	0.835	0.837	0.837	0.837 (BS)
		GB	0.805	0.746	0.815	0.815	0.855	0.855	0.635	0.742	0.797	0.863	0.890	0.890 (BS)
	HQ UEQ	KNN	0.755	0.815	0.815	0.815	0.815	0.815	0.776	0.815	0.815	0.815	0.815	0.815 (RS)
		SVM	0.772	0.848	0.866	0.866	0.866	0.866	0.735	0.865	0.865	0.866	0.866	0.866 (RS)
		MLP	0.823	0.856	0.874	0.874	0.874	0.875	0.784	0.848	0.857	0.857	0.874	**0.875 (RS)**
		RF	0.741	0.672	0.742	0.807	0.814	0.818	0.682	0.844	0.844	0.844	0.876	0.876 (BS)
		ADA	0.818	0.850	0.852	0.852	0.852	0.852	0.804	0.850	0.850	0.863	0.863	0.863 (BS)
		GB	0.769	0.746	0.796	0.796	0.817	0.817	0.698	0.713	0.809	0.841	0.848	0.848 (BS)
	HQ AttrakDiff	KNN	0.757	0.829	0.829	0.829	0.829	0.829	0.779	0.803	0.803	0.803	0.803	0.829 (RS)
		SVM	0.821	0.845	0.857	0.857	0.857	0.869	0.795	0.834	0.834	0.834	0.845	0.869 (RS)
		MLP	0.846	0.868	0.880	0.880	0.880	0.880	0.843	0.843	0.880	0.880	0.881	**0.881 (BS)**
		RF	0.723	0.751	0.750	0.751	0.783	0.783	0.720	0.752	0.792	0.809	0.828	0.828 (BS)
		ADA	0.722	0.770	0.775	0.782	0.782	0.796	0.737	0.768	0.768	0.768	0.768	0.796 (RS)
		GB	0.615	0.699	0.776	0.776	0.779	0.779	0.651	0.768	0.811	0.867	0.867	0.867 (BS)
Website 3	PQ UEQ	KNN	0.584	0.741	0.741	0.741	0.743	0.743	0.631	0.739	0.741	0.743	0.743	0.743 (BS)
		SVM	0.584	0.932	0.947	0.952	0.966	0.966	0.810	0.947	0.966	0.966	0.966	**0.966 (X)**
		MLP	0.584	0.891	0.907	0.907	0.907	0.907	0.818	0.838	0.854	0.874	0.874	0.907 (RS)
		RF	0.547	0.742	0.795	0.795	0.795	0.795	0.672	0.797	0.797	0.797	0.810	0.810 (BS)
		ADA	0.689	0.742	0.746	0.746	0.746	0.746	0.689	0.746	0.746	0.746	0.746	0.746 (X)
		GB	0.540	0.669	0.762	0.762	0.778	0.781	0.756	0.756	0.798	0.815	0.868	0.868 (BS)
	PQ AttrakDiff	KNN	0.583	0.632	0.634	0.634	0.634	0.634	0.609	0.634	0.634	0.634	0.634	0.634 (X)
		SVM	0.675	0.890	0.890	0.910	0.910	0.910	0.764	0.877	0.877	0.877	0.877	**0.910 (RS)**
		MLP	0.730	0.848	0.848	0.848	0.856	0.856	0.820	0.832	0.832	0.832	0.832	0.856 (RS)
		RF	0.559	0.658	0.679	0.679	0.763	0.763	0.638	0.691	0.691	0.691	0.691	0.763 (RS)
		ADA	0.568	0.711	0.763	0.763	0.763	0.763	0.691	0.712	0.712	0.712	0.744	0.763 (RS)
		GB	0.553	0.674	0.674	0.674	0.711	0.730	0.582	0.646	0.667	0.793	0.833	0.833 (BS)
	HQ UEQ	KNN	0.569	0.669	0.718	0.718	0.733	0.733	0.666	0.669	0.669	0.669	0.733	0.733 (X)
		SVM	0.569	0.826	0.826	0.826	0.879	0.879	0.770	0.810	0.810	0.821	0.821	**0.879 (RS)**
		MLP	0.729	0.841	0.841	0.841	0.861	0.861	0.736	0.794	0.822	0.855	0.855	0.861 (RS)
		RF	0.516	0.667	0.667	0.691	0.697	0.719	0.696	0.696	0.729	0.729	0.736	0.736 (BS)
		ADA	0.687	0.595	0.599	0.599	0.658	0.658	0.580	0.590	0.652	0.652	0.652	0.658 (RS)
		GB	0.585	0.567	0.633	0.633	0.670	0.688	0.624	0.624	0.718	0.718	0.735	0.735 (BS)
	HQ AttrakDiff	—	—	—	—	—	—	—	—	—	—	—	—	—

GPT-4, https://chatgpt.com/) to assist in the formulation of this document. These tools were used only for language refinement or during the coding processes, not to generate content or ideas. Those originated solely from the authors or are based on the cited literature.

DATA

If you have any questions regarding the dataset, eye movement metric calculations or the python sklearn Machine Learning implementation, feel free to contact Fabian Engl using the contact information provided.

REFERENCES

[1] M. Hassenzahl, A. Platz, M. Burmester, and K. Lehner, "Hedonic and *ergonomic quality aspects determine a software's appeal*," en, in *Proceedings of the SIGCHI conference on Human Factors in Computing Systems*, ACM, Apr. 2000, pp. 201–208.

[2] E. Mortazavi, P. Doyon-Poulin, D. Imbeau, M. Taraghi, and J.-M. Robert, "Exploring the landscape of ux subjective evaluation tools and ux dimensions: A systematic literature review (2010–2021)," *Interacting with Computers*, vol. 36, no. 4, pp. 255–278, 2024.

[3] J. Š. Novák, J. Masner, P. Benda, P. Šimek, and V. Merunka, "Eye tracking, usability, and user experience: A systematic review," *International Journal of Human–Computer Interaction*, vol. 40, no. 17, pp. 4484–4500, 2024.

[4] R. Zemblys, D. C. Niehorster, and K. Holmqvist, "Gazenet: End-to-end eye-movement event detection with deep neural networks," *Behavior Research Methods*, vol. 51, no. 2, pp. 840–864, Apr. 2019.

[5] K. Koonsanit, T. Tsunajima, and N. Nishiuchi, "Evaluation of strong and weak signifiers in a web interface using eye-tracking heatmaps and machine learning," in *Computer Information Systems and Industrial Management*, K. Saeed and J. Dvorský, Eds., Cham: Springer International Publishing, 2021, pp. 203–213.

[6] Y. Cao *et al.*, "Detecting users' usage intentions for websites employing deep learning on eye-tracking data," *Information Technology and Management*, vol. 22, no. 4, pp. 281–292, Dec. 1, 2021.

[7] P. Wang, H. Yang, J. Hou, and Q. Li, "A machine learning approach to primacy-peak-recency effect-based satisfaction prediction," *Information Processing & Management*, vol. 60, no. 2, p. 103 196, Mar. 1, 2023.

[8] I. O. Pappas, K. Sharma, P. Mikalef, and M. N. Giannakos, "How quickly can we predict users' ratings on aesthetic evaluations of websites? employing machine learning on eye-tracking data," in *Responsible Design, Implementation and Use of Information and Communication Technology*, M. Hattingh *et al.*, Eds., Cham: Springer International Publishing, 2020, pp. 429–440.

[9] M. Moshagen and M. T. Thielsch, "Facets of visual aesthetics," *International journal of human-computer studies*, vol. 68, no. 10, pp. 689–709, 2010.

[10] M. Öder, Ş. Eraslan, and Y. Yeslida, "Automatically classifying familiar web users from eye-tracking data: A machine learning approach," *Turkish Journal of Electrical Engineering and Computer Sciences*, vol. 30, no. 1, pp. 233–248, Jan. 1, 2022.

[11] M. Hassenzahl, M. Burmester, and F. Koller, "AttrakDiff: Ein Fragebogen zur Messung wahrgenommener hedonischer und pragmatischer Qualität," de, in *Mensch & Computer 2003: Interaktion in Bewegung*, G. Szwillus and J. Ziegler, Eds., Wiesbaden: Vieweg+Teubner Verlag, 2003, pp. 187–196.

[12] T. Ezer, M. Greiner, L. Grabinger, F. Hauser, and J. Mottok, "Eye tracking as technology in education: Data quality analysis and improvements," in *16th annual International Conference of Education, Research and Innovation*, ser. ICERI 2023, Seville, Spain: IATED, Nov. 2023, pp. 4500–4509.

[13] T. Ezer, L. Grabinger, F. Hauser, S. Staufer, and J. Mottok, "Eye tracking as technology in education: Further investigation of data quality and improvements," in *18th International Technology, Education and Development Conference*, ser. INTED 2024, Valencia, Spain: IATED, Mar. 2024, pp. 2955–2961.

[14] M. Kristen, F. Engl, and J. Mottok, "Enhancing phishing detection: An eye-tracking study on user interaction and oversights in phishing emails," in *SECURWARE 2024, The Eighteenth International Conference on Emerging Security Information, Systems and Technologies*, 2024.

[15] K. Holmqvist, *Eye Tracking: A Comprehensive Guide to Methods and Measures*. Oxford University Press, 2017, pp. 440–527.

[16] Y. Yin, M. P. McGuire, Y. Alqahtani, J. H. Feng, and J. Chakraborty, "Classification of information display types using graph neural networks," in *2023 International Conference on Computational Science and Computational Intelligence (CSCI)*, Dec. 2023, pp. 130–136.

[17] G. Kootstra, B. de Boer, and L. R. Schomaker, "Predicting eye fixations on complex visual stimuli using local symmetry," *Cognitive computation*, vol. 3, pp. 223–240, 2011.

[18] P. Blignaut, "Fixation identification: The optimum threshold for a dispersion algorithm," *Attention, Perception, & Psychophysics*, vol. 71, pp. 881–895, 2009.

[19] M. Millecamp, C. Conati, and K. Verbert, "Classifeye: Classification of personal characteristics based on eye tracking data in a recommender system interface," in *Joint Proceedings of the ACM IUI 2021 Workshops*, CEUR Workshop Proceedings, vol. 2903, 2021.

[20] A. Bulling, J. A. Ward, H. Gellersen, and G. Tröster, "Eye movement analysis for activity recognition using electrooculography," *IEEE transactions on pattern analysis and machine intelligence*, vol. 33, no. 4, pp. 741–753, 2010.

[21] A. Jung, *Machine Learning: The Basics*. Springer Nature, 2022, pp. 21–25.

[22] M. A. Hall, "Correlation-based feature selection for discrete and numeric class machine learning," Ph.D. dissertation, University of Waikato, Department of Computer Science, 1999.

[23] D. Chicco and G. Jurman, "The advantages of the matthews correlation coefficient (mcc) over f1 score and accuracy in binary classification evaluation," *BMC Genomics*, vol. 21, no. 1, p. 6, Jan. 2020.

[24] D. Chicco, M. J. Warrens, and G. Jurman, "The matthews correlation coefficient (mcc) is more informative than cohen's kappa and brier score in binary classification assessment," *IEEE Access*, vol. 9, pp. 78 368–78 381, May 2021.

[25] D. J. Hand, P. Christen, and N. Kirielle, "F*: an interpretable transformation of the f-measure," *Machine Learning*, vol. 110, no. 3, pp. 451–456, 2021.

[26] M. Startsev and R. Zemblys, "Evaluating eye movement event detection: A review of the state of the art," *Behavior Research Methods*, vol. 55, no. 4, pp. 1653–1714, Jun. 2023.

[27] C. Albon, *Python Machine Learning Cookbook: Practical Solutions from Preprocessing to Deep Learning*. 2018, pp. 210–213.

[28] J. Snoek, H. Larochelle, and R. P. Adams, "Practical bayesian optimization of machine learning algorithms," *Advances in Neural Information Processing Systems*, vol. 4, pp. 2951–2959, 2012. arXiv: 1206.2944.

[29] F. Nogueira, *Bayesian Optimization: Open source constrained global optimization tool for Python*, 2014.

Evaluating Diffusion-Based Image Generation for Easy Language Accessibility

Christoph Johannes Weber *†, Dominik Beyer †, Sylvia Rothe *
*University of Television and Film Munich, Munich, Germany
†LMU Munich, Munich, Germany
e-mail: c.weber@hff-muc.de, dominikbeyer711@gmail.com, s.rothe@hff-muc.de,

***Abstract*—Easy Language is a linguistic resource designed to facilitate comprehension for individuals with learning impairments and non-native speakers. Utilizing simplification of text, the restriction of vocabulary, and layout adjustments, Easy Language texts are constructed to ensure accessibility. Furthermore, Easy Language texts have the capacity to incorporate visual aids, such as images or symbols, to enhance comprehension. Although the use of imagery has been shown to improve understanding, it remains unclear whether visuals generated by artificial intelligence (AI) can meet the specific stylistic and semantic requirements of Easy Language. This paper investigates the potential of diffusion-based image generation to address these needs. A Stable Diffusion model was fine-tuned to produce images in a minimal, symbol-like style. Two user studies were conducted to assess the model's ability to replicate a consistent visual style and to determine whether the generated images effectively conveyed the intended meanings. The results show that participants were generally unable to distinguish AI-generated from original symbols and correctly interpreted most of the illustrated concepts. The findings suggest that diffusion models, when properly fine-tuned, are capable of producing illustrations that align with the stylistic conventions and semantic clarity required in Easy Language. However, certain abstract or emotionally nuanced concepts remain challenging to represent accurately. These results indicate that, when guided by stylistic constraints, AI-generated visuals can offer a scalable approach to producing accessible visual content.**

Keywords-image generation; accessibility; easy language.

I. Introduction

Communication is a central aspect of everyday life, whether it is necessary to coordinate daily activities, interact socially, or communicate information to broader audiences. Depending on the context and recipients, the mode and complexity of communication are adapted accordingly. However, in public domains, such as government websites, the audience often includes individuals with various cognitive and linguistic abilities. For this reason, ensuring broad accessibility becomes a key concern.

An approach to making written content more accessible is *Easy Language*, a simplified form of communication designed primarily for people with cognitive or learning difficulties. It is governed by a set of formal rules that emphasize short sentences, familiar vocabulary, and the use of supportive visuals, such as symbols or images [1][2]. According to the cognitive theory of multimedia learning, the combination of verbal and visual information can improve comprehension and reduce cognitive load [3]. However, the visuals used in Easy Language must adhere to strict stylistic conventions: they must be consistent in style, placed near the corresponding text, and avoid redundancy or ambiguity [1].

In practice, creating these images is a complex and iterative process. Translators usually begin by drafting a visual concept for a specific word or phrase. This is given to a designer who produces an initial sketch that is reviewed by a test group, often people with learning difficulties. The image is reviewed multiple times based on user feedback until the intended meaning is clearly understood [4]. While this process ensures clarity, it is time-consuming and may limit the timely dissemination of accessible information.

Previous research has examined the role of visuals in Easy Language using methods, such as comprehension tests [5], eye-tracking [6], and reading speed analysis [7]. These studies have also evaluated different visual formats, from realistic photographs to symbolic representations [8]. However, the potential role of AI in automating this process has not yet been explored.

Recent advances in AI-based image generation, particularly diffusion models, such as Stable Diffusion [9], DALL-E [10][11] or Midjourney [12] have shown that machines can generate visually coherent and stylistically adaptive images based on text prompts. These models can be further fine-tuned to reflect specific visual styles, making them promising candidates for generating accessible visuals. Previous work has shown that some AI-generated images are indistinguishable from real images [13], but their applicability in accessibility contexts, such as Easy Language remains unclear.

This paper investigates whether AI-generated images, produced via a fine-tuned Stable Diffusion model, can support Easy Language communication. Specifically, we assess (1) whether the model can reproduce a consistent visual style aligned with existing symbol sets, and (2) whether the generated images are expressive enough to unambiguously convey intended meanings.

To this end, a Stable Diffusion model was fine-tuned using Low-Rank Adaptation (LoRA) [14] on a minimalist black-and-white pictogram data set derived from Picto-Selector [15]. Two user studies were conducted: one to test style fidelity, the other to evaluate semantic expressiveness. Participants were generally unable to distinguish the AI-generated images from originals and correctly interpreted most of the illustrated concepts.

Our findings suggest that AI-generated imagery, when guided by specific stylistic constraints, can support the goals of Easy Language and may offer a scalable alternative to manual illustration processes.

The remainder of this paper is structured as follows: Section II introduces Easy Language. Section III reviews related work. Section IV describes the model fine-tuning. Section V presents two user studies. Section VI reports the findings. Section VIII discusses future work and concludes.

II. Background

Easy Language emerged as a means to promote inclusion and equal access to information, especially for people with cognitive or learning difficulties. Originating in the 1960s and gaining traction in Germany in the 1990s, it encompasses simplified versions of the standard language [16]. It reduces linguistic complexity through short sentences, simple vocabulary, minimal use of connectors, and the inclusion of images and adjusted layouts [1]. Terms, such as easy-to-read, clear language, or simplified language are often used interchangeably across countries. "Leichte Sprache" is the German adaptation, with this work focusing on its regulations [2][17]. Easy Language is distinct from Plain Language, which is less formalized and aims to reduce stigmatization. An intermediate form, "Easy Language Plus", has also been proposed [18].

Target Groups: Easy Language serves a diverse population, including people with learning disabilities, low literacy, sensory impairments, or those affected by migration [16][19]. However, its implementation varies between countries. While often developed for people with intellectual disabilities, it also benefits those facing temporary or situational communication barriers. Despite its accessibility goals, Easy Language sometimes faces resistance due to its distinct appearance or simplified style, potentially leading to stigmatization or rejection by target users [18]. Therefore, texts should be neutral in tone and format and provided across various media formats, not just online.

Guidelines: Rulebooks for Easy Language differ by country and context. In Germany, the *Netzwerk Leichte Sprache e.V.* and *Duden Leichte Sprache* offer key guidance [2][17]. These include linguistic, textual, and visual rules, often influenced by international frameworks, such as *Inclusion Europe* [20] or the *International Organization for Standardization* (ISO) [21]. Despite wide application, many of these rules lack a scientific basis. Current regulations, such as those defined in the *German web accessibility regulation* (BITV) [22] and in emerging national standards from the German Institute for Standardization (DIN) [23], govern accessibility on official websites. However, inconsistencies and vague formulations in these rulebooks challenge objective evaluation and implementation.

Research: Empirical research on Easy Language remains limited but is growing. Existing studies have evaluated rules through text simplification, word frequency, or visual aids [19][24], but many current guidelines are based on expert opinion rather than data. Research centers, such as the University of Hildesheim, are working to establish a scientific foundation [25]. Three main areas are being explored: text production, user perception, and translation practices [26]. Interdisciplinary perspectives also examine social and economic dimensions.

Image Support: Visuals, such as symbols and photographs, are widely used to support comprehension in Easy Language, particularly for individuals with cognitive or learning difficulties [5][27][8]. Symbols can vary in clarity, ranging from easily guessable (transparent) to learnable (translucent) and abstract (opaque) [5]. As illustrated in Figure 1, these categories reflect different levels of intuitiveness. Transparent symbols, for example a simple drawing of a dog to represent the word "dog", are generally the most effective, especially for individuals with intellectual disabilities [28][29]. Photographs are often seen as more transparent than symbols because they resemble real-life objects and actions more closely. Studies suggest they may be more effective in supporting comprehension, particularly for abstract or complex concepts [30][8]. However, both symbols and photographs can cause misinterpretation if poorly chosen or overly abstract. Their effectiveness depends on factors, such as user familiarity, visual processing ability, and attention span [31]. The cognitive theory of multimedia learning supports the use of visuals, stating that multi-modal information presentation reduces cognitive load and improves understanding [3]. However, visuals can also lead to overload or hinder comprehension if used excessively or without context [32][19]. Research findings remain mixed [24], highlighting the need to apply images with careful consideration of the target audience and communicative intent.

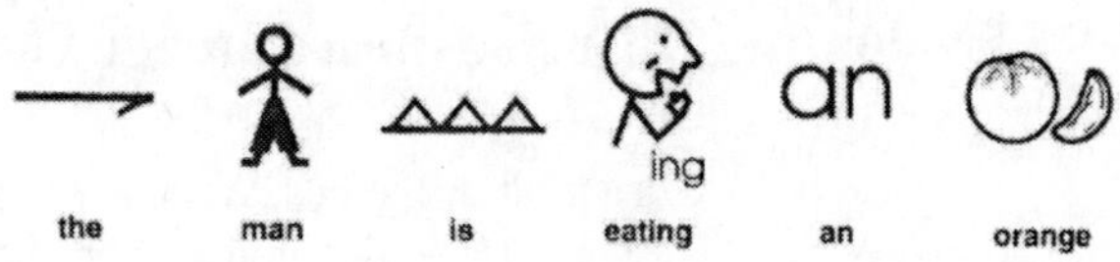

Figure 1. Illustration of opaque ("the", "is"), translucent ("eating"), and transparent ("man", "orange") symbols used to support sentence comprehension [5].

III. Related Work

Several studies have examined whether humans can distinguish AI-generated images from real photographs. Lu et al. [13] conducted a large-scale study using Midjourney-generated images and internet photos, finding that participants correctly identified real images 66.9% of the time and AI-generated ones 55.8% of the time. Notably, prior exposure to AI-generated content improved classification accuracy, and images featuring people were easier to assess than object-based images. Gal et al. [33] and Ruiz et al. [34] compared different fine-tuning methods for diffusion models. While Ruiz et al. found DreamBooth to outperform Textual Inversion in terms of fidelity and subject likeness, these studies did not include real images or measure human ability to distinguish image sources.

Research into symbol comprehension has highlighted the role of visual resemblance and familiarity. Mirenda et al. [29] showed that symbols more closely resembling real objects were easier for non-speaking individuals with cognitive impairments to interpret. Similar findings were reported by Bloomberg et al. [35], who ranked symbol sets based on participant ratings. Dada et al. [36] demonstrated that children with mild intellectual disabilities could successfully match high-iconicity symbols with labels. Hartley et al. [37] emphasized that colored images improved symbolic understanding in children with autism.

Schlosser et al. [38] found that animated symbols enhanced interpretability, particularly when paired with text.

Research on the effectiveness of image-supported Easy Language remains limited and somewhat inconsistent. Rivero-Contreras et al. [6] used eye-tracking to study dyslexic readers and found that simplified text and illustrative support both contributed to improved processing. Jones et al. [27] reported improved comprehension in adults with learning disabilities when symbols were placed above individual words. Noll et al. [8] found that photo-supported Easy Language enhanced performance in mathematical tasks for students with and without special needs, whereas symbols showed no such effect, which suggests that the benefits may depend on the specific task. Poncelas and Murphy [5] observed no immediate benefit from symbols in manifestos but noted improved comprehension after repeated exposure, which highlights the importance of symbol familiarity. Conversely, Hurtado et al. [28] compared Easy Language leaflets with and without images and found no significant difference in information retention. Similarly, Parsons and Sherwood [39] implemented Widgit symbols in legal information leaflets for detainees with learning disabilities but relied solely on stakeholder satisfaction rather than comprehension metrics. Cardone [40] questioned the reliability of visual-based questioning methods and cautioned against assuming pictures always enhance understanding. A more recent user study systematically evaluated how well different AI-generated images illustrate simplified texts for accessibility purposes [41]. Involving participants from the target group, the study found that while visual fidelity was often high, semantic clarity varied greatly depending on the model and prompt formulation. These findings underline the need for human-in-the-loop approaches when using AI imagery in Easy Language.

Overall, while some studies support the potential of image support in Easy Language, results are mixed and highly dependent on task, audience, and design choices. This study extends prior work by introducing AI-generated imagery as a new visual support modality for Easy Language.

IV. Implementation

Data Set: The dataset used for fine-tuning was sourced from the Picto-Selector application, which contains over 34,000 pictograms (see Figure 2) for creating visual schedules [15]. Specifically, the Pictogenda symbol set was used due to its consistent black-and-white, minimalist visual style. This style is visually similar to Widgit symbols [42], which have been successfully used in Easy Language contexts. From the original set of 420 symbols, a total of 99 images were selected for fine-tuning. The reduction was based on two main criteria: (1) stylistic consistency, as images that diverged visually from the core set were excluded, and (2) prompt suitability, as symbols with overly complex content, such as overlapping objects or difficult pose, could not be described effectively in simple prompts. Since each image is accompanied by a textual prompt during training, inadequate or ambiguous prompts could compromise learning quality. The final set reflects a balance between visual homogeneity and prompt clarity. Each image was manually captioned to guide training, using a structured prompt format that included a unique style identifier ("pl41nl4ng"), a detailed description of the image, and stylistic tags (e.g., "black background").

Figure 2. Sample images from the Pictogenda data set [15] used for fine-tuning. From left to right: (1) person waving, (2) wrapped gift box, (3) dog, (4) coastal scene with lighthouse and sailboat, (5) two people standing together. Each image is rendered in a simplified black-and-white style.

Fine-Tuning: Stable Diffusion v1.5 [43], trained on LAION-Aesthetics v2 5+ [44], was selected as the base model due to its open-source availability and robust latent diffusion architecture [9]. A fine-tuned autoencoder [45] was used for latent space transformations. LoRA was applied to fine-tune both the U-Net and the text encoder with reduced parameter overhead. DreamBooth's prior preservation [34] was not necessary due to the single-style training objective.

The U-Net was trained with a learning rate of 5e-6, the text encoder with 2.5e-6, and a rank of 256. AdamW8bit optimization was used. Training ran for 29,700 steps over 30 epochs, with each image used ten times per epoch on a Tesla T4 GPU. During training, one image per epoch was sampled to monitor the model's progress. Of the 30 total epochs, images from the first six were discarded due to low visual quality, leaving 24 candidate models for evaluation. The full training configuration, model weights, and dataset are available on Hugging Face [46]. The training script was based on an adapted notebook [47], using the kohya-trainer repository [48].

Image Generation: Images were generated via the *Stable Diffusion Web UI* implementation for Google Colab [49][50], using the same base model, LoRA weights, and autoencoder as during training. Prompts closely followed the training captions. A consistent negative prompt containing terms like "deformed" or "bad art" was used to suppress undesired output, alongside three quality-enhancing embeddings [51][52][53]. Most images were generated with 30 diffusion steps, the "Euler a" sampler, a Classifier-Free Guidance (CFG) scale of 8, and a resolution of 512x512 pixels. ControlNet [54] was used to control human poses and ensure structural consistency across styles.

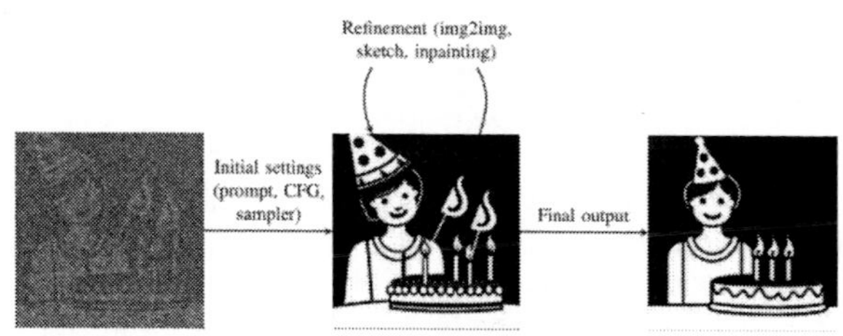

Figure 3. Illustration of the workflow for generating the images used in the user studies. An initial image was created using text2img. The image was then refined, e.g., with img2img. The final output was used in the user studies.

Since initial outputs were often imperfect, a multi-step refinement process followed. Sketching was used to remove elements, inpainting to add or replace content, and img2img to enhance visual quality. These were applied with denoising strengths between 0.1 and 0.9. To generate both black and white background versions, ControlNet was used to transfer structure, and prompts were adjusted accordingly. The full generation workflow is shown in Figure 3, and all final images (and their training counterparts) are included in Appendix A Figures 6–24.

V. User Studies

To evaluate the suitability of AI-generated images for Easy Language, two user studies were conducted. The first study examined whether diffusion models can replicate a consistent visual style, while the second explored whether the generated images are expressive enough to clearly convey specific meanings.

A. Study 1: Visual Distinctiveness

The first study assessed whether participants could distinguish between AI-generated images and original pictograms from the Pictogenda set [15]. Since Easy Language materials should maintain a consistent image style throughout [1], it is important to determine whether fine-tuned diffusion models can replicate a given visual aesthetic. This is particularly relevant because conventional diffusion models are unlikely to be familiar with Easy Language imagery.

Fifteen participants, mostly computer science students, took part in this web-based study. The experiment was conducted via an online survey platform and presented in two parts. In part one, participants were shown 40 images: 20 generated by the fine-tuned diffusion model and 20 original Pictogenda icons. Each generated image had a content-matched original counterpart. The image sets were equally divided between transparent and translucent symbols, following classification schemes, such as those by Poncelas and Murphy [5]. Participants were asked to judge whether each image was AI-generated or not. In part two, image pairs were shown again and participants had to select which image better illustrated a given concept, or mark both as equally good, similar to the setup used by Lu et al. [13].

Before the task, participants viewed a short introduction and example images to become familiar with the Pictogenda style. Their judgments were recorded, and optional text input fields captured the reasoning behind classification choices.

B. Study 2: Expressiveness for Easy Language

The second study evaluated whether AI-generated images could effectively convey meanings to people with cognitive impairments, a key requirement for Easy Language illustrations. A total of 42 participants took part, many of whom were members of the *Netzwerk Leichte Sprache e.V.* [17]. The group included both Easy Language translators and testers, some with learning difficulties.

The study was designed in consultation with an Easy Language expert and implemented using the same online survey platform. To reduce cognitive load, only 20 images were shown, half transparent, half translucent, and all instructions were written and verified in Easy Language. Images were displayed with white backgrounds, based on accessibility recommendations from the translator. Participants were asked to type what they thought each image meant, using simple text responses limited to 100 characters. To reduce frustration and mitigate the risk of participants guessing, all answers were optional.

To evaluate the answers, a three-level scoring system was applied: correct (1), partially correct (0.5), and incorrect (0). Blank responses were scored as incorrect. Partially correct answers either correctly described the image without identifying the intended meaning or mixed correct and incorrect concepts.

VI. Results

A. Fine-Tuning Stable Diffusion

To determine the best model checkpoint, one image was generated after each of the 30 training epochs. The first six epochs were excluded due to insufficient visual quality, leaving 24 candidate models. For each candidate, 10 images were generated with LoRA strength values between 0.0 and 1.0 in steps of 0.1, resulting in a total of 240 images (see an excerpt in Figure 4). All generations used the same prompt, seed, and settings to allow for consistent comparison. The final model, from epoch 19 with a strength value of 0.8, was selected based on visual evaluation. It produced images with correct composition, no unintended features such as eyebrows or detailed fingers, and strong alignment with the input prompt.

B. Visual Distinctiveness Study

This study investigated whether participants could distinguish between AI-generated and original images. Among 15 participants, the overall classification accuracy was 47.7%, which is not significantly better than random guessing. Prior experience with AI-generated images had no significant effect on performance. Filtering for image quality (e.g., blurred lines) or focusing on human-centered images also yielded no improvements. These findings are consistent with Lu et al. [13], who reported that participants struggled to distinguish AI-generated from real images, although their study suggested that human-centered imagery may be slightly easier to classify, which was not confirmed here. Participants reported relying on features, such as line sharpness, object proportions, facial expressions, and finger details in their decision-making. However, these cues did not result in reliable classification. In a follow-up task, participants compared image pairs (AI vs. original) and indicated which better conveyed the intended concept. Across 20 comparisons, AI-generated images were preferred 120 times, while original images were chosen 31 times; 149 comparisons were rated as equally good.

Figure 4. An overview of the training results: Rows represent epochs, columns represent influence strength.

C. *Evaluation of AI-Generated Images for Easy Language*

In the second study, 42 participants, including Easy Language users and translators, were asked to describe the meaning of 20 AI-generated images. The overall mean accuracy (acc) was high (acc = 0.898), with transparent images recognized significantly better (acc = 0.946) than translucent ones (acc = 0.851). This difference was confirmed by a Wilcoxon signed-rank test ($p < 0.001$). A concept-level analysis showed that 17 out of 20 concepts had a mean accuracy above 0.85. *Fish* and *sad* were recognized perfectly by all participants (Figures 15 and 23). *Headache* showed the lowest recognition rate with a mean accuracy of (acc = 0.367), followed by *coffee* (acc = 0.756) and *angry* (acc = 0.767) (Figures 16, 12, and 7).

To assess how consistently participants interpreted each concept, we calculated mean accuracy scores and 95% confidence intervals. These help evaluate the reliability of the results and highlight differences in interpretive agreement (see Figure 5).

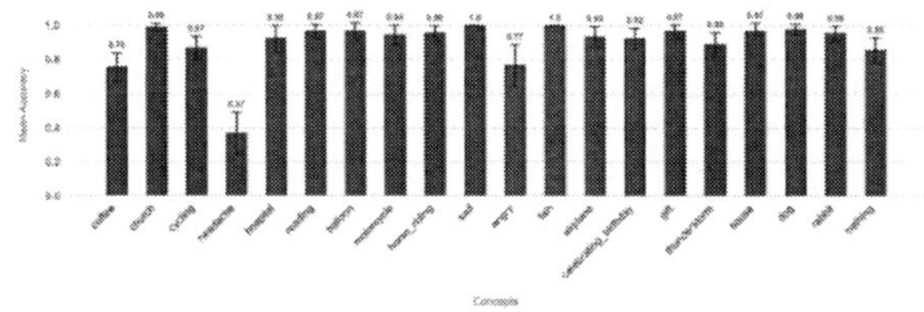

Figure 5. Mean accuracy per concept with 95% confidence intervals across all participants.

A Friedman test ($p < 0.001$) revealed significant differences between concepts. A Nemenyi post hoc test further showed that *headache* differed significantly from nearly all other concepts, and *coffee* differed from *church*, *fish*, and *sad* (Figures 16, 12, 11, 15, and 23). To identify differences between high and low performers, the 25% bottom and 25% top participants were compared using Mann–Whitney U tests. Significant differences were found for *headache*, *angry*, *thunderstorm*, *cycling*, and *hospital*, with lower scores in the bottom group for all these concepts (Figures 24, 13, and 17). To further examine individual variation among lower-performing participants, the 50% and 25% with the lowest mean accuracy were analyzed separately ($n = 21$ and $n = 11$). Both groups still achieved relatively high average scores (acc = 0.830) and (acc = 0.777), but showed more variation between concepts. In the 50% group, *headache* differed significantly from 14 other concepts. In the 25% group, although the Friedman test remained significant ($p < 0.001$), the Nemenyi test showed no pairwise differences, likely due to the small sample. Participants also provided free-text feedback. One noted that some images appeared too childlike, while another questioned the necessity of visualizing certain concepts at all.

Overall, results indicate that fine-tuned diffusion models can generate images that are visually consistent and semantically meaningful enough to support Easy Language, though with clear limitations for certain abstract or emotionally nuanced concepts.

VII. Discussion

The overarching goal of this work was to investigate whether AI-generated images can support Easy Language. Two main conditions were examined: first, whether diffusion models can replicate the visual style of existing image sets, and second, whether they can generate images that are expressive and unambiguous enough to convey meaning. These goals were addressed through two user studies.

The visual style used in the studies was not explicitly designed for Easy Language but was selected based on expert recommendation and its similarity to successful sets like *Widgit* [42]. While this choice introduces a potential limitation, the focus was on the model's ability to replicate and express a given style consistently. Some participants commented that the tested concepts were too simple or did not require visualization. However, widely recognizable concepts were chosen deliberately to isolate image expressiveness from concept familiarity. Although the studies reused some concepts seen during training, the prompts and generation settings were altered, reducing the risk of overfitting.

In the first study on visual distinctiveness, participants were unable to reliably distinguish between AI-generated and non-AI-generated images. Mean accuracy remained around 0.5, indicating chance-level performance. No significant difference was observed between participants with or without prior experience with AI-generated images. These findings suggest that diffusion models can successfully mimic the style of existing image sets using relatively small datasets (~100 images). However, high variance in individual performance and the small sample size (15 participants) make it difficult to draw general conclusions. A larger sample is needed to further investigate whether certain groups are more capable of this task. Many participants reported relying on image sharpness as a distinguishing factor, as AI-generated images were consistently sharp while non-AI images varied in clarity. Although blurred images were excluded from part of the analysis, results remained non-significant. This supports prior findings by Lu et al. [13], who also observed that participants struggled to identify AI-generated images, especially for people-centered content.

The second study, focused on expressiveness, showed that AI-generated images achieved high recognition accuracy (acc = 0.898). Transparent images were understood more reliably than translucent ones, mostly due to low scores on a few specific concepts like *headache* and *angry*, which involve emotional or abstract meaning. Participants with lower overall scores particularly struggled with these concepts, suggesting that emotional content remains a challenge for current diffusion models. At the same time, concepts like *sad* were correctly identified by all participants, underscoring the importance of content and design choices. Since the study included translators and experts rather than exclusively people with learning difficulties, the results provide only limited insight into Easy Language's target audience. However, subgroup analysis of lower-performing participants offered useful indications of where comprehension breaks down and where image refinement may be needed.

Overall, the fine-tuned diffusion model was effective in reproducing the visual style and conveying meaning for a majority of tested concepts. Abstract or emotional concepts proved more difficult, highlighting the importance of iterative testing with target users. While AI-generated images show promise for supporting Easy Language, human feedback remains essential. In practice, generating effective images often requires additional tools, such as ControlNet [54], in combination with text prompts, which may limit accessibility for non-technical users, such as Easy Language translators.

VIII. Conclusion and Future Work

AI-generated images show significant potential for supporting Easy Language by providing scalable, on-demand visual content tailored to accessibility needs. This study evaluated whether a fine-tuned diffusion model can (1) replicate the coherent visual style required for Easy Language and (2) produce illustrations that clearly convey intended meanings. A Stable Diffusion model was fine-tuned using the LoRA method [14] on a minimalist pictogram dataset derived from Picto-Selector [15], and tested in two user studies. Results indicate that participants were generally unable to distinguish the AI-generated images from original symbols [13], and that most generated images were interpreted correctly, with an overall accuracy of nearly 90%. This suggests that diffusion models can effectively support the visual dimension of Easy Language communication. However, challenges remain for abstract or emotional concepts, such as *headache* or *angry*, particularly among lower-performing participants. These limitations highlight the need for more expressive and semantically aware generation techniques. Interpretation of the findings must consider certain constraints: the visual style was deliberately minimalist, and the participant pool, while diverse, was small and only partially representative of the Easy Language target audience. Generalizing the results to other styles or broader user groups requires further validation. Importantly, the study shows that with appropriate fine-tuning, diffusion models can produce illustrations that align with key stylistic and semantic expectations in Easy Language contexts. This balance of visual consistency and conceptual clarity is essential for accessible communication and positions AI-generated imagery as a viable component in inclusive design workflows.

Future work should build on these findings by exploring several open directions. One area of interest is whether the lower recognition rates observed among certain user subgroups (e.g., the lowest-performing 25%) are due to limitations in the model or to user-related factors such as concept familiarity or cognitive load. Dedicated studies focusing on individuals from the Easy Language target group could yield deeper insights. The current findings are specific to a minimalist visual style. It remains unclear whether diffusion models can maintain semantic clarity and stylistic consistency when applied to more complex or detailed styles. Comparative studies involving varying visual styles would help assess the generalizability of these results. Additionally, testing whether humans can still distinguish AI-generated from non-AI images in more detailed styles would be valuable. To improve the robustness of the findings, future research should increase the sample size and diversity of tested concepts. A broader participant pool and concept range could help validate the expressiveness and stylistic fidelity of AI-generated images more comprehensively. Recent developments in controllable image generation, such as ControlNet, StyleAlign, or prompt-to-prompt editing, could further enhance the expressiveness and clarity of visuals in accessibility contexts [54]. These tools offer fine-grained control over layout, pose, and visual style, making them promising for generating context-aware illustrations in Easy Language workflows. Finally, integrating user-driven image generation into Easy Language workflows may enable adaptive support. By allowing users to highlight parts of a text and generate matching illustrations, accessibility could become more personalized. However, this requires robust text-to-prompt models that can convert vague or minimal text into meaningful image prompts, an area where current text-based guidance still has limitations. To fully realize this potential, image generation must remain embedded in iterative, human-centered design processes. As controllable generation tools continue to evolve, they offer new opportunities for generating personalized and context-sensitive visual supports for diverse user needs.

References

[1] U. Bredel and C. Maaß, *Easy Language: Theoretical Foundations and Practical Guidance*. Berlin: Dudenverlag, 2016, Original title: *Leichte Sprache: theoretische Grundlagen – Orientierung für die Praxis*, ISBN: 3411756160.

[2] C. Maaß, *Easy Language: The Rulebook*. Münster: Lit-Verlag, 2015, Original title: *Leichte Sprache. Das Regelbuch*, ISBN: 978-3-643-12907-9.

[3] R. E. Mayer, "Cognitive theory of multimedia learning," in *The Cambridge Handbook of Multimedia Learning*, ser. Cambridge Handbooks in Psychology, R. E. Mayer, Ed., 2nd ed., Cambridge: Cambridge University Press, 2014, pp. 43–71. DOI: 10.1017/CBO9781139547369.005.

[4] *Lebenshilfe for people with intellectual disabilities bremen (registered association)*, https://www.leichte-sprache.de/, Accessed: 2025-05-31.

[5] A. Poncelas and G. Murphy, "Accessible information for people with intellectual disabilities: Do symbols really help?" *Journal of Applied Research in Intellectual Disabilities*, vol. 20, pp. 466–474, 2007. DOI: 10.1111/j.1468-3148.2006.00334.x.

[6] M. Rivero-Contreras, P. Engelhardt, and D. Saldaña, "An experimental eye-tracking study of text adaptation for readers with dyslexia: Effects of visual support and word frequency," *Annals of Dyslexia*, vol. 71, pp. 1–18, 2021. DOI: 10.1007/s11881-021-00217-1.

[7] S. Schmutz, A. Sonderegger, and J. Sauer, "Easy-to-read language in disability-friendly web sites: Effects on nondisabled users," *Applied Ergonomics*, vol. 74, pp. 97–106, 2019. DOI: 10.1016/j.apergo.2018.08.013.

[8] A. Noll, J. Roth, and M. Scholz, "Overcoming reading barriers in inclusive mathematics education – a comparative study of visual and linguistic support measures," *Journal für Mathematik-Didaktik*, vol. 41, pp. 157–190, 2020, Original title: *Lesebarrieren im inklusiven Mathematikunterricht überwinden – visuelle und sprachliche Unterstützungsmaßnahmen im empirischen Vergleich*. DOI: 10.1007/s13138-020-00158-z.

[9] R. Rombach, A. Blattmann, D. Lorenz, P. Esser, and B. Ommer, "High-resolution image synthesis with latent diffusion models," in *Proceedings of the IEEE Conference on Computer Vision and Pattern Recognition (CVPR)*, 2022. arXiv: 2112.10752 [cs.CV].

[10] A. Ramesh *et al.*, *Zero-shot text-to-image generation*, 2021. arXiv: 2102.12092 [cs.CV]. [Online]. Available: https://arxiv.org/abs/2102.12092.

[11] A. Ramesh, P. Dhariwal, A. Nichol, C. Chu, and M. Chen, *Hierarchical text-conditional image generation with clip latents*, 2022. arXiv: 2204.06125 [cs.CV]. [Online]. Available: https://arxiv.org/abs/2204.06125.

[12] *Midjourney*, https://www.midjourney.com/, Accessed: 2025-05-31.

[13] Z. Lu *et al.*, *Seeing is not always believing: Benchmarking human and model perception of ai-generated images*, 2023. arXiv: 2304.13023 [cs.AI].

[14] E. J. Hu *et al.*, *Lora: Low-rank adaptation of large language models*, 2021. arXiv: 2106.09685 [cs.CL].

[15] *Picto-selector*, https://www.pictoselector.eu/, Accessed: 2025-05-31.

[16] C. Lindholm and U. Vanhatalo, *Handbook of Easy Languages in Europe* (Easy - Plain - Accessible). Berlin: Frank & Timme, 2021, ISBN: 9783732907717.

[17] *Netzwerk leichte sprache e.v.* https://www.leichte-sprache.org/, Accessed: 2025-05-31.

[18] S. Hansen-Schirra and C. Maaß, *Easy Language - Plain Language - Easy Language Plus: Perspectives on Comprehensibility and Stigmatisation* (Easy – Plain – Accessible). Berlin: Frank & Timme, 2020, ISBN: 9783732906918.

[19] M. González-Sordé and A. Matamala, "Empirical evaluation of easy language recommendations: A systematic literature review from journal research in catalan, english, and spanish," *Universal Access in the Information Society*, 2023. DOI: 10.1007/s10209-023-00975-2.

[20] *Inclusion europe*, https://www.inclusion-europe.eu/, Accessed: 2025-05-31.

[21] I. J. 1. 35, "Information technology – user interfaces – requirements and recommendations on making written text easy to read and understand," International Organization for Standardization, Standard ISO/IEC 23859:2023, 2023.

[22] *Regulation for the creation of accessible information technology (bitv 2.0)*, https://www.bmas.de/DE/Service/Gesetze-und-Gesetzesvorhaben/barrierefreie-informationstechnik-verordnung-2-0.html, Original title: *Verordnung zur Schaffung barrierefreier Informationstechnik nach dem Behindertengleichstellungsgesetz (BITV 2.0)*. Accessed: 2025-05-31, 2023.

[23] D. e. V., "E din spec 33429:2023-04 "recommendations for german easy language"," DIN Deutsches Institut für Normung e. V., Standard E DIN SPEC 33429:2023-04, 2023, Original title: *E DIN SPEC 33429:2023-04 "Empfehlungen für Deutsche Leichte Sprache"*.

[24] I. Fajardo *et al.*, "Easy-to-read texts for students with intellectual disability: Linguistic factors affecting comprehension," *Journal of applied research in intellectual disabilities : JARID*, vol. 27, 2013. DOI: 10.1111/jar.12065.

[25] C. Maaß, I. Rink, and S. Hansen-Schirra, "Easy language in germany," *Handbook of Easy Languages in Europe*, p. 191, 2021. DOI: 10.26530/20.500.12657/52628.

[26] S. Hansen-Schirra and C. Maaß, *Easy Language Research: Text and User Perspectives* (Easy – Plain – Accessible). Berlin: Frank & Timme, 2020, ISBN: 978-3-7329-0688-8.

[27] F. Jones, K. Long, and W. Finlay, "Symbols can improve the reading comprehension of adults with learning disabilities," *Journal of intellectual disability research : JIDR*, vol. 51, pp. 545–550, 2007. DOI: 10.1111/j.1365-2788.2006.00926.x.

[28] B. Hurtado, L. Jones, and F. Burniston, "Is easy read information really easier to read?" *Journal of intellectual disability research : JIDR*, vol. 58(9), pp. 822–829, 2013. DOI: 10.1111/jir.12097.

[29] P. Mirenda and P. A. Locke, "A comparison of symbol transparency in nonspeaking persons with intellectual disabilities," *The Journal of speech and hearing disorders*, vol. 54(2), pp. 131–140, 1989. DOI: 10.1044/jshd.5402.131.

[30] R. Sutherland and T. Isherwood, "The evidence for easy-read for people with intellectual disabilities: A systematic literature review: The evidence for easy-read for people with intellectual disabilities," *Journal of Policy and Practice in Intellectual Disabilities*, vol. 13, 2016. DOI: 10.1111/jppi.12201.

[31] P. Mirenda, "Designing pictorial communication systems for physically able-bodied students with severe handicaps," *Augmentative and Alternative Communication*, vol. 1, pp. 58–64, 1985. DOI: 10.1080/07434618512331273541.

[32] J. Sweller, J. J. G. Van Merrienboer, and F. Paas, "Cognitive architecture and instructional design," *Educational Psychology Review*, vol. 10, 1998. DOI: 10.1023/a:1022193728205.

[33] R. Gal *et al.*, *An image is worth one word: Personalizing text-to-image generation using textual inversion*, 2022. arXiv: 2208.01618 [cs.CV].

[34] N. Ruiz *et al.*, *Dreambooth: Fine tuning text-to-image diffusion models for subject-driven generation*, 2023. arXiv: 2208.12242 [cs.CV].

[35] K. Bloomberg, G. R. Karlan, and L. L. Lloyd, "The comparative translucency of initial lexical items represented in five graphic symbol systems and sets," *Journal of speech and hearing research*, vol. 33(4), pp. 717–725, 1990. DOI: 10.1044/jshr.3304.717.

[36] S. Dada, A. Huguet, and J. Bornman, "The iconicity of picture communication symbols for children with english additional language and mild intellectual disability," *Augmentative and alternative communication (Baltimore, Md. : 1985)*, vol. 29, pp. 360–373, 2013. DOI: 10.3109/07434618.2013.849753.

[37] C. Hartley and M. Allen, "Symbolic understanding of pictures in low-functioning children with autism: The effects of iconicity and naming," *Journal of autism and developmental disorders*, vol. 45, pp. 15–30, 2013. DOI: 10.1007/s10803-013-2007-4.

[38] R. Schlosser *et al.*, "Animation of graphic symbols representing verbs and prepositions: Effects on transparency, name agreement, and identification," *Journal of speech, language, and hearing research : JSLHR*, vol. 55, pp. 342–58, 2011. DOI: 10.1044/1092-4388(2011/10-0164).

[39] S. Parsons and G. Sherwood, "A pilot evaluation of using symbol-based information in police custody," *British Journal of Learning Disabilities*, 2015. DOI: 10.1111/bld.12140.

[40] D. Cardone, "Exploring the use of question methods: Pictures do not always help people with learning disabilities," *The British Journal of Development Disabilities*, vol. 45, no. 89, pp. 93–98, 1999. DOI: 10.1179/096979599799155894.

[41] M. Anschütz, T. Sylaj, and G. Groh, *Images speak volumes: User-centric assessment of image generation for accessible communication*, 2024. arXiv: 2410.03430 [cs.CV]. [Online]. Available: https://arxiv.org/abs/2410.03430.

[42] *Widgit symbols*, https://www.widgit.com/, Accessed: 2025-05-31.

[43] *Stable diffusion v1.5*, https://huggingface.co/stable-diffusion-v1-5/stable-diffusion-v1-5, Accessed: 2025-05-31.

[44] C. Schuhmann, *Laion-aesthetics v2 5+*, https://web.archive.org/web/20230331034058/https://huggingface.co/datasets/ChristophSchuhmann/improved_aesthetics_5plus, Accessed: 2025-05-31.

[45] S. AI, *Sd-vae-ft-mse-original autoencoder*, https://huggingface.co/stabilityai/sd-vae-ft-mse-original, Accessed: 2025-05-31.

[46] Hugging Face, *PlainLang Collection*, https://huggingface.co/collections/bomdey/plainlang-65663ad0f450504854ce6145, Accessed: 2025-05-31, 2025.

[47] F. Taqwa, *Fine-tuning notebook*, https://colab.research.google.com/github/Linaqruf/kohya-trainer/blob/main/kohya-LoRA-dreambooth.ipynb, Accessed: 2025-05-31.

[48] F. Taqwa, *Fine-tuning repository*, https://github.com/Linaqruf/kohya-trainer/tree/main, Commit: 3d494d8.

[49] *Stable diffusion web ui colab*, https://github.com/camenduru/stable-diffusion-webui-colab, Accessed: 2025-05-31.

[50] *Stable diffusion web ui*, https://github.com/AUTOMATIC1111/stable-diffusion-webui, Accessed: 2025-05-31.

[51] *Verybadimagenegative - stable diffusion embedding*, https://huggingface.co/nolanaatama/embeddings/blob/main/verybadimagenegative_v1.3.pt, Accessed: 2025-05-31.

[52] *Bad-artist - stable diffusion embedding*, https://civitai.com/models/5224/bad-artist-negative-embedding, Accessed: 2025-05-31.

[53] *Bad-hands-5 - stable diffusion embedding*, https://civitai.com/models/116230/bad-hands-5, Accessed: 2025-05-31.

[54] L. Zhang, A. Rao, and M. Agrawala, *Adding conditional control to text-to-image diffusion models*, 2023. arXiv: 2302.05543 [cs.CV].

APPENDIX

Figure 6. Concept *airplane* (transparent). Left to right: original reference, text2img, refined black, refined white.

Figure 7. Concept *angry* (transparent). Left to right: original reference, text2img, refined black, refined white.

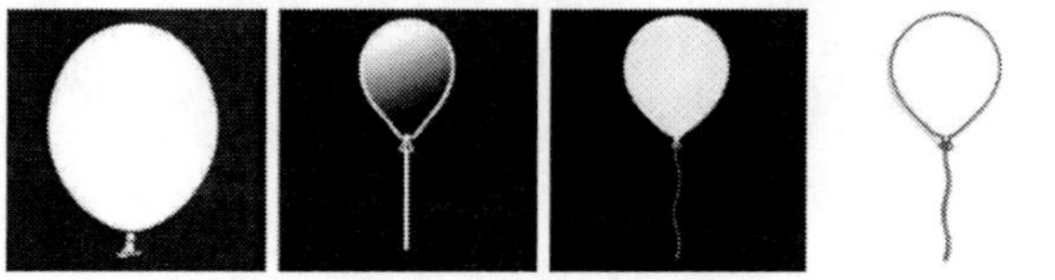

Figure 8. Concept *balloon* (transparent). Left to right: original reference, text2img, refined black, refined white.

Figure 9. Concept *bathing* (transparent). Left to right: original reference, text2img, refined black, refined white.

Figure 10. Concept *birthday* (transparent). Left to right: original reference, text2img, refined black, refined white.

Figure 11. Concept *church* (transparent). Left to right: original reference, text2img, refined black, refined white.

Figure 12. Concept *coffee* (translucent). Left to right: original reference, text2img, refined black, refined white.

Figure 13. Concept *cycling* (translucent). Left to right: original reference, text2img, refined black, refined white.

Figure 14. Concept *dog* (transparent). Left to right: original reference, text2img, refined black, refined white.

Figure 15. Concept *fish* (transparent). Left to right: original reference, text2img, refined black, refined white.

Figure 16. Concept *headache* (translucent). Left to right: original reference, text2img, refined black, refined white.

Figure 17. Concept *hospital* (translucent). Left to right: original reference, text2img, refined black, refined white.

Figure 18. Concept *motorcycle* (transparent). Left to right: original reference, text2img, refined black, refined white.

Figure 19. Concept *present* (transparent). Left to right: original reference, text2img, refined black, refined white.

Figure 20. Concept *rabbit* (transparent). Left to right: original reference, text2img, refined black, refined white.

Figure 21. Concept *reading* (translucent). Left to right: original reference, text2img, refined black, refined white.

Figure 22. Concept *riding* (transparent). Left to right: original reference, text2img, refined black, refined white.

Figure 23. Concept *sad* (transparent). Left to right: original reference, text2img, refined black, refined white.

Figure 24. Concept *thunderstorm* (translucent). Left to right: original reference, text2img, refined black, refined white.

Grounding on Shaky Ground: Wikipedia's Legal Articles, Editorial Integrity, and the Risk of Data Poisoning in Artificial Intelligence

An Empirical Study of Contributor Bans and Knowledge Reliability

Matthias Harter
Faculty of Engineering
Hochschule RheinMain - University of Applied Sciences
Rüsselsheim, Germany
e-mail: matthias.harter@hs-rm.de

***Abstract*—Analyzing revision histories of over 15,000 articles in the German-language Wikipedia legal domain from 2004 to 2025, this study examines the persistent infiltration of entries by contributors later permanently banned for vandalism, extremist propaganda, promotional editing, or uncooperative conduct. We quantify a non-trivial proportion of edits originating from compromised accounts, demonstrating how such editorial contamination degrades Wikipedia's reliability as a training corpus for Large Language Models (LLMs) in legal and media-content generation contexts where factual precision is critical. Our investigation further reveals that Retrieval-Augmented Generation (RAG) architectures, which ground outputs in external data, risk propagating inaccuracies if their source repositories are compromised. These findings have direct implications for trust and disinformation in AI media, ethical considerations in AI-generated content, and the evaluation of LLM-based tools, by highlighting vulnerabilities in open-source knowledge pipelines. Ultimately, our findings challenge assumptions about swarm intelligence and demonstrate the urgent need for robust safeguards to ensure reliable AI-driven media production workflows.**

Keywords*—*Wikipedia; Data poisoning; LLM; AI training data; Trustworthiness in AI; Crowdsourced content; Disinformation.

I. Introduction

Wikipedia has become a cornerstone of online knowledge dissemination, widely used not only by individuals seeking accessible explanations but increasingly as a foundational dataset for LLMs. Legal articles on Wikipedia, in particular, play a critical role in public access to complex statutory language and jurisprudence, often bridging the gap between technical legal terminology and lay understanding. Yet, despite its openness being a strength, Wikipedia remains vulnerable to bad-faith editorial behavior.

A. Related Work

The integrity of training data has emerged as a central concern in the development of LLMs. A growing body of research addresses the vulnerability of such models to *data poisoning*—intentional contamination of training or grounding data with misleading content. Reference [1] demonstrates that even a few hundred adversarial examples injected during instruction tuning can cause persistent and targeted misbehavior in LLMs. Similar risks were identified by [2], who show that in medical domains, poisoned inputs comprising less than 0.001% of training data can significantly distort output while maintaining benchmark performance.

Benchmarking frameworks such as PoisonBench [3] confirm these vulnerabilities at scale across multiple architectures and highlight the insufficiency of current alignment mechanisms to guard against subtle data corruption. These findings emphasize a broader pattern: scaling models does not inherently confer robustness.

Wikipedia plays a notable role in LLM training corpora. It accounts for approximately 3–5% of tokens in foundational models such as GPT-3 [4], LLaMA [5], and BERT [6]. Its inclusion is often motivated by its structured factual content and perceived reliability. However, sociotechnical investigations [7] question this assumption, arguing that the sustainability and neutrality of Wikipedia are increasingly threatened by automation, declining editor activity, and external exploitation.

Reference [8] in *Nature* compared 42 science articles and showed that Wikipedia's accuracy was broadly comparable to *Encyclopædia Britannica*. Yet later studies nuance this optimism. Using matched U.S. political topics, Greenstein and Zhu find Wikipedia to be more slanted toward Democratic viewpoints than Britannica and overall more biased, though the gap narrows with successive edits [9]. Extending the lens from content to contributors, persuasion [10] show that roughly 80–90% of the observed moderation in article slant is driven by the exit of highly partisan editors rather than by on-platform. Most recently, [11] employs large-scale sentiment analysis over 1,600 politically charged terms and documents a systematic tendency for right-of-centre public figures to be associated with more negative sentiment than their left-leaning counterparts. Together, these works suggest that while Wikipedia can rival expert sources on factual accuracy, ideological asymmetries persist and are shaped by community composition over time; our focus on banned-user infiltration builds on this line of inquiry by foregrounding the durability of partisan edits in a specific domain.

Empirical research on Wikipedia manipulation reveals that a subset of hoax articles—despite being rare—persist long enough to influence downstream systems [12]. Further, disinformation is often opportunistic: [13] find that spikes in public interest precede the creation of manipulative content.

Detection of covert influence operations remains an open problem, though approaches for identifying undisclosed paid editing show promise [14].

To mitigate hallucinations—factual errors generated by LLMs despite fluent output—researchers have explored RAG [15]. By conditioning responses on external sources, RAG systems can improve factuality. However, as shown by [16] and by [17] on "RAG poisoning", these systems are only as trustworthy as their underlying retrieval corpora. If sources, such as Wikipedia, are compromised, even grounded systems may propagate misinformation.

In summary, while LLMs benefit from open knowledge sources like Wikipedia, current research points to systemic risks related to editorial integrity, data poisoning, and trust calibration. These vulnerabilities are particularly consequential in sensitive domains, such as law and medicine, where both AI outputs and their citations must be held to a high standard of factual rigor.

B. Overview of this paper

This paper presents an empirical study of long-term editorial manipulation within the German-language Wikipedia's legal category. By tracing the revision and discussion histories of over 15,000 articles described in Section II, we document the involvement of users who were later permanently banned from the platform due to rule violations—excluding voluntary account closures and deceased editors. The findings in Section III indicate a systematic pattern of infiltration even in domains typically considered neutral or apolitical. As discussed in Section IV, these insights carry serious implications for artificial intelligence systems. Wikipedia is frequently cited as a critical component of LLM training corpora and serves as a common grounding source in RAG frameworks. However, when the integrity of that source is compromised, AI outputs become vulnerable not only to hallucinations but also to factual contamination—a double-layered risk that undermines both answer reliability and user trust. This study sheds light on the hidden risks of relying on crowdsourced platforms for factual grounding in AI systems, calling for a re-evaluation of data hygiene practices in the machine learning pipeline.

II. Methodology

Figure 10 provides a visual overview of the five-step procedure for constructing the article database. Each step relied on the Wikipedia REST API, coupled with Python scripts:

1) *Maintenance-Category Retrieval.* In the first pass, maintenance categories used by Wikipedia to tag outdated or problematic pages were downloaded (175 in total). These categories served as one filtering criterion to exclude articles from subsequent steps if they were deemed insufficiently maintained or not in compliance with editorial standards.
2) *Recursive Download of Legal Subcategories.* The second pass started at the top-level category "Recht" (German for "Law") in the German-language Wikipedia. All subcategories were recursively traversed, collecting any articles placed under these nested categories (15,295 total). These articles were then added to the database.
3) *Template-Based Retrieval.* In the third pass, the scripts identified all articles that utilized one of 24 law-specific templates (e.g., infoboxes or structured references) designed to provide a uniform layout for legal topics. Any article that belonged to a maintenance category or that did *not* map to a legal category was excluded. A brief manual review of categories followed to ensure that peripheral topics (e.g., chemicals or pharmaceuticals) were omitted if they were tangentially but not substantively related to the legal domain. The full text of these articles (17,183 in sum) was downloaded.
4) *Keyword-based Title Search.* The fourth pass used a list of legal terms from a specialized law dictionary ("Weber kompakt" [18]), performing a title-based search in Wikipedia. Although about 9,000 articles were initially returned, roughly 4,000 were filtered out because they discussed aspects (often technical or historical) not relevant to the dictionary's legal perspective. About 5,000 articles passed the filtering, with 854 of those being genuinely new to the database; the remainder were duplicates of already-collected articles.
5) *Expansion via Internal Links.* Finally, from all articles in the database, the 10,000 most frequently occurring internal Wikipedia links were extracted and subjected to the same category-based filtering. This step added about 1,500 articles, bringing the total to 15,344 articles. A final manual review process then excluded categories that were still not strictly related to the legal domain, ensuring the final dataset was as specific as possible to topics in law.

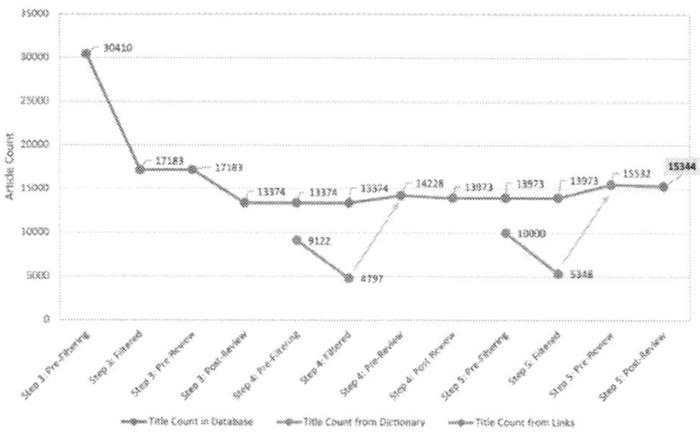

Figure 1. Progression of the database size in pages (articles) in blue depending on the steps in the download process.

As shown in Figure 1, the initial corpus grew substantially during the second and third steps, when the "Recht" root category and legal templates were harvested. In the fourth step (lexical title matching with a legal dictionary), the net increase in articles was relatively modest, because many of the newly found candidate pages were already present or failed the filter. Finally, the link-expansion step further added around

1,500 articles, though a minor decrease is visible after each "post-review" process, which eliminated pages affiliated with irrelevant or borderline categories.

Throughout the steps in the download process, each article was stored in a SQLite database along with all associated metadata, including internal links, revision histories, discussion pages, external references, and page-view statistics. In addition, a second SQLite database was populated with 185,555 permanently blocked (banned) users (April 27, 2004 to March 20, 2025). Reasons for indefinite blocks provided as free-text by Wikipedia administrators, were parsed via regular expressions and grouped into broader categories (e.g., vandalism, sockpuppetry). Any article revision or discussion post by a user in this second database was flagged, enhancing the main database with ban-related columns.

III. Findings

The goal of this study was to assess the extent of editorial infiltration in the German-language Wikipedia's legal domain. The results indicate a non-trivial overlap between legal articles and contributors who were subsequently banned.

A. Banning of Users

Table I shows that over 180,000 users were permanently banned from Wikipedia for reasons other than their own request or death, while Table II and Figure 2 highlight the principal violation categories. Among these, "sockpuppetry" stands out as a clear strategy for infiltration: the term references manipulated accounts operated under pseudonyms, sometimes identified through investigations documented by both investigative journalism and Wikipedia itself [19] [20] [21]. In early 2025, a German public broadcaster (ARD) devoted a podcast to exposing a "Sockenpuppenzoo" (zoo of sockpuppetry) [22], revealing how pervasive and coordinated such efforts can be.

TABLE I
Number of Banned Users (last 21 years).

	No. of Users	Percentage
Non-Compliance	183,756	99%
At Own Request	1,455	0.8%
Deceased	344	0.2%
All Permanently Blocked Users	185,555	100%

TABLE II
Reasons for Banning of Users (last 21 years).

	No. of Users	Percentage
"Clearly not being here to build an encyclopedia"	52,656	29%
Vandalism	12,427	7%
Sockpuppetry	9,724	5%
Edit Wars	1,915	1%
Other Reasons	107,034	58%
Non-Compliance	183,756	100%

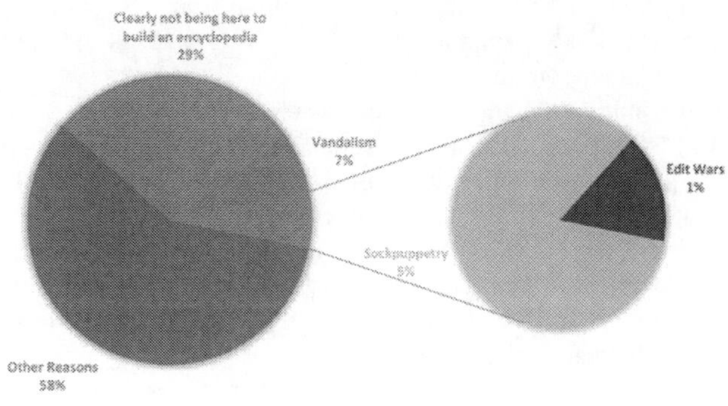

Figure 2. Reasons for permanently banning of users. See also Table II.

Figure 3 visualizes how the number of bans per month has fluctuated over the past two decades. During the project's early years, bans rose sharply, possibly due to a combined effect of increased Wikipedia participation and improved moderator capacity. Although monthly bans have remained high overall, there is no obvious surge specifically attributable to the advent of large language models or AI-generated content.

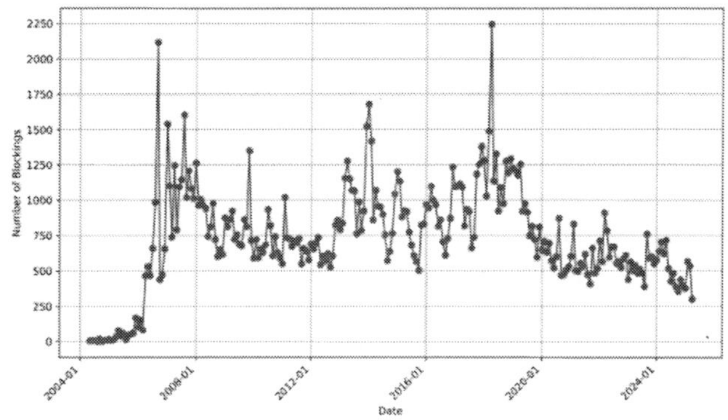

Figure 3. Number of permanently banned users per month until March 20, 2025.

Meanwhile, Figure 4 compares monthly bans against the number of new user registrations, revealing that in some months—particularly in the pre-2008 era—over 10% of newly registered users ended up permanently banned. More recently, this percentage has stabilized between 2% and 4%, indicating a persistent but somewhat reduced infiltration rate.

For the subset of 15,344 legal articles, analysis of the revision history and associated discussion pages reveals that roughly 70% have at least one revision by a permanently banned user, and about 21% of the discussion pages contain contributions from permanently banned users (Tables III and IV, Figures 5 and 6). Of notable concern is the group of articles (0.83% of the total) whose most recent revision was authored by a user later banned. Their content may remain compromised if not superseded by a good-faith edit.

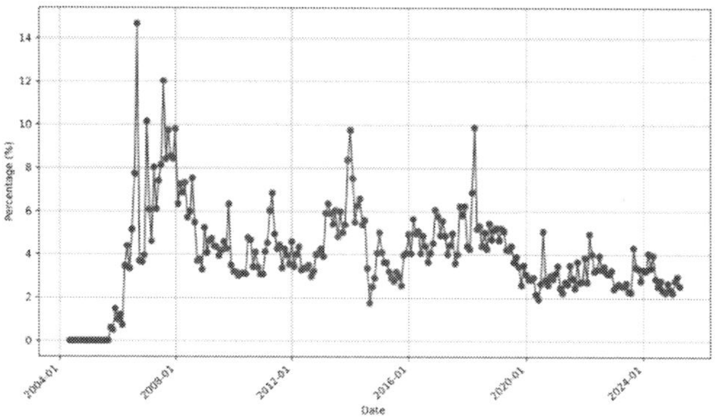

Figure 4. Number of permanently banned users in relation to the number of new registrations per month until March 20, 2025.

TABLE III
BANNING RATIO IN REVISIONS IN ABSOLUTE AND RELATIVE NUMBERS. SEE ALSO FIGURE 5.

Banning Ratio	Articles	Percentage
0% (no infiltration / banned authors)	4,682	30.51%
between 0% and 10%	9,216	60.00%
between 10% and 20%	978	6.37%
between 20% and 30%	261	1.70%
between 30% and 40%	125	0.81%
between 40% and 50%	52	0.34%
more than 50%	30	0.20%
	15,344	100%

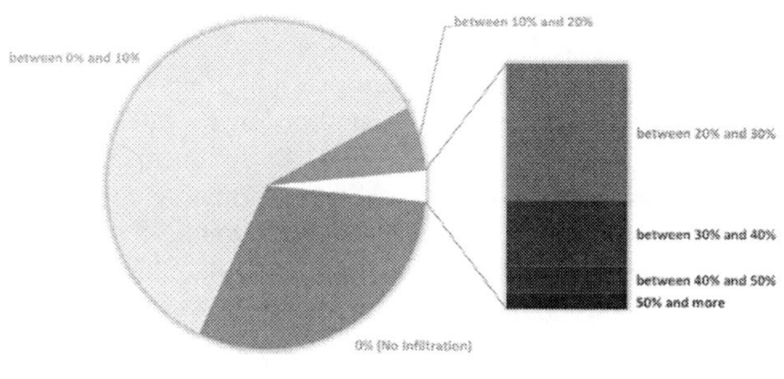

Figure 5. Banning ratio in revisions. For roughly one third of the articles, no revision originates from a banned author (0% banning ratio). See also Table III.

TABLE IV
BANNING RATIO IN DISCUSSIONS IN ABSOLUTE AND RELATIVE NUMBERS. SEE ALSO FIGURE 6.

Banning Ratio	Articles	Percentage
no discussions for these articles	4,572	29.80%
0% (no infiltration / banned contributors)	7,517	48.99%
between 0% and 10%	1,818	11.85%
between 10% and 20%	792	5.16%
between 20% and 30%	266	1.73%
between 30% and 40%	166	1.08%
between 40% and 50%	107	0.70%
more than 50%	106	0.69%
	15,344	100%

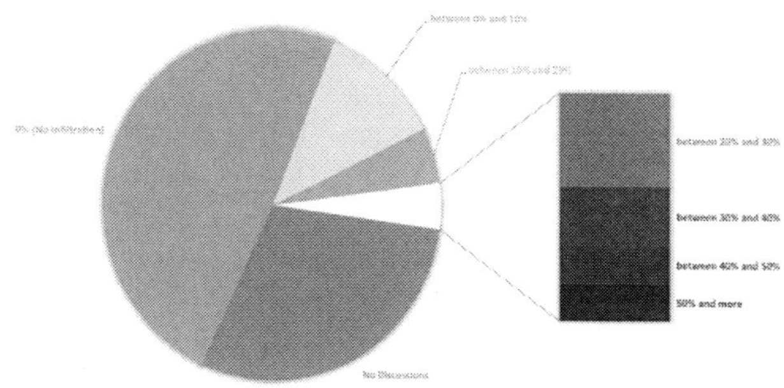

Figure 6. Banning ratio in discussions. For approximately one third of the articles, no discussion was recorded at all, and for nearly half of them no contributor was banned. See also Table IV.

B. Correlation with Page Views

A quantitative rank correlation analysis (using Spearman's correlation coefficient) revealed that the relationship between average daily page views and the banning ratio (in both revisions and discussions) is weakly positive and statistically significant: the coefficient was determined to be $\rho = 0.369$ for revisions and $\rho = 0.272$ for discussion pages. Figure 7 illustrates a more nuanced insight when articles are grouped by their daily page views. Four scenarios are compared:

- All articles (no filter on page views)
- Articles with daily page views $\geq Q1$ (the 25% quartile)
- Articles with daily page views $\geq$ median
- Articles with daily page views $\geq Q3$ (the 75% quartile)

For each of these four subsets, the figure tracks the proportion of articles that have *no banned authors* in their revision histories (banning ratio = 0%) versus those that have *banned authors involved* (> 0% banning ratio). A clear trend emerges as the minimum threshold of daily page views increases: the percentage of articles showing at least some infiltration steadily grows. This indicates that articles drawing higher traffic—be they prominent legal topics or controversial issues—tend to accumulate more edits overall, which in turn raises the likelihood of encountering disruptive contributors.

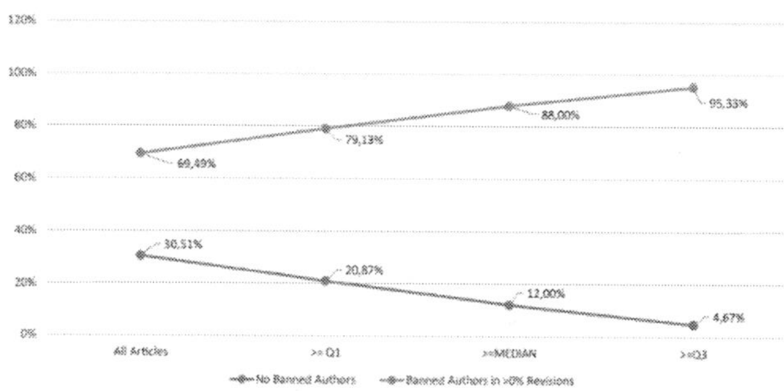

Figure 7. Proportion of articles w/ and w/o banned authors as a function of minimum number of daily page views.

Figure 8 depicts a histogram of the average daily page views *exclusively* for articles that are entirely free from banned contributors (in both revisions and discussions). A majority of these "clean" articles attract fewer than five views per day, suggesting they may be of limited interest to either casual readers or would-be manipulators. The histogram is right-skewed, indicating that while most articles remain unnoticed, a small subset does register higher traffic. The absence of permanently blocked (banned) authors among these pages compared to those pages with solely banned users in Figure 9 aligns with the notion that low-visibility pages tend to experience fewer conflict-driven edits. Of course, it does not guarantee editorial quality in an absolute sense.

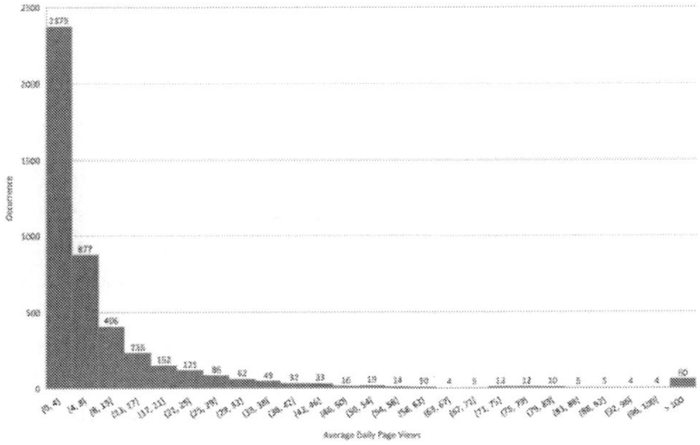

Figure 8. Distribution of average daily page views for all articles that do *not* have permanently banned authors.

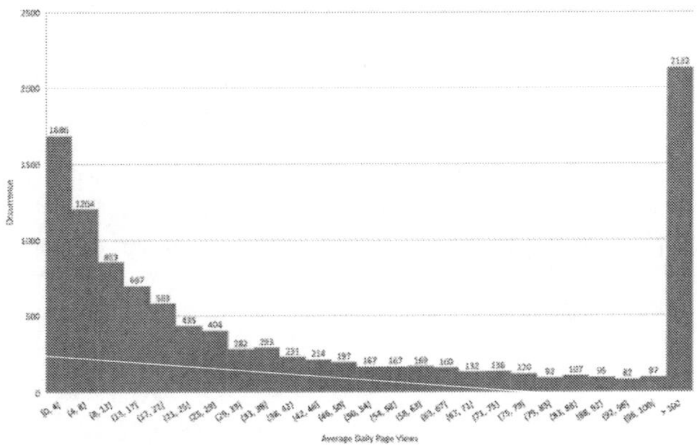

Figure 9. Distribution of average daily page views for all articles that *do* have permanently banned authors.

These findings confirm that even a relatively narrow, less politically charged topic, such as law, is not immune to data poisoning efforts. The prevalence of sockpuppet accounts emphasizes the sophistication of such adversarial behavior, while the long duration of this infiltration—spanning more than two decades—points to a systemic issue of editorial integrity in open knowledge platforms.

Across the corpus of 15,344 legal articles, our quantitative analysis demonstrated that approximately 70% of pages include at least one revision by a permanently banned user, and about 21% of associated discussion pages show contamination. While roughly one third of articles remain free of compromised edits, a small but significant fraction exhibit banning ratios exceeding 20–30% in their revision histories. Spearman correlation coefficients reveal a clear trend: articles with higher daily page views are more likely to have been infiltrated, whereas "clean" articles tend to register fewer than five views per day. This pattern highlights how visibility amplifies vulnerability, reinforcing the need to account for both editor behavior and page popularity when assessing the reliability of open-source knowledge for AI applications.

IV. Conclusion and Future Work

The following section discusses the key findings and draws conclusions. The subsequent section summarizes the outcome of this study.

This study highlights the persistent vulnerability of Wikipedia's German-language legal domain to infiltration by malicious actors. Despite extensive administrative and community-driven oversight, more than two-thirds of legal articles show traces of editorial input from subsequently banned users. Although the legal field may appear apolitical, the data highlight that infiltration and opinion manipulation are not confined to typically controversial areas.

Furthermore, the findings raise important concerns about using Wikipedia articles as a grounding source in RAG systems. As widely documented, large language models can hallucinate when faced with gaps in their training data. RAG mitigates this risk by drawing upon external documents. However, if those external sources harbor inaccuracies or manipulations—intentionally introduced by users with malicious or extremist agendas—hallucinations may be replaced by confidently stated falsehoods. In the context of legal advice, such errors can have serious practical consequences, undermining public trust in both open-source knowledge and AI systems.

The present results recommend the following directions for future work on the topic:

- *Broader Multi-Domain Analysis.* Replicating this methodology for additional subject areas would clarify whether the observed infiltration patterns are specific to the legal sphere or mirrored across other domains.
- *Automated Quality Ratings.* Integrating a rating scheme that accounts for a page's infiltration history (e.g., via the "Banning Ratio") could inform downstream usage for training or grounding. This may include a large-language-model-based sentiment analysis of discussion pages to identify constructive versus adversarial engagement.
- *Refined Filtering for AI Data.* For RAG-based systems or training pipelines, removing or downweighting articles that show high infiltration scores and introducing a reliability metric into prompts can reduce the risk of providing manipulated content to end users.
- *Ongoing Community Oversight.* As infiltration continues to evolve, a coordinated effort by Wikipedia administrators and community volunteers is essential. Studies like

this may help sharpen the focus on identifying emerging patterns and closing loopholes that enable repeated sockpuppetry.

In summary, even a specialized, seemingly neutral topic, such as "Recht" (law) on the German Wikipedia, exhibits clear patterns of infiltration by permanently banned contributors. This study has documented both the extent of that infiltration and its implications for data reliability and AI systems that rely on Wikipedia for training or reference. The belief that crowdsourced content will always self-correct through sheer volume of contributors is challenged by the persistent manipulation attempts observed here. As large language models become more ingrained in everyday applications—particularly in legally sensitive contexts—the urgency to shore up editorial quality and counter data poisoning grows. Countermeasures, including refined scraping, filtering processes, and real-time oversight, are crucial steps toward ensuring the continued integrity of open knowledge ecosystems.

ACKNOWLEDGEMENTS

I would like to thank the referees for very useful comments on the original submission. This research did not receive any specific grant from funding agencies in the public, commercial, or not-for-profit sectors.

REFERENCES

[1] A. Wan, E. Wallace, S. Shen, and D. Klein, "Poisoning language models during instruction tuning," in *Proceedings of the 40th International Conference on Machine Learning*, ICML'23, pp. 35413–35425, JMLR.org, 2023.

[2] D. Alber *et al.*, "Medical large language models are vulnerable to data-poisoning attacks," *Nature Medicine*, vol. 31, pp. 618–626, 01 2025.

[3] T. Fu, M. Sharma, P. Torr, S. B. Cohen, D. Krueger, and F. Barez, "Poisonbench: Assessing large language model vulnerability to data poisoning," *ArXiv*, vol. abs/2410.08811, 2024.

[4] T. B. Brown *et al.*, "Language models are few-shot learners," in *Advances in Neural Information Processing Systems* (H. Larochelle, M. Ranzato, R. Hadsell, M. Balcan, and H. Lin, eds.), vol. 33, pp. 1877–1901, Curran Associates, Inc., 2020.

[5] H. Touvron *et al.*, "Llama: Open and efficient foundation language models," *ArXiv*, vol. abs/2302.13971, 2023.

[6] J. Devlin, M.-W. Chang, K. Lee, and K. Toutanova, "Bert: Pre-training of deep bidirectional transformers for language understanding," *ArXiv*, vol. abs/1810.04805, 2019.

[7] M. Vetter, J. Jiang, and Z. McDowell, "An endangered species: how llms threaten wikipedia's sustainability," *AI & SOCIETY*, pp. 1–14, 02 2025.

[8] J. Giles, "Internet encyclopaedias go head to head," *Nature*, vol. 438, no. 7070, pp. 900–901, 2005.

[9] S. Greenstein and F. Zhu, "Do experts or crowd-based models produce more bias? evidence from encyclopædia britannica and wikipedia," *MIS Quarterly*, vol. 42, pp. 945–959, Sept. 2018.

[10] S. Greenstein, G. Gu, and F. Zhu, "Ideology and composition among an online crowd: Evidence from wikipedians," *Management Science*, vol. 67, no. 5, pp. 3067–3086, 2021.

[11] D. Rozado, "Is wikipedia politically biased?," *Manhattan Institute*, June 2024. Published June, 20th, 2024.

[12] S. Kumar, R. West, and J. Leskovec, "Disinformation on the web: Impact, characteristics, and detection of wikipedia hoaxes," in *Proceedings of the 25th International Conference on World Wide Web*, WWW '16, (Republic and Canton of Geneva, CHE), pp. 591–602, International World Wide Web Conferences Steering Committee, 2016.

[13] A. Elebiary and G. L. Ciampaglia, "The role of online attention in the supply of disinformation in wikipedia," *ArXiv*, vol. abs/2302.08576, 2023.

[14] N. Joshi, F. Spezzano, M. Green, and E. Hill, "Detecting undisclosed paid editing in wikipedia," in *Proceedings of The Web Conference 2020*, WWW '20, (New York, NY, USA), pp. 2899–2905, Association for Computing Machinery, 2020.

[15] P. Lewis *et al.* NIPS '20, (Red Hook, NY, USA), Curran Associates Inc., 2020.

[16] L. Huang *et al.*, "A survey on hallucination in large language models: Principles, taxonomy, challenges, and open questions," *ACM Transactions on Information Systems*, vol. 43, pp. 1–55, Jan. 2025.

[17] W. Zou, R. Geng, B. Wang, and J. Jia, "Poisonedrag: Knowledge corruption attacks to retrieval-augmented generation of large language models," *ArXiv*, vol. abs/2402.07867, 2024.

[18] K. Weber, T. Aichberger, and R. Werner, *Weber compact, Law Dictionary*. Beck-online : Bücher, München: Verlag C.H. Beck, 11. edition, stand: 01.08.2024 ed., 2024.

[19] Wikipedia contributors, "Sock puppet account." https://en.wikipedia.org/wiki/Sock_puppet_account, 2025. Accessed: 2025-05-15.

[20] Wikipedia contributors, "Wikipedia:sockpuppet investigations." https://en.wikipedia.org/wiki/Wikipedia:Sockpuppet_investigations, 2025. Accessed: 2025-05-15.

[21] Wikipedia contributors, "Wikipedia:sockpuppetry." https://en.wikipedia.org/wiki/Wikipedia:Sockpuppetry, 2025. Accessed: 2025-05-15.

[22] C. Schattleitner and D. Laufer, "Sock puppet zoo – attack on wikipedia." https://www.ardaudiothek.de/sendung/sockenpuppenzoo-angriff-auf-wikipedia/13996869/, 2025. Podcast.

APPENDIX

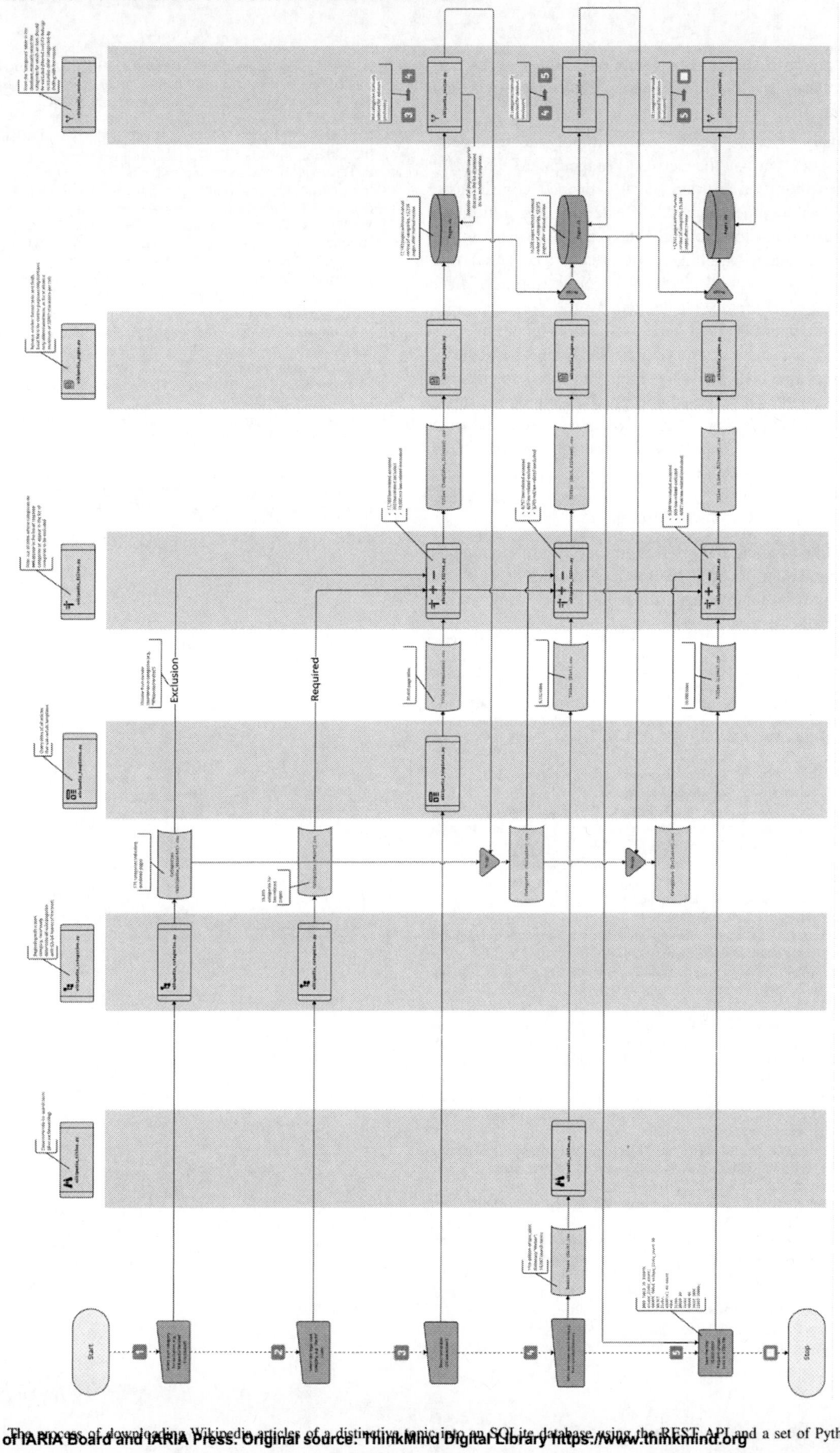

Figure 10. The process of downloading Wikipedia articles of a distinctive topic into an SQLite database using the REST API and a set of Python scripts.

A Novel Synthetic Dataset for Broadcast Motorsports Scene Understanding

Luca Francesco Rossi [1,2], Andrea Sanna [1], Federico Manuri [1]
[1]Department of Control and Computer Engineering
Politecnico di Torino
Corso Duca degli Abruzzi, 24, 10129, Torino, TO, Italy
e-mail: {lucafrancesco.rossi | andrea.sanna | federico.manuri}@polito.it

Mattia Donna Bianco[2]
[2]netventure R&D S.r.l.
Software Engineer
Via della Consolata, 1\bis, 10122, Torino, TO, Italy
e-mail: m.donnabianco@netventure.tv

Abstract*—The paper introduces a foundational approach to motorsports scene understanding by investigating the role of synthetic data generation in advancing scene understanding for high-speed broadcast scenarios. Utilizing the CARLA (Car Learning to Act) simulation environment, the study constructs a high-fidelity dataset incorporating diverse lighting conditions, occlusions, and dynamic camera perspectives to enhance model generalization. A multi-stage data refinement pipeline is introduced to mitigate the impact of extreme occlusions and irrelevant samples while preserving the complexity of real-world challenges. Possible applications include 3D real-world understanding from a single monocular 2D image, which could open up interesting possibilities for augmented reality in broadcast media by allowing seamless integration of virtual elements, interactive graphics and dynamic visual effects, enhancing storytelling, audience engagement, and production flexibility. The efficacy of the dataset is further evaluated via transfer learning to the real-world domain, with the model pretrained on synthetic data demonstrating a significantly superior performance compared to its counterpart.

Keywords-computer vision; augmented reality; synthetic data generation; transfer learning.

I. Introduction

Computer Vision (CV) algorithms based on Artificial Intelligence (AI) are revolutionizing the sports industry, offering advanced analytical capabilities that enhance performance evaluation, officiating accuracy, and fan engagement. By leveraging AI-driven techniques, such as player tracking, ball trajectory estimation and action recognition, these algorithms provide real-time insights that were previously considered unattainable [1]. Coaches and analysts can use this technology to refine strategies, optimize training regimens and prevent injuries by closely monitoring player movements and biomechanics. Referees benefit from automated decision-making tools that minimize human error and ensure fair play, while broadcasters utilize computer vision to generate augmented replays, statistical overlays and personalized viewing experiences. Yet, while a noticeable surge of interest towards these techniques has been observed in a multitude of sports [2]–[4], the specific field of motorsports has traditionally been regarded as exclusively linked to industrial applications, with minimal to no scholarly research available in the literature addressing the analysis and comprehension of event dynamics and racing scenarios.

Therefore, this study was undertaken to address this gap by introducing a synthetic dataset that includes 3D information on ABB FIA Formula E Gen3 racing car models in urban environments, considering as underlying objective to establish a foundation for advancing research in motorsports scene understanding.

The structure of the paper is as follows: Section II reviews relevant literature pertinent to the present study; Section III outlines the methodology and technical details employed in constructing the synthetic dataset, discussing both its advantages and limitations; Section IV assesses the reliability of the dataset by examining synthetic-to-synthetic and synthetic-to-real performance, exploring potential applications of the work; and Section V concludes the paper, summarizing the findings and suggesting avenues for future research.

II. Related work

The increasing popularity of AI, particularly in subfields like Machine Learning (ML) and Deep Learning (DL), has led to a significant challenge in the limited size (or lack) of training datasets. This limitation is primarily due to high workloads and privacy concerns, which hinder the model's ability to generalize effectively [5]. Synthetic Data Generation (SDG) arose as a viable solution to address such an issue: by generating artificial data and labels that closely emulate authentic samples, it alleviates constraints imposed by traditional datasets. This approach proves highly valuable when real data is insufficient, costly to label or exhibits biased distributions, and its advantages go beyond cost reduction, contributing to reduced computational time and addressing bias in data distribution. Eventually, synthetic data can also be generated on the fly during training, eliminating the need for storage, and can be made to be as photorealistic as possible, allowing models to transfer from synthetic training sets to real test sets.

A. Synthetic data generation for sports

Cerqueira and Kenwright [6] introduced a novel approach to CV-based feature extraction in football by leveraging entirely synthetic training data. Differently from conventional machine learning models in sports analytics that typically depend on real-world images, such a study investigates instead the feasibility of training machine learning models exclusively on synthetic datasets generated through computer graphics, with the objective of minimizing the domain gap between synthetic and real-world data [7]. By generating high-fidelity, labeled synthetic images of football matches and by incorporating a diverse range of viewpoints, lighting conditions, occlusions, and visual artifacts, the authors demonstrate that models trained exclusively on synthetic data can generalize effectively to real-world football imagery, accurately identifying pitch markers and player positions. The study validates the potential of synthetic data to address key limitations of real-world datasets, demonstrating its efficacy in the application of synthetic data for sports analytics.

Bhargavi et al. [8] demonstrated that the integration of synthetic data with lightweight deep learning models can achieve state-of-the-art results in jersey number identification while minimizing the need for extensive manual annotations or large-scale datasets. The proposed method involves an initial step of detecting and segmenting players from video frames using a pretrained person detection model [9]. Subsequently, a human pose estimation model [10] is employed to localize jersey numbers by identifying torso key points, thereby obviating the need for manual annotation of bounding boxes. Given the constraints of real-world datasets in terms of sample size and class imbalance, the study introduces two synthetic datasets – Simple2D and Complex2D.

Qin et al. [11] presented SoccerSynth-Detection, a novel synthetic dataset specifically designed for soccer player detection, addressing the limitations of existing real-world datasets, such as SoccerNet-Tracking [12] and SportsMoT [13]. To construct the dataset, the authors augmented a previously developed soccer stadium simulator by integrating a central camera with configurations derived from real-world match footage. They employed assets from the Unreal Engine Marketplace to model player appearances and animations, while movement logic was implemented through AI-controlled Behavior Trees. The simulation environment was further enhanced by incorporating dynamic lighting, randomized textures and motion blur, thereby mitigating the domain gap between synthetic and real-world data to improve model generalization. In the transfer learning experiment, a model trained on SoccerSynth-Detection was evaluated against real-world datasets. While it exhibited a slight reduction in AP50 performance [14] compared to real datasets, it demonstrated superior results in more stringent detection settings (mAP50-95), particularly in handling motion blur, suggesting that the synthetic dataset can either match or surpass real datasets under specific conditions.

B. Scene understanding in motorsports

Boiarov et al. [15] presented RaceLens, a novel application that utilizes deep learning and computer vision models to automatically analyze racing photos. It is designed to maximize the potential of racing photographs by identifying and interpreting crucial elements in the images, such as detecting racing cars, recognizing car numbers, and detecting and quantifying car details. The proposed method employs a Metric Learning [16] approach to tackle the task, where the main encoder model takes a 3-channel image as input and outputs a 1-D vector representing the color scheme of the car in the image. The embeddings are trained to be closer to each other for images of the same class and farther apart for different classes, using a triplet loss and a fully connected layer with cross-entropy loss. During the inference phase, clusters can be created using the embeddings, and the so-called Car Number Recognition Model [17] is utilized to assign the corresponding team names to the clusters. The method allows for clustering of images based on color scheme and uses the Car Number Recognition Model to assign team names to the clusters, enabling the affiliation of cars with their respective teams. It has been deployed for NASCAR teams and has processed over 200 race events, with an average of 7000 photos per event, and has achieved high accuracy in its analysis, with an average percent of photos without cars being less than 1%. The framework uses a combination of models, including Keypoint R-CNN with ResNet-50 backbone [18], and has been evaluated using COCO metrics, achieving high average precision and recall.

Tyo et al. [19] presented the Racer Number Dataset (RnD), a novel and challenging dataset aimed at advancing research in Optical Character Recognition (OCR) within the domain of off-road motorsports. The dataset comprises 2,411 images collected from professional motorsports photographers across 50 distinct off-road competitions, encompassing a total of 5,578 manually annotated bounding boxes that delineate visible motorcycle racer numbers. These images present a range of conditions that pose significant challenges to OCR systems, including occlusions caused by mud, motion blur, glare, complex backgrounds, and non-standardized fonts. To assess the efficacy of contemporary OCR techniques in this domain, the authors conducted a benchmarking study using two state-of-the-art OCR models [20][21] – both in their pre-trained configurations and after fine-tuning on the RnD dataset – underscoring the necessity for domain-specific OCR techniques that are robust to extreme visual conditions, particularly in the context of motorsports.

Tyo et al. [22] further extended their work by presenting the Muddy Racer re-iDentification Dataset (MUDD), similarly designed to advance research in computer vision applications for off-road motorsports. The MUDD dataset consists of 3,906 images depicting 150 distinct riders across ten competitions, specifically curated for the task of rider re-identification (ReID). In line with their previous findings, empirical results underscore the necessity for domain-specific adaptations to enhance OCR and ReID performance in real-world motorsports applications, with benchmark evaluations conducted using state-of-the-art OCR and ReID models [23] revealing that existing pre-trained models perform inadequately in such a domain. Promising results are nonetheless retrieved via a Contrastive Multiple Instance Learning (CMIL) framework [24] which introduces a new formulation that enables contrastive learning at the bag level: instead of focusing on individual image representations, CMIL optimizes entire bag representations, encouraging similar bags to have closer representations while pushing apart dissimilar ones.

III. Method

CARLA (Car Learning to Act) is an open-source urban driving simulator specifically designed to facilitate research in autonomous driving [25]. Developed through a collaboration between Intel Labs, the Toyota Research Institute, and the Computer Vision Center in Barcelona, it provides a sophisticated simulation environment for the development, testing, and validation of autonomous driving systems. A distinguishing characteristic of CARLA is its fully open-source nature, which includes an extensive collection of freely available digital assets, encompassing urban layouts, vehicles, pedestrians, and environmental elements. The platform enables the customization of sensor configurations, incorporating RGB cameras, depth sensors, and semantic segmentation, thereby allowing for comprehensive experimentation with perception systems. Furthermore, CARLA offers a dynamic simulation environment, supporting variable weather conditions, lighting scenarios, and traffic situations involving both autonomous and non-player vehicles as well as pedestrians, thus ensuring a high degree of realism and adaptability. The interested reader is recommended to discover more about CARLA in [26].

The rationale behind this work is that pose estimation for rigid bodies provides a fundamental approach to inferring three-dimensional (3D) spatial relationships from two-dimensional (2D) image data, enabling a deeper understanding of object orientation and motion within a scene. By leveraging keypoint detection and geometric transformations, pose estimation algorithms recover essential structural information, with consequent mapping of 2D projections to 3D coordinates through Perspective-n-Point (PnP) methods [27] leading to spatial understanding. Considering broadcasting applications, a 6-keypoints pose representation for race cars is proposed, selecting those keypoints that remain predominantly visible under typical viewing conditions. These keypoints include the four wheels, the top of the front wing, and the camera mount, ensuring robust and consistent pose estimation in dynamic racing environments.

A. *Dataset preparation*

Since originally developed for autonomous driving scenarios, the first extension required for modeling realistic motorsports images in CARLA consists in decoupling recording sensors and cameras from the ego vehicle to simulate possible broadcasting-level panoramic views. This is obtained by synchronously moving all cameras and sensors from one vehicle to the other at each world tick by applying a geometric transformation $\mathbb{T}_\tau$ to the camera position c_τ and orientation ρ_τ at tick time τ, i.e.,

$$\begin{bmatrix} c \\ \rho \end{bmatrix}_{\tau+1} = \mathbb{T}_\tau \left(\begin{bmatrix} c \\ \rho \end{bmatrix}_\tau \right) \tag{1}$$

where the geometric transformation is computed in such a way that

$$\mathbb{T}_\tau = \bar{\mathbb{T}}_\tau + \mathbb{X}_\tau \tag{2}$$

with $\bar{\mathbb{T}}_\tau$ being the transformation that would precisely bring the camera to point towards the chosen vehicle, and $\mathbb{X}_\tau$ is the instantiation at tick time τ of possible noisy operating camera movements observable in the real setting, such as zoom in, zoom out or random rotations that force the camera to drift away from always having the target exactly at the center of the image. Qualitatively, the optimal results were achieved by configuring the camera's field of view to 90° and letting $\bar{\mathbb{T}}_\tau$ positioning it along a circular trajectory with a radius of 7.5 meters, centered on the target vehicle's position. The camera was placed at a height of 3.5 meters above ground level and oriented directly toward the vehicle, irrespective of the specific point along the circumference. The transformation noise $\mathbb{X}_\tau$ is introduced to simulate zooming effects by applying a random shift within the interval $[-2, 2]$ meters to both the radius and height. Additionally, imprecision in camera orientation is incorporated by applying random variations in the yaw and pitch angles within the interval $[-15°, 15°]$ and in the roll angle within the interval $[-5°, 5°]$.

Three distinct lighting conditions – noon, sunset, and evening – were considered, with $1,500$ images generated for each setting, resulting in a total of $4,500$ frames at a resolution of 1920 × 1080 pixels.

B. *Data refinement*

One of the primary advantages of utilizing synthetic data is the availability of precise ground-truth information regarding the 3D spatial distribution at every stage. However, data processed by neural networks typically resides within the camera coordinate system, necessitating a transformation pipeline between the real 3D world and its abstracted 2D sensor representation. Figure 1 provides a step-by-step visual representation of the proposed approach discussed here:

A) the RGB frame is captured at world tick time τ;
B) real-world coordinates are employed to project the 3D bounding box coordinates onto the image plane;
C) an initial estimation of the 2D bounding boxes is obtained by identifying the extreme coordinates of the original 3D bounding boxes;
D) these preliminary 2D bounding boxes are further refined by computing the minimal enclosing rectangle of the vehicle's mask convex hull, extracted through semantic segmentation;
E) pose and keypoint visibility are filtered using a point cloud generated by a LiDAR sensor, distinguishing visible points from occluded ones relative to the camera perspective;

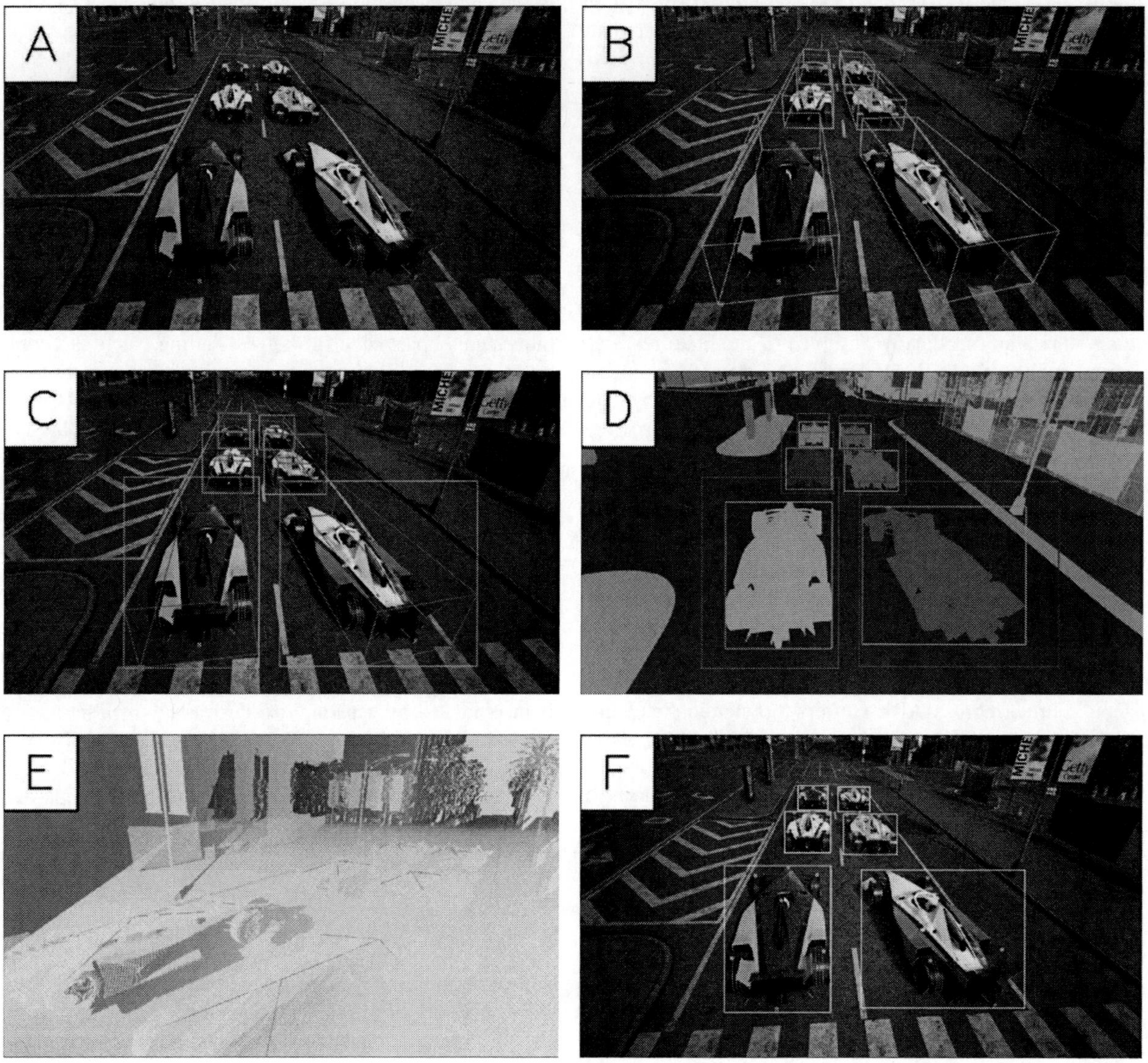

Figure 1. Qualitative visualization of the iterative SDG pipeline in CARLA.

F) the final dataset consists of the refined 2D bounding boxes, along with the corresponding poses and keypoints' visibility.

To minimize the presence of pure background images in the dataset, frames in which the relevant pixel area—defined as the number of pixels labeled by semantic segmentation as belonging to the actor of interest—was less than 1% of the total image size were automatically discarded during the data generation pipeline. Likewise, a maximum distance of 150 meters between an actor and the camera was established as a threshold for determining its relevance. A final criterion for actor inclusion was based on the ratio between its pixel area and the size of its refined 2D bounding box: if this ratio fell below 10%, the actor was automatically excluded by the SDG pipeline. Despite being qualitatively determined, these thresholds were kept very loose in order to just remove noisy information, such as complete occlusions or extreme aspect ratios and bounding box sizes. With respect to keypoint visibility, a threshold of 0.3 meters was established. More in detail, a spherical region with this radius, centered at the actual 3D location of the keypoint, is defined in the point cloud: if no other point is detected within such neighborhood, the keypoint is considered as not visible.

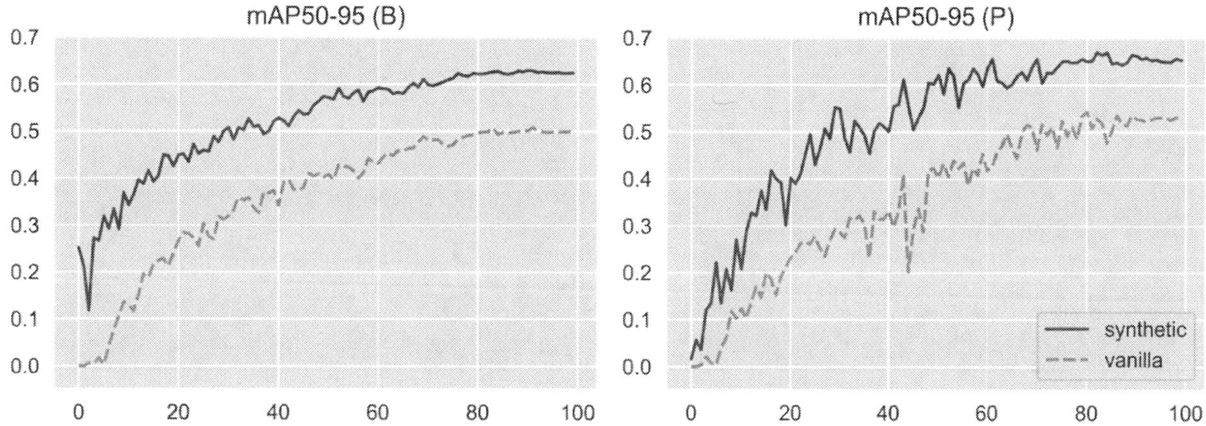

Figure 2. Validation mAP50-95 box (B) and pose (P) metrics gap on real data with and without transfer learning from the proposed synthetic dataset.

C. Limitations

Given the significant variability in camera orientations and the impact of partial environmental occlusions, certain deficiencies of such a fully automated approach must be acknowledged. First, when refining the 2D bounding box via semantic segmentation, it is assumed that the convex hull of the most frequently labeled vehicle pixels corresponds to the actor of interest. This assumption is generally robust, but some care has to be taken in those rare cases of strong occlusions among vehicles, where mis-classifications might occur.

Second, in order to build the point cloud for visibility computation, a static ray-casting should ideally be set from the camera perspective. This is not exactly what is done by CARLA LiDAR sensor [26], which behaves as a solid approximation but few (ideally not visible) points might still be present in the cloud. For such a reason, a strategy of hidden point removal [28] is implemented: by identifying the points located on the convex hull of a transformed cloud, visibility can be determined without neither the need for surface reconstruction nor normal estimation [29].

IV. Evaluation and Discussion

This section presents empirical results obtained using the dataset introduced thus far. Given the inherently fast-moving dynamics of motorsports scenarios, the You Only Look Once (YOLO) framework [30][31] has been chosen to simulate inference under real-time constraints. From the entire dataset, 3,150 images (70%) were allocated for training, 900 images (20%) for validation, and 450 images (10%) for testing.

More in detail, the whole training process was executed on a single NVIDIA Tesla V100 SXM2 GPU (32 GB, 5120 CUDA cores), inside a Python 3.7.7 environment with PyTorch 1.31.1 for CUDA 11.6. A YOLOv8x model was trained for 100 epochs with mixed precision on batches of eight 1280×1280 resized images. A cosine scheduler was set, progressively reducing the learning rate from its initial value of 1e-4 to a hundredth of it.

Table I and Table II highlight the best COCO metric values – on both validation and test splits – for vehicle bounding box detection and keypoints pose estimation, respectively. Concerning such results, a peculiar disparity between precision and recall is evident, likely attributable to a non-negligible presence of false negatives, as inferred from the high precision value. The suboptimal performance observed on the dataset may partially stem from the loosely-defined exclusion criteria applied during its construction. If the exclusion process fails to properly eliminate all borderline cases, i.e., ground truth vehicles under challenging occlusions or strong out-of-frame – the overall recall metric may as results be negatively impacted by the dataset's compromised quality rather than the inherent limitations of the model itself. Yet, while such exclusion criteria may introduce very challenging scenarios for the model, this characteristic can be seen as an advantage rather than a deficiency. By retaining most borderline cases, the dataset better reflects the complexities of real-world scenarios, where perfect visibility and ideal conditions are rarely guaranteed. Instead of filtering out these challenging instances, their inclusion provides a more comprehensive evaluation of the model's robustness and generalization ability. This approach ensures that the model is trained and tested on a diverse range of conditions, ultimately possibly leading to improved performance in practical broadcasting applications where imperfect data is the norm.

TABLE I. SYNTHETIC DATASET METRICS FOR BBOX DETECTION.

Split	P_B	R_B	*mAP50*$_B$	*mAP50-95*$_B$
Validation	0.952	0.793	0.897	0.793
Test	0.962	0.773	0.884	0.784

TABLE II. SYNTHETIC DATASET METRICS FOR POSE ESTIMATION.

Split	P_P	R_P	*mAP50*$_P$	*mAP50-95*$_P$
Validation	0.924	0.728	0.842	0.816
Test	0.918	0.716	0.827	0.795

Figure 3. Qualitative illustration of dataset samples with 3D space reconstruction after PnP computation.

A. Synthetic to real adaptation

The disparity in performance between synthetic and real-domain data remains a subject of ongoing discussion within the research community [32]. Reducing this gap is crucial to enhance both the reliance on and the applicability of synthetic data [33]. Given that models trained exclusively on synthetic data continue to exhibit suboptimal performance when applied to real-world scenarios [34], this study conducts a qualitative evaluation of the proposed dataset via transfer learning from the synthetic domain to the real one, with the objective of determining whether this approach leads to any improvement in model performance.

For this purpose, a proprietary dataset consisting of broadcast images from the 2023-2024 ABB FIA Formula E World Championship has been assembled from official broadcast racing highlights: 293 training frames from the Mexico City ePrix and 42 validation frames from the Portland ePrix were provided to five independent annotators to generate manually-labeled ground-truth annotations for bounding boxes and pose keypoints, including visibility information.

In accordance with the previously described experimental setup, two distinct YOLOv8x models – one pretrained on the synthetic dataset and the other initialized from scratch – were trained on the real data. Figure 2 presents the evolution of the mAP50-95 metric over 100 epochs for both bounding box detection (on the left) and keypoints pose estimation (on the right) for the two models, emphasizing the disparity between the two performance trends. The results clearly illustrate the impact of synthetic pretraining, with the pretrained model demonstrating an improvement of 24.56% in mAP50-95 for bounding box detection and 23.08% for keypoints pose estimation, compared to its "vanilla" counterpart.

Table III offers a detailed summary of key statistics, providing an overview of the performance improvements observed across all training epochs.

TABLE III. RELEVANT STATISTICS CONCERNING mAP50-95 GAP.

Task	*AVG*	*STD*	*MIN*	*25%*	*50%*	*75%*	*MAX*
Box	0.161	0.042	0.113	0.127	0.149	0.183	0.317
Pose	0.164	0.056	0.016	0.128	0.152	0.205	0.354

B. PnP computation

The PnP problem consists in solving for the rotation and translation that minimizes the reprojection error from 3D-2D point correspondences. By reverse engineering the well-known problem [35]

$$\lambda \begin{bmatrix} u \\ v \\ 1 \end{bmatrix} = \mathbf{K}[\mathbf{R}|\mathbf{t}] \begin{bmatrix} x \\ y \\ z \\ 1 \end{bmatrix} \tag{3}$$

one is therefore able to abstract the real-world 3D representation from the given 2D frame. Figure 3 qualitatively illustrates some dataset samples with corresponding 3D understanding reconstruction.

When transposed to the real setting, this approach could open up a whole set of opportunities: for example, understanding the 3D world from a single 2D image unlocks transformative possibilities for Augmented Reality (AR) in broadcast TV, enhancing storytelling, audience engagement, and real-time visual effects. By reconstructing 3D scenes from standard camera feeds, broadcasters can seamlessly integrate virtual objects, dynamic graphics, and interactive overlays into live or pre-recorded footage without requiring complex depth-sensing equipment. Real-time depth estimation also facilitates more natural occlusion handling, ensuring AR elements interact convincingly with on-screen subjects. Additionally, AI-driven 3D scene understanding allows broadcasters to create adaptive, personalized content, such as interactive replays or custom viewing perspectives. These advancements reduce production costs, increase creative flexibility, and redefine audience engagement, making AR-enhanced broadcasting more accessible and compelling across news, sports, and entertainment.

V. Conclusion and Future Work

Through the adoption of simulation platforms, such as CARLA, this study introduces the feasibility of constructing a high-fidelity dataset that encapsulate real-world complexities, including variable lighting conditions, partial occlusions, and non-static camera viewpoints. The empirical findings indicate that, while synthetic datasets may introduce challenges associated with domain adaptation, they serve as a robust framework for enhancing model generalization and performance in real-world deployment scenarios. Given the inherently time-consuming and costly nature of manual data annotation, the proposed work aims to address this limitation in the domain of motorsports scene understanding. Empirical results on real-world data demonstrate the effectiveness of the proposed dataset in minimizing the reliance on extensive labeled datasets, thereby offering a robust foundation for further analysis, and a structured way to address 3D scene reconstruction in broadcast media images.

Future research should prioritize the refinement of exclusion criteria, the development of advanced domain adaptation strategies, and the integration of physics-based simulations to further mitigate the domain gap between synthetic and real-world data. Ultimately, continued innovation in synthetic data generation methodologies will be instrumental in fostering the development of more reliable, scalable, and adaptable AI-driven vision systems for motorsports analytics and beyond.

Future work will indeed focus on advancing the end-to-end synthetic data generation pipeline, with the objective of increasing the fidelity, diversity, and domain-relevance of the generated data. Enhancements in procedural generation, domain randomization, and photorealistic rendering could significantly improve model generalization and robustness, particularly in scenarios where annotated real-world data is limited or biased. Another potential extension involves the integration of additional semantic classes, specifically targeting vehicle livery recognition. Incorporating livery as a distinct detection class would enable the system to differentiate between visually similar vehicle instances based on team or sponsor-specific visual attributes. This capability could help mitigate the inherent class imbalance and representation bias present in existing real-world datasets, thereby improving fairness and reliability in downstream perception tasks, and leading to models even more suitable for broadcasting purposes. Furthermore, a re-examination of the CARLA simulation framework presents valuable opportunities for domain-specific augmentation. By introducing racing-oriented dynamics – such as high-speed maneuvers, competitive interactions, and tactical behavior patterns – the simulation environment can be tailored to better reflect the operational context of racing environments. In this context, incorporating (inter)action recognition becomes particularly salient. Beyond static object detection, the ability to model and infer temporal and relational dynamics among agents (e.g., overtaking, blocking, cooperative maneuvers) can facilitate higher-level scene understanding and event prediction. This shift from instance-level perception to spatiotemporal reasoning has the potential to significantly enhance the decision-making capabilities of those agents operating in competitive, high-speed environments.

The generated synthetic dataset is made publicly accessible to foster further research in this field and is available for download [36].

References

[1] G. Thomas, R. Gade, T. B. Moeslund, P. Carr, and A. Hilton, "Computer vision for sports: Current applications and research topics", *Computer Vision and Image Understanding*, vol. 159, pp. 3–18, 2017, Computer Vision in Sports, ISSN: 1077-3142. DOI: https://doi.org/10.1016/j.cviu.2017.04.011.

[2] B. T. Naik, M. F. Hashmi, and N. D. Bokde, "A comprehensive review of computer vision in sports: Open issues, future trends and research directions", *Applied Sciences*, vol. 12, no. 9, p. 4429, 2022, ISSN: 2076-3417. DOI: 10.3390/app12094429.

[3] K. Host and M. Ivašić-Kos, "A comprehensive review of computer vision in sports: Open issues, future trends and research directions", *Heliyon*, vol. 8, no. 6, 2022, ISSN: 2405-8440. DOI: 10.1016/j.heliyon.2022.e09633.

[4] T. Mendes-Neves, L. Meireles, and J. Mendes-Moreira, "A survey of advanced computer vision techniques for sports", *arXiv e-prints*, arXiv:2301.07583, arXiv:2301.07583, Jan. 2023. DOI: 10.48550/arXiv.2301.07583. arXiv: 2301.07583 [cs.CV].

[5] S. I. Nikolenko, *Synthetic Data for Deep Learning*. Springer Cham, 2022. DOI: 10.1007/978-3-030-75178-4.

[6] J. Cerqueira Fernandes and B. Kenwright, "Identifying and extracting football features from real-world media sources using only synthetic training data", *arXiv e-prints*, arXiv:2209.13254, arXiv:2209.13254, Sep. 2022. DOI: 10.48550/arXiv.2209.13254. arXiv: 2209.13254 [cs.AI].

[7] G. Paulin and M. Ivasic-Kos, "Review and analysis of synthetic dataset generation methods and techniques for application in computer vision", *Artif. Intell. Rev.*, vol. 56, no. 9, pp. 9221–9265, Jan. 2023, ISSN: 0269-2821. DOI: 10.1007/s10462-022-10358-3.

[8] D. Bhargavi, E. Pelaez Coyotl, and S. Gholami, "Knock, knock. who's there? – identifying football player jersey numbers with synthetic data", *arXiv e-prints*, arXiv:2203.00734, arXiv:2203.00734, Sep. 2022. DOI: 10.48550/arXiv.2203.00734. arXiv: 2203.00734 [cs.AI].

[9] K. Duan *et al.*, "Centernet: Keypoint triplets for object detection", in *2019 IEEE/CVF International Conference on Computer Vision (ICCV)*, 2019, pp. 6568–6577. DOI: 10.1109/ICCV.2019.00667.

[10] H.-S. Fang *et al.*, "Alphapose: Whole-body regional multi-person pose estimation and tracking in real-time", *IEEE Trans. Pattern Anal. Mach. Intell.*, vol. 45, no. 6, pp. 7157–7173, Jun. 2023, ISSN: 0162-8828. DOI: 10.1109/TPAMI.2022.3222784.

[11] H. Qin, C. Yeung, R. Umemoto, and K. Fujii, "Soccersynth-detection: A synthetic dataset for soccer player detection", *arXiv e-prints*, arXiv:2501.09281, arXiv:2501.09281, Jan. 2025. DOI: 10.48550/arXiv.2501.09281. arXiv: 2501.09281 [cs.CV].

[12] A. Cioppa *et al.*, "Soccernet-tracking: Multiple object tracking dataset and benchmark in soccer videos", in *2022 IEEE/CVF Conference on Computer Vision and Pattern Recognition Workshops (CVPRW)*, 2022, pp. 3490–3501. DOI: 10.1109/CVPRW56347.2022.00393.

[13] Y. Cui *et al.*, " SportsMOT: A Large Multi-Object Tracking Dataset in Multiple Sports Scenes ", in *2023 IEEE/CVF International Conference on Computer Vision (ICCV)*, Los Alamitos, CA, USA: IEEE Computer Society, Oct. 2023, pp. 9887–9897. DOI: 10.1109/ICCV51070.2023.00910.

[14] T.-Y. Lin *et al.*, "Microsoft coco: Common objects in context", in *Computer Vision – ECCV 2014*, D. Fleet, T. Pajdla, B. Schiele, and T. Tuytelaars, Eds., Cham: Springer International Publishing, 2014, pp. 740–755, ISBN: 978-3-319-10602-1.

[15] A. Boiarov, D. Bleklov, P. Bredikhin, N. Koritsky, and S. Ulasen, " RaceLens: A Machine Intelligence-Based Application for Racing Photo Analysis ", in *2023 IEEE 28th Pacific Rim International Symposium on Dependable Computing (PRDC)*, Los Alamitos, CA, USA: IEEE Computer Society, 2023, pp. 352–355. DOI: 10.1109/PRDC59308.2023.00057.

[16] E. Hoffer and N. Ailon, "Deep metric learning using triplet network", in *Similarity-Based Pattern Recognition*, A. Feragen, M. Pelillo, and M. Loog, Eds., Cham: Springer International Publishing, 2015, pp. 84–92.

[17] M. Tan and Q. Le, "EfficientNet: Rethinking model scaling for convolutional neural networks", in *Proceedings of the 36th International Conference on Machine Learning*, K. Chaudhuri and R. Salakhutdinov, Eds., ser. Proceedings of Machine Learning Research, vol. 97, PMLR, Sep. 2019, pp. 6105–6114.

[18] K. He, X. Zhang, S. Ren, and J. Sun, "Deep residual learning for image recognition", in *2016 IEEE Conference on Computer Vision and Pattern Recognition (CVPR)*, 2016, pp. 770–778. DOI: 10.1109/CVPR.2016.90.

[19] J. Tyo, Y. Chung, M. Olarinre, and Z. C. Lipton, "Reading Between the Mud: A Challenging Motorcycle Racer Number Dataset", *arXiv e-prints*, arXiv:2311.09256, arXiv:2311.09256, Nov. 2023. DOI: 10.48550/arXiv.2311.09256. arXiv: 2311.09256 [cs.CV].

[20] I. Krylov, S. Nosov, and V. Sovrasov, "Open images v5 text annotation and yet another mask text spotter", in *Proceedings of The 13th Asian Conference on Machine Learning*, V. N. Balasubramanian and I. Tsang, Eds., ser. Proceedings of Machine Learning Research, vol. 157, PMLR, 17–19 Nov 2021, pp. 379–389.

[21] M. Huang *et al.*, "Swintextspotter: Scene text spotting via better synergy between text detection and text recognition", in *2022 IEEE/CVF Conference on Computer Vision and Pattern Recognition (CVPR)*, 2022, pp. 4583–4593. DOI: 10.1109/CVPR52688.2022.00455.

[22] J. Tyo, M. Olarinre, Y. Chung, and Z. C. Lipton, "Beyond the Mud: Datasets and Benchmarks for Computer Vision in Off-Road Racing", *arXiv e-prints*, arXiv:2402.08025, arXiv:2402.08025, Feb. 2024. DOI: 10.48550/arXiv.2402.08025. arXiv: 2402.08025 [cs.CV].

[23] K. Zhou, Y. Yang, A. Cavallaro, and T. Xiang, "Omni-scale feature learning for person re-identification", in *2019 IEEE/CVF International Conference on Computer Vision (ICCV)*, 2019, pp. 3701–3711. DOI: 10.1109/ICCV.2019.00380.

[24] J. Tyo and Z. C. Lipton, "Contrastive Multiple Instance Learning for Weakly Supervised Person ReID", *arXiv e-prints*, arXiv:2402.07685, arXiv:2402.07685, Feb. 2024. DOI: 10.48550/arXiv.2402.07685. arXiv: 2402.07685 [cs.CV].

[25] A. Dosovitskiy, G. Ros, F. Codevilla, A. Lopez, and V. Koltun, "CARLA: An open urban driving simulator", in *Proceedings of the 1st Annual Conference on Robot Learning*, S. Levine, V. Vanhoucke, and K. Goldberg, Eds., ser. Proceedings of Machine Learning Research, vol. 78, PMLR, 13–15 Nov 2017, pp. 1–16.

[26] S. Malik, M. A. Khan, and H. El-Sayed, "Carla: Car learning to act — an inside out", *Procedia Computer Science*, vol. 198, pp. 742–749, 2022, 12th International Conference on Emerging Ubiquitous Systems and Pervasive Networks / 11th International Conference on Current and Future Trends of Information and Communication Technologies in Healthcare, ISSN: 1877-0509. DOI: 10.1016/j.procs.2021.12.316.

[27] X. X. Lu, "A review of solutions for perspective-n-point problem in camera pose estimation", *Journal of Physics: Conference Series*, vol. 1087, no. 5, p. 052009, Sep. 2018. DOI: 10.1088/1742-6596/1087/5/052009.

[28] S. Katz, A. Tal, and R. Basri, "Direct visibility of point sets", *ACM Trans. Graph.*, vol. 26, no. 3, 24–es, Jul. 2007, ISSN: 0730-0301. DOI: 10.1145/1276377.1276407.

[29] R. Mehra, P. Tripathi, A. Sheffer, and N. J. Mitra, "Visibility of noisy point cloud data", *Computers & Graphics*, vol. 34, no. 3, pp. 219–230, 2010, Shape Modelling International (SMI)

Conference 2010, ISSN: 0097-8493. DOI: https://doi.org/10.1016/j.cag.2010.03.002.

[30] P. Jiang, D. Ergu, F. Liu, Y. Cai, and B. Ma, "A review of yolo algorithm developments", *Procedia Computer Science*, vol. 199, pp. 1066–1073, 2022, The 8th International Conference on Information Technology and Quantitative Management (ITQM 2020 & 2021): Developing Global Digital Economy after COVID-19, ISSN: 1877-0509. DOI: https://doi.org/10.1016/j.procs.2022.01.135.

[31] J. Terven, D.-M. Córdova-Esparza, and J.-A. Romero-González, "A comprehensive review of yolo architectures in computer vision: From yolov1 to yolov8 and yolo-nas", *Machine Learning and Knowledge Extraction*, vol. 5, no. 4, pp. 1680–1716, 2023, ISSN: 2504-4990. DOI: 10.3390/make5040083.

[32] X. Bai *et al.*, "Bridging the domain gap between synthetic and real-world data for autonomous driving", *ACM J. Auton. Transport. Syst.*, vol. 1, no. 2, Apr. 2024. DOI: 10.1145/3633463.

[33] M. S. Werda *et al.*, "Towards minimizing domain gap when using synthetic data in automotive vision control applications", *IFAC-PapersOnLine*, vol. 58, no. 19, pp. 522–527, 2024, 18th IFAC Symposium on Information Control Problems in Manufacturing INCOM 2024, ISSN: 2405-8963. DOI: https://doi.org/10.1016/j.ifacol.2024.09.265.

[34] K. Singh, T. Navaratnam, J. Holmer, S. Schaub-Meyer, and S. Roth, "Is synthetic data all we need? benchmarking the robustness of models trained with synthetic images", in *Proceedings of the IEEE/CVF Conference on Computer Vision and Pattern Recognition (CVPR) Workshops*, Jun. 2024, pp. 2505–2515.

[35] E. Marchand, H. Uchiyama, and F. Spindler, "Pose estimation for augmented reality: A hands-on survey", *IEEE Transactions on Visualization and Computer Graphics*, vol. 22, no. 12, pp. 2633–2651, Dec. 2016. DOI: 10.1109/TVCG.2015.2513408.

[36] L. F. Rossi, *A Novel Synthetic Dataset for Broadcast Motorsports Scene Understanding*, version V1, 2025. DOI: 10.7910/DVN/DHX380.

Evaluating AI Editing Algorithms for Video News Reporting

Caspian J. Moosburner
RheinMain University of Applied Sciences
Wiesbaden, Germany
email: caspianjade.moosburner@hs-rm.de

Dennis Quandt
RheinMain University of Applied Sciences
Wiesbaden, Germany
email: dennis.quandt@hs-rm.de

Matthias Kowald
RheinMain University of Applied Sciences
Wiesbaden, Germany
email: matthias.kowald@hs-rm.de

Wolfgang Ruppel
RheinMain University of Applied Sciences
Wiesbaden, Germany
email: wolfgang.ruppel@hs-rm.de

Till Dannewald
RheinMain University of Applied Sciences
Wiesbaden, Germany
email: till.dannewald@hs-rm.de

Matthias Narroschke
RheinMain University of Applied Sciences
Wiesbaden, Germany
email: matthias.narroschke@hs-rm.de

Abstract-With video news gaining more and more popularity, Artificial Intelligence (AI) video editing tools could be implemented to accelerate video news production. A challenging issue, however, is the quality of AI-edited video news and the acceptance of such news by media consumers. A survey with 143 participants is conducted in Germany in order to evaluate the quality of video news clips edited by AI models in comparison to news clips produced by professional human editors. All survey participants are recruited by a commercial survey company. The evaluation of the survey reveals that AI editing is widely undetected by the participants. Overall, the evaluation shows that the quality difference of AI edited video new clips and human edited ones is negligible as confidence intervals of measured quality features overlap. Future research can benefit from investigating the influence of clearly labelled AI content in user evaluations.

Keywords-Artificial Intelligence; AI; video editing; video news; algorithms.

I. INTRODUCTION

Video news has been established as a strong contender for attention in the digital landscape, aided by the rise of TikTok and their short form video content that is making a jump to other social media platforms [1]. This creates a need for quick video news reporting, a need that could be aided by implementing Artificial Intelligence (AI) editing tools.

With 40% of young people preferring social media search engines over traditional means [1], the market share of video news reporting on social platforms will continue to grow. This is aided by media publishers who put a bigger focus on digital video production [1] making it clear that the video news reporting demand will increase, and the market is preparing to supply by offering more and more AI tools. One example for this is the launch of the AI writing tool "ChatGPT" in 2022, establishing AI tools as more and more popular and expected to reach a global market share of "more than 2.5 trillion USD by 2032" [2]. Creative industries have implemented generative AI and AI algorithms, for example Adobe Photoshop offering options like generative fill [3], Canva that has its own AI image generation [4] or on countless social media websites via algorithmic AI [5].

The conducted survey is part of a larger survey study. A total of three survey waves are being collected with this paper focussing on the first wave. The first wave aims to gather some general information and results evaluating the algorithm performance.

A second survey wave is planned, aiming to investigate the implications of disclosing AI for quality evaluation in detail by testing audience reception to flagging clips explicitly as AI-edited or human-edited in two different groups. A third wave offers the chance to test further improvements of AI editing algorithms or to re-evaluate the audience reception to AI disclosure.

The here reported first wave questions were designed and conducted with 143 participants to investigate whether the tedious process of editing video news clips could be delegated to AI models and how AI editing technology is perceived by humans. In detail, the study measures subjective receptions of video news and survey participants' evaluation of the quality of editing algorithms.

In Section 2, the algorithms utilised for video editing will be explained, and a previous experiment will be addressed. Section 3 delves into the survey protocol and video experiment while Section 4 illustrates the results. Finally, Section 5 discusses the survey findings and gives a brief outlook into potential future proceedings.

II. Background

Editing video news clips comprises two main steps. In a first step, typically 10 to 15 most suitable scenes for a news story are selected from up to 200 scenes in raw footage. In the second step, the selected scenes are compiled into a video sequence, which is then accompanied by a voice over of a news text to create the final video news clip.

The core of the conducted first survey wave investigates how automated AI-based editing of video news clips scores against human news editing as a high anchor and a random editing as a low anchor. Hereby, two AI models are considered, which both are described in detail in [6]. The first AI model is the CLIP (Contrastive Language–Image Pre-training) model [7], pairing images of video shots with snippets of news text. The second AI model is denoted as KIGVI and has been developed by the RheinMain University of Applied Sciences [6]. The KIGVI model was trained using a dataset of 12354 video clips from news segments that ranged from 30 seconds to 5 minutes covering multiple categories of news from the years 2012 to 2025. The KIGVI model uses shot detection to split footage into scenes and follows learned professional video editing rules. These rules include varying shot sizes, an initial establishing shot illustrating the main topic and the inclusion of a human-like editing rhythm when composing the video news clip. This marks a major improvement over previous algorithms that failed to align information sourced in the visual component as well as the textual one.

A previous experiment with a small sample size ($n = 38$ participants) scored the KIGVI algorithm against human edits based on professionality of the edit, choice of scenes and how well the video sequences illustrated the voiceover. The findings of this experiment warranted further investigation with a bigger sample size and a larger survey that asks respondents about their opinion on AI, video news consumption habits and general media reception. Thus, a more comprehensive survey was developed.

For the analysis of the first survey wave, CLIP and KIGVI have been combined into the category AI and collectively compared to human video editing and random video editing. Human edited news clips were produced by professional editors. In random editing, scenes are randomly selected and compiled into a video news clip. All edited video news clips are voiced over by a professional German recording studio.

III. Survey Protocol

A. Basic principle

The survey is designed as an online survey. The participants of the survey are asked to assess video news clips according to a list of criteria, and to identify the editor of the respective video clip.

B. Samples

The greater RheinMain area is used as survey area. A market research institute was tasked to recruit survey participants living in or around the RheinMain area aged from 16 to 70+ for a first wave of the survey. From this first wave, 150 interviews were conducted between December 2024 and January 2025. The responses of the participants are evaluated in this paper. Surveying the second half of the first wave will continue in the second half of April 2025.

The RheinMain area is a multi-state area in southern Germany including major cities like Frankfurt and Wiesbaden, mid-sized cities such as Russelsheim, as well as a number of smaller municipalities. Since the KIGVI algorithm might improve as it continues being trained on more and more video clips, a future second wave may account for the expected improvements. Completing the online survey took participants 12 minutes on average. The questionnaires were distributed via online links hosted on the platform Qualtrics. The sample size of validly completed questionnaires was 143, with seven interviews that had to be excluded due to incomplete answers and high amounts of item non-response.

C. Survey Structure

In an experiment portion of the questionnaire video news clips are shown, which cover three overall categories of news. These are:

- *Traffic news*
- *Local news*
- *News concerning politics.*

Each of these three categories of news consists of four video news clips, and each video news clip is edited in four different variants, which are:

- *Human editing*
- AI-based editing using the *KIGVI model*
- AI-based editing using the model based on *CLIP*
- *Random editing.*

This results in a pool of 48 video news clips (3 categories × 4 video news clips × 4 variants) as illustrated in Figure 1.

Prior to the experiment portion, the participants received a short introduction before facing a screen-out question that determines whether they agreed to data collection and were inhabitants of the greater RheinMain area. Succeeding led the participants being asked about their news consumption habits and preferences, how familiar they are with AI in general as well as attitudes towards the technology in general, accounting for both algorithmic and generative AI. The experiment portion was introduced to ensure participants understood the task of evaluating the algorithmic AI technology utilised in the editing process.

Matrix questions followed each editing variant in order to assess the quality of a video news clip. A matrix question is the judgement of a specific statement on the Likert-Scale.

Eight statements are used in the survey, which are shown in Table 1. They were inherited from a previous quality survey conducted in [6] with additional questions such as whether participants noticed technical errors like flickering, black screens, timing errors, etc. Furthermore, they were asked whether the video offered additional value to the news report or evoked emotions.

TABLE I. STATEMENTS BEING JUDGED BY A PARTICIPANT ON A LIKERT-SCALE TO ASSESS THE QUALITY OF A VIDEO NEWS CLIP.

Number	Statement
(1)	The voiceover matches the visual material
(2)	The scenes in the video illustrate all the important information in the program
(3)	The video looks professionally edited
(4)	The video is similar to video news I've seen before
(5)	Aspects of the report seem inconsistent / incorrect
(6)	I will probably remember the video report
(7)	The video makes the report more interesting to me
(8)	The report triggers emotion in me

D. Choice Experiment

Responses of the participants to the experiment portion as well as to general attitudes towards news, news reception, artificial intelligence and AI in news are measured on a six-point Likert-scale, which ranges from *Strongly Disagree* (1) to *Strongly Agree* (6). The experiment potion was randomised. A first randomisation assigned a category of news per participant while a second randomisation within each category selected one video news clip per editing variant meaning every participant was shown one random editing variant, one human editing variant, one AI editing variant using the KIGVI model and one AI editing variant using the model based on CLIP.

The video news clips were embedded in the experiment in a way that the participants were able to view them multiple times to secure the responses. Participants were tasked to evaluate the presented video news clip via the matrix questions. Following this evaluation, a choice was presented whether participants believed a human or an AI to be the editor of the before seen video news clip and how confident they were in their choice via Likert scale. Tracking the time, the participants spent on a specific page aimed to make sure that they at least viewed each video news clip once.

IV. RESULTS

In the sample of 143 individuals, 50.4% of survey participants reported identifying as female. A high number of participants, 22.3%, selected an age group of 41-50 years old, 15.8% selected 61-70 years old, 13.7% selected 31-35 years old, and only 10.8% selected ages of 22-25. Ages of 16-22 and 71+ were rare with under 5% of answers. Education levels culminated in 40.6% of participants reporting having passed their A-levels or owning a university degree of some kind while 25.4% completed vocational training.

A key finding of the conducted survey is that human editing and AI editing are rated almost identically on average. Both were ranked much higher than random editing.

When forced to assign a "human-edited" or "AI-edited" label to the different variants, a majority of the participants

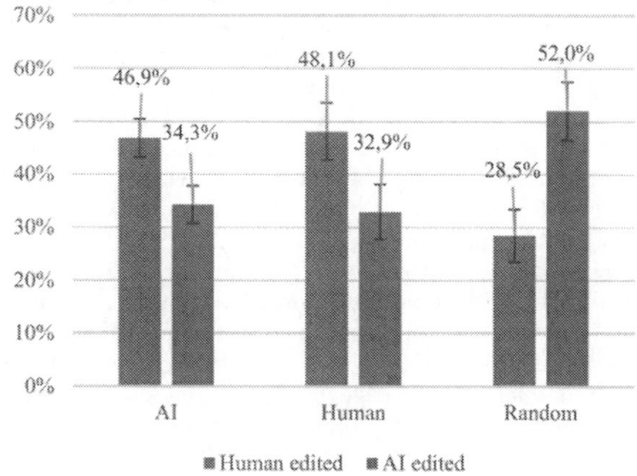

Fig 1. Percentage of survey participants voting either "human edited" (orange) or "AI edited" (blue) for each editing variant.

assigned the label "human-edited" to both, AI edited video news clips and human edited video news clips. Surprisingly, the human edited video news clips were assigned the "AI-edited" label too, as shown in Figure 1. All results shown are

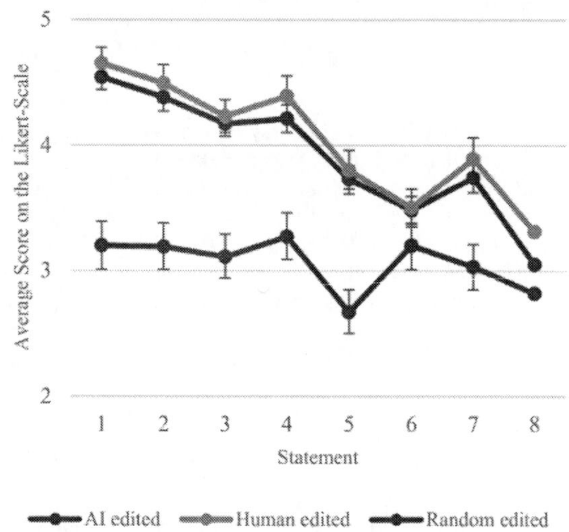

Fig. 2. Average scores on the Likert-Scale versus judged statement of Table 1.

depicted with a corresponding 95% confidence interval.

In Figure 2, the average Likert-Score is illustrated for each of the eight judged statements, (compare Table 1), alongside the corresponding 95% confidence intervals. The Likert-Scores were rounded towards whole values to allow for interpretation.

Overall, AI edited, and human edited video news clips delivered similar average scores on the Likert-scale, recording stronger agreement with the statements except for the inconsistency/incorrectness potential (5) whereas the randomly edited video news clips were scored lower in average for most statements. The more content-related statements are scored highest in average for AI edited and human edited video news clips. Especially the matching of the voiceover to the visual material (1) received highest scores in average, closely followed by the scene selection illustrating the categories of news well (2). Professionality of the edit (3) and resemblance to other news programs (4) also received high scores with AI editing and human editing performing almost identical in average. Inconsistencies / incorrectness (5) were scored much lower than random and met more disagreement. Memorability (6) was scored lower in average than other aspects with the smallest difference between all three editing variants. The human editing scores slightly higher in average when it comes to making the video interesting (7) and emotionality (8) was scored low across all three variants.

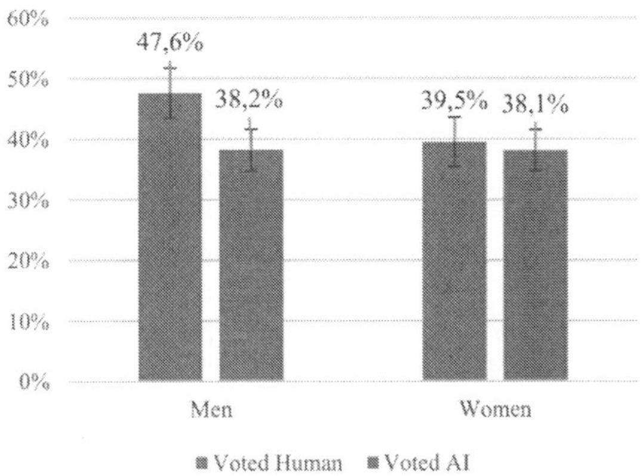

Fig. 3. Percentage of voting for "Human-edited" and "AI-edited" versus the gender of the participants.

Figure 3 illustrates the voting behaviour differentiated into women and men with a 95% confidence interval, showing a higher overall likeliness of men to vote for human-editing as the editor of the video news clip. For women, the choice between AI editing and human editing is much more evenly split. However, a high number of recipients who reported the usage of AI in media as positive assumed the creator of the videos as human rather than AI whereas all other stances had a more even distribution of creator assumptions. Since participants were given the option to cast a neutral vote in addition to the options "Human" or "AI", Figures 1, 3 and 4 do not sum up to 100%.

Figure 4 details the attitude of the participants towards AI in media landscapes ranging from *positive* to *negative* on a four-point scale combined with the likeliness to identify the video editor as human or AI.

Generally, the attitude towards AI in media industries was evaluated as rather positive and rather negative much more

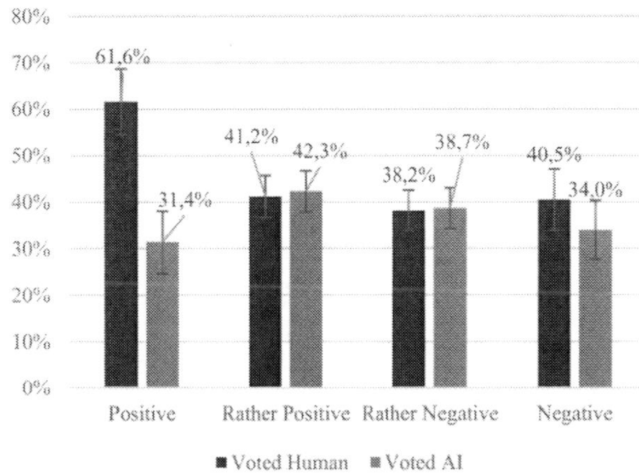

Fig. 4. Attitude of the survey participants towards AI usage in media spaces and voting behaviour.

than the definitive stances of positive or negative as shown in Table 2.

TABLE II. OPINIONS TOWARDS AI IN MEDIA IN PERCENTAGE.

Opinion towards AI	Number of Answers (%)
Positive	13,6
Rather Positive	34,6
Rather Negative	36,0
Negative	15,8

It is noted that Figures 4 and 5 display voting behaviour without accounting for whether the selected choice (human-edited or AI-edited) corresponds to the actual editor of the video news clips. Furthermore, Figure 5 shows that a negative attitude towards AI does not influence the rating of the participants supporting the evaluation results. However, a high number of recipients that reported the usage of AI in media as positive assumed the creator of the videos as human rather than AI whereas all other stances had a more even distribution of creator assumptions.

V. Conclusion

In this paper, a survey is designed and conducted with 143 recruited participants in order to evaluate the quality of video news clips edited by AI models in comparison to the one of news clips produced by professional human editors. A total of 48 video news clips is used in the study, containing three categories of news, four video news clips per category, and four editing variants of each video news clip. Two AI editing variants are applied. In addition, two anchor variants are used. The professionally human edited video news clips serve as a high anchor. Randomly edited video news clips serve as a low anchor. The participants were asked to judge eights statements on a Likert-Scale to assess the quality of a video news clip.

Overall, the evaluation shows that the quality difference of AI edited video news clips and human edited ones is statistically insignificant as confidence intervals of measured quality features overlap. AI editing is widely undetected by the participants.

The evaluation results point towards the conclusion that an AI can already perform the task of video editing as well as, or at least similarly to a professional editor in the industry. The lower evaluation of results for statements (6) to (8) of the question matrix question the relevance of these statements when it comes to the performance of the algorithms since the strictly technical evaluation generally scored higher provided a high separation of AI editing and Human editing versus random editing.

Additionally, the low scoring random edit could indicate faithful responses, as the random variant videos were lower in quality and included clips that did not fit the categories of news of the overall videos. Seeing this represented in the matrix questions allows to interpret, that users filled out the video experiment portion genuinely paying attention to the videos.

Reference [8] already found social media users to be incapable of distinguishing AI and human made content, in their case generative AI created images and Instagram captions. These findings align with our findings of recipients not being able to distinguish the AI from the human edit.

As of the present, results are based on a first wave of data of $n = 147$ participants. A second survey wave is currently in the field. For this second wave, the video experiment portion was pulled up in the survey flow to precede the questions about news habit and co. in an effort to potentially rule out effects of fatigue on the data. Furthermore, the two AI editing tools, the CLIP and the KIGVI algorithm, were combined in this paper to focus only on the performance of AI versus human. However, the evaluation in the surveys were separated into each algorithm to ensure the possibility of a separate assessment as well.

Additionally, the survey asks for user's socio-demographic characteristics, individual habits of news and video consumption, as well as views on AI. The according information allows deeper and group specific analysis in the future. For example, it will be possible to analyse whether bias towards AI exists, how it shows in the evaluation of the videos, and whether disclosing the use of AI influences audiences' perception of it.

VI. Outlook

The present research gives a brief outline of key findings from a first survey wave. Data collection is ongoing and will allow for more in-depth results concerning the multitude of topics (news habits, attitudes towards AI) recorded in the survey later on. The present findings already highlight the improvements of AI editing in news broadcasting and pave the way towards bigger strides of the technology. As of now, statistical choice models determining the author of the clips are being estimated, aided by the aforementioned matrix with the addition of sociodemographic factors and attitudes towards AI. Employing a logistic regression model will inform about multiple effects and contributing factors affecting the recipient's assumed identification of the creator of the videos whether it be human or AI.

Acknowledgment

The authors thank the German Federal Ministry of Research, Technology and Space, and Qvest GmbH for funding this work via the program FH-Kooperativ 2-2019, contract number 13FH544KX9.

References

[1] N. Newman, "Journalism, media and technology trends and predictions 2023," Reuters Institute for the Study of Journalism. https://doi.org/10.5287/bodleian:NokooZeEP [retrieved: 2025-06-05]

[2] Y. Hayashi, "Prospects for Revolutionary and Popular AI Technology following the Launch of ChatGPT in 2023," Electronics, 13(2), 290, pp. 1–2. https://doi.org/10.3390/electronics13020290 [retrieved: 05, 2025]

[3] J. O. Adigun et al., "Enhancing Academic Performance with AI-Powered Tools: A Comparative Study of Adobe Photoshop and Lightroom in Educational Technology Photography," Journal of Science Research and Reviews, 1(1), pp. 43–48. http://dx.doi.org/10.70882/josrar.2024.v1i1.9 [retrieved: 2025-06-05]

[4] Free online AI image Generator. (n.d.). Canva. https://www.canva.com/ai-image-generator/ [retrieved: 05, 2025]

[5] E. Theophilou et al., "AI and narrative scripts to educate adolescents about social media algorithms: insights about AI overdependence, trust and awareness," In European Conference on Technology Enhanced Learning, pp. 415–429. Cham: Springer Nature Switzerland. http://dx.doi.org/10.1007/978-3-031-42682-7_28 [retrieved: 2025-06-05]

[6] D. Quandt, P. Altmeyer, W. Ruppel, and M. Narroschke, "Automatic Text-based Clip Composition for Video News," In Proceedings of the 2024 9th International Conference on Multimedia and Image Processing (ICMIP '24). Association for Computing Machinery, New York, NY, USA, pp. 106–112. https://doi.org/10.1145/3665026.3665042 [retrieved: 2025-06-05]

[7] A. Radford et al., " Learning Transferable Visual Models from Natural Language Supervision," In Proceedings of the 38th International Conference on Machine Learning, in Proceedings of Machine Learning Research 139, pp. 8748–8763, Available from https://proceedings.mlr.press/v139/radford21a.html [retrieved: 05, 2025]

[8] J. Park, C. Oh, and H. Y. Kim, "AI vs. human-generated content and accounts on Instagram: User preferences, evaluations, and ethical considerations," Technology in Society, 79, 102705, pp. 10–11. http://dx.doi.org/10.1016/j.techsoc.2024.102705 [retrieved: 2025-06-05]

The Future of Learning as a Path to Meaning: AI-Enhanced Immersive Foresight for Purpose Discovery

Iuliana Adina Apostol
Imagination-driven foresight | AI content creator
Independent Consultant and Innovator
Hannover, Germany
e-mail: apostol.adina@gmail.com

https://orcid.org/0009-0005-7458-9457

Normen Schack
Co-Founder | Scientific Director of the Institute for NeuroMeditation Germany
Hannover, Germany
e-mail: normen.schack@email.de

Abstract—**This paper introduces the Resonant Future Self Framework, an experimental methodology that integrates strategic foresight, neuroscience, and immersive storytelling to support purpose discovery through experiential learning. Participants engage with personalized, audiovisual simulations of future selves generated with the assistance of Artificial Intelligence. These simulations are combined with real-time biometric feedback, including electroencephalography and heart rate variability, to assess emotional and physiological resonance with alternative future life paths. Rather than relying on abstract analysis or verbal reflection alone, the framework enables individuals to rehearse future identities in embodied, emotionally charged scenarios. The multi-phase process includes expanded self-inquiry, narrative construction supported by Artificial Intelligence, immersive simulation, physiological monitoring, and behavioral anchoring in daily life. Early findings from a single-participant case study show distinct neurophysiological responses across scenarios and strong alignment between subjective emotional feedback and biometric data. This approach reframes learning and self-development as dynamic, affective processes. The long-term vision is to develop a scalable toolkit for use in education, research, and purpose-driven learning environments, supporting individuals in navigating identity, career, and meaning in a future defined by the presence of Artificial Intelligence.**

Keywords-Immersive foresight; AI-generated futures; biofeedback; embodied simulation; purpose discovery; experiential learning.

I. INTRODUCTION

As Artificial Intelligence (AI) changes how media is created and consumed, it also introduces new possibilities for how individuals engage with questions of identity and purpose. Traditional education focuses primarily on knowledge acquisition, often overlooking the deeper question of meaning—why individuals learn and how imagined futures feel from within. At the same time, strategic foresight offers tools for thinking about possible futures, but these approaches are typically analytical and detached from direct emotional experience.

This paper introduces immersive foresight as an experimental method for purpose discovery. The approach combines computer-generated simulations of possible future selves with physiological feedback to support experiential learning. By shifting foresight from external speculation to embodied exploration, the study aims to examine whether individuals can feel into a meaningful future identity, rather than only reason about it.

II. CONCEPTUAL FRAMEWORK

This work builds on recent developments in strategic foresight, embodied cognition, and immersive media design. It is based on the premise that meaning is not solely a cognitive construct but also an embodied and emotional experience. The proposed framework, titled the Resonant Future Self Method, integrates multiple interdisciplinary components to support experiential purpose discovery.

First, the method incorporates Artificial Intelligence (AI)-assisted foresight. Generative systems are used to produce personalized narrative representations of potential future selves, grounded in participant-specific reflections and biographical data.

Second, these narratives are translated into immersive audiovisual simulations. Although not necessarily requiring virtual reality, the goal is to create emotionally rich and sensorially engaging experiences that support identification with different future identities.

Third, the framework includes real-time physiological monitoring. Biofeedback data, such as heart rate variability and other biometric indicators, are collected during the experience to detect moments of emotional resonance or dissonance. These responses serve as intuitive markers of alignment between the individual and a given future scenario.

The central hypothesis is that this combination of narrative immersion, emotional embodiment, and physiological feedback allows individuals to access futures that feel intrinsically meaningful. Rather than selecting futures through abstract reasoning, participants are invited to sense and test which paths generate a coherent, internal sense of "rightness."

III. SIMILAR APPROACHES

A. Immersive Future-Self Simulations in Education and Career Guidance

Virtual Reality (VR) tools like *VRChances* let students try out careers in immersive environments, improving their understanding of job roles. While the experience corrected misconceptions (e.g., about being an electrician), it didn't increase interest in pursuing the job. Experts see it as a valuable addition to career guidance, though broader career options and better accessibility are needed for wider impact [1].

Beyond career trials, immersive tech is being applied to general education and professional training. A case study by explored a VR+AI simulation for teacher training. In their system, pre-service teachers practiced giving lessons in a virtual classroom where AI-driven student avatars could ask questions and react. The simulation provided realistic classroom challenges (e.g. answering unexpected student queries) in a safe environment. Feedback from 17 participants indicated that the high-immersion VR, combined with AI interactivity, was valuable for building confidence and translating content knowledge into practice [2].

B. Immersive AI and Biofeedback Tools in Therapy and Well-Being

Future You is an AI-based tool developed at Massachusetts Institute of Technology (MIT) that lets users chat with a personalized avatar of their older self (age-progressed from a photo). In a study with 344 young adults, just one 15-minute conversation with this future-self avatar significantly reduced anxiety and increased emotional connection to their future. The tool is fully web-based, making it scalable and accessible, and shows strong potential for use in therapy and coaching to support well-being and long-term decision-making [3].

A 2023 study introduced an AI-enhanced VRET system for public-speaking anxiety that uses brain and heart data to detect stress and adapt the VR experience in real time. Though not yet tested with patients, it shows potential for personalized, self-guided therapy [4].

DEEP is a VR biofeedback game that teaches deep breathing for stress and anger reduction by letting users control movement in a calming underwater world through their breath. In a 2024 study with forensic psychiatric patients, some showed clear improvements, while others did not. Though effective for some, DEEP is not universally engaging or transformative, highlighting the need for personalized support and real-life skill transfer [5].

IV. EXPERIMENTAL ROADMAP

The study is organized into three sequential phases, progressing from individual exploration to group dynamics and questions of scalability.

A. Single-Participant Immersive Foresight (April 2025)

The initial phase involves one participant engaging with personalized, computer-generated future self-simulations delivered in an immersive audiovisual format. During these sessions, physiological data—such as heart rate variability and other biometric signals—are recorded to identify somatic markers of emotional alignment (e.g., calmness, coherence, or activation). Narrative journaling immediately follows to support reflective integration. These first sessions are being conducted to assess system usability and to gather preliminary emotional and physiological response data. Selected early findings will be presented at the AIMEDIA 2025 - The First International Conference on AI-based Media Innovation.

B. Group-Based Resonance Testing

In this phase, participants engage in shared immersive foresight experiences, followed by group discussion. The goal is to investigate whether witnessing and reflecting on others' future scenarios enhances self-understanding. This phase explores the potential for resonance not only within individuals but also across a shared, social context.

C. Scalability and Application Feasibility

The final phase addresses the question of scalability. The study will examine whether the method can be adapted for broader use through mobile-friendly, lightweight immersive tools. The long-term vision is a flexible platform where individuals can explore, compare, and emotionally test multiple future pathways—offering a personalized, embodied alternative to conventional career and life planning models.

V. METHODOLOGICAL FOUNDATIONS

The Resonant Future Self Framework is designed as a structured yet flexible methodology that integrates strategic foresight, immersive narrative design, emotional cognition, and physiological tracking. The goal is to enable participants to move beyond abstract scenario analysis and engage with imagined futures as lived, emotional, and somatic experiences. The framework consists of nine interconnected steps, each supporting cognitive, emotional, and behavioral dimensions of self-development.

A. Discover

Participants begin by engaging in an expanded inquiry process that combines structured reflection and open-ended exploration. This phase maps six key aspects of the self: personal strengths, past aspirations, shadow desires, current internal conflicts, daily rhythms, and emotional anchors. The goal is to gather a psychologically rich and emotionally relevant dataset from which meaningful future scenarios can later be generated.

B. Reflect

Using the inputs from the discovery phase, six distinct future self-scenarios are created with the support of artificial intelligence systems. These scenarios vary in tone, pace, lifestyle, and existential positioning. They are not predictive but are designed to provoke emotional response, challenge assumptions, and present alternative visions of personal fulfillment, identity, and purpose.

C. Select

After experiencing all six scenarios, participants engage in a resonance mapping process. They are asked to assess each future not through analytical ranking, but through intuitive and embodied sensing—identifying which ones feel most alive, aligned, or emotionally charged. The two most resonant scenarios are selected, which may represent distinct paths or emerge as a hybridized, integrative vision.

D. Embody

The selected scenarios are then transformed into immersive narrative experiences, presented in formats such as personalized video, guided audio, or visual storyboards. Participants engage with these materials twice—once in a detached observer role, and once as a fully embodied protagonist. During these sessions, biometric data are collected, including electroencephalography (EEG), heart rate, respiration, skin conductance, and peripheral temperature. These measurements are intended to identify physiological signals of resonance, resistance, or cognitive-emotional conflict.

E. Review

After the embodiment session, both biometric data and self-reported emotional responses are analyzed and compared. Participants receive interpretive feedback that integrates these data points into a cohesive emotional profile. This stage supports the integration of intuitive insight with measurable signals, helping participants to understand which elements of the future self experience triggered alignment or dissonance.

F. Activate

Participants are then guided to begin incorporating the chosen future identity into their daily life through behavioral anchoring. This includes micro-practices such as writing, movement, breathwork, or symbolic gestures that serve to reinforce the emotional memory of the chosen future. Additionally, they are encouraged to spend one hour per week intentionally "living as" their future self in a real-world context.

G. Backcast

In this phase, participants co-develop a narrative roadmap that links their chosen future state to the present. This process involves identifying key milestones, decisions, habits, or relational shifts required to move toward that future. Backcasting allows participants to frame long-term visions as a series of actionable, near-term steps.

H. Revisit

After a predefined integration period—typically six to eight weeks—a guided reflection session is conducted. Participants review any behavioral, emotional, or perceptual shifts that have occurred since their initial engagement. This phase evaluates how the imagined future has influenced their real-world sense of purpose, identity, or direction.

I. Second Test

In the final phase, participants re-engage with the immersive simulations under the same biometric recording conditions as in the first session. The goal is to compare physiological and emotional responses over time, assessing whether greater congruence, coherence, or clarity is present. This serves as a measurable indicator of internal transformation and embodied alignment with the selected future identity.

The nine-step framework positions foresight not only as a cognitive tool for long-range thinking, but as a lived, multisensory practice. By integrating narrative, embodiment, and feedback, the Resonant Future Self Framework offers a novel methodology for facilitating deep personal insight and purpose-driven learning.

VI. PRELIMINARY RESULTS

A pilot study was conducted in April 2025 with one participant to test the feasibility, experiential depth, and neurophysiological responsiveness of the Resonant Future Self Framework. The objective was to assess whether personalized immersive scenarios could produce distinct biometric patterns and whether those patterns would align with subjective emotional feedback.

The participant engaged with two personalized simulations of imagined future selves, generated using artificial intelligence. Each scenario was experienced twice: once as a passive observer and once with the participant featured as the protagonist. During these sessions, electroencephalography (EEG), heart rate, respiration, skin conductance, and temperature were continuously recorded.

Results revealed clear physiological differences between the scenarios. One future, involving a scene with the participant's child, triggered elevated gamma activity in the left prefrontal cortex, along with increased heart rate—both associated with emotional engagement and empathy. In contrast, music-driven segments produced elevated alpha wave activity, often interpreted as markers of calm attention or emotional integration. These biometric responses corresponded closely with the participant's reflections, which highlighted moments of emotional clarity and discomfort.

The participant reported that certain scenes, especially those blending realistic and imagined content, felt both unfamiliar and deeply resonant—suggesting access to subconscious emotional material. The use of self-image in the video generated strong identification, but also cognitive overload in some cases, underscoring the complexity of self-representation in immersive futures.

While this early result is limited in scope, it demonstrates the technical viability of the method, the emotional depth of the experience, and the potential of biometric resonance as a measurable indicator of inner alignment. These findings support continued exploration, with a focus on future group-based testing and formal outcome studies.

VII. COMPARISON AND POSITIONING

The Resonant Future Self Framework shares goals with a range of immersive tools aimed at fostering self-awareness and future readiness. However, it differs significantly in intent and design.

Whereas systems like Future You use chatbot-guided prompts to reduce anxiety and support short-term decision-making, and VRChances offers gamified career simulations, this framework provides a more introspective, emotionally immersive experience. It invites participants to co-create and explore deeply personal future narratives based on their own values, dilemmas, and aspirations.

Rather than focusing on skill-building or vocational exposure, the framework emphasizes emotional resonance, identity development, and meaning-making. It treats the future not as a set of external options to choose from, but as an inner space to inhabit, reflect on, and embody.

While still in an early exploratory stage, the framework is grounded in established foresight and neuroscience methods. Its strength lies in depth over scale: prioritizing personal transformation through emotion-driven immersion, supported by real-time physiological feedback. This positions it as a complementary alternative to more standardized, task-focused tools—expanding the role of immersive media from instruction toward inner alignment and purpose discovery.

VIII. SIGNIFICANCE AND INNOVATION

This work introduces a novel methodology at the intersection of strategic foresight, immersive narrative design, and biometric sensing. Unlike traditional foresight tools, which rely on cognitive analysis or scenario planning, the Resonant Future Self Framework enables individuals to feel their way into different futures—transforming abstract projections into lived, embodied experiences.

The framework's primary innovation lies in its ability to integrate three dimensions rarely combined in current research:

- AI-assisted narrative personalization, allowing for scalable and tailored future scenario generation.
- Immersive emotional engagement, enabling participants to experience future selves in a sensorially rich format.
- Biometric feedback, which introduces a measurable, physiological layer of validation and reflection.

In doing so, the method addresses an unmet need in learning and development contexts: how to support individuals not just in imagining or planning their futures, but in emotionally identifying with them. This capacity to evoke and track inner alignment could have wide-reaching implications for personalized education, career guidance, mental well-being, and identity formation.

Furthermore, the use of iterative testing and post-session behavioral anchoring distinguishes the framework from conventional immersive experiences, making it a potentially transformative tool for future-ready learning in an AI-mediated society.

IX. CONCLUSION

This paper introduced the Resonant Future Self Framework, a novel methodology that integrates strategic foresight, immersive narrative design, and biometric feedback to support purpose discovery through experiential learning. The nine-phase process enables individuals to engage with imagined futures not only as abstract possibilities, but as embodied, emotionally resonant experiences. Preliminary findings from a pilot session suggest that the approach can produce measurable neurophysiological differences across future scenarios and align these with subjective emotional responses.

While the current work is exploratory and based on a single participant, it demonstrates conceptual viability and offers early support for the framework's potential impact. Unlike existing immersive learning tools focused on task performance or anxiety reduction, this method centers on meaning-making, identity development, and future alignment. Its emphasis on emotional depth, self-authorship, and embodied feedback distinguishes it as a reflective, personalized complement to more standardized interventions.

Future work will focus on expanding the participant base, refining automation tools, and exploring integration into educational and coaching environments. In doing so, the framework aims to contribute to the evolving landscape of immersive learning—one that not only teaches, but transforms.

REFERENCES

[1] M. Holly, C. Weichselbraun, F. Wohlmuth, F. Glawogger, M. Seiser, P. Einwallner, and J. Pirker, "VRChances: An Immersive Virtual Reality Experience to Support Teenagers in Their Career Decisions," Multimodal Technologies and Interaction, vol. 8, no. 3, pp. 1–15, Sep. 2024, DOI:10.3390/mti8090078

[2] J. Pitura, R. Kaplan-Rakowski, and Y. Asotska-Wierzba, "The VR-AI–Assisted Simulation for Content Knowledge Application in Pre-Service EFL Teacher Training," TechTrends, vol. 69, pp. 100–110, 2025, https://doi.org/10.1007/s11528-024-01022-4

[3] P. Pataranutaporn, K. Winson, P. Yin, A. Lapapirojn, P. Ouppaphan, M. Lertsutthiwong, P. Maes, and H. E. Hershfield, "Future You: A Conversation with an AI-Generated Future Self Reduces Anxiety, Negative Emotions, and Increases Future Self-Continuity," arXiv preprint arXiv:2405.12514, May 2024.

[4] M. A. Rahman, D. J. Brown, M. Mahmud, et al., "Enhancing biofeedback-driven self-guided virtual reality exposure therapy through arousal detection from multimodal data using machine learning," Brain Informatics, vol. 10, no. 14, 2023. https://doi.org/10.1186/s40708-023-00193-9.

[5] L. Klein Haneveld, T. Dekkers, Y. H. A. Bouman, H. Scholten, J. Weerdmeester, S. M. Kelders, and H. Kip, "The Effect of the Virtual Reality–Based Biofeedback Intervention DEEP on Stress, Emotional Tension, and Anger in Forensic Psychiatric Inpatients: Mixed Methods Single-Case Experimental Design," JMIR Formative Research, vol. 9, p. e65206, Feb. 2025.

Empowered or Exposed? The Tension Between Human Agency and Automation in GenAI-Driven Creative Work

Laura Hesse, Paul Muschiol, Reinhard E. Kunz
Department of Media Management
Bauhaus-Universität Weimar
Weimar, Germany
e-mail: laura.hesse@uni-weimar.de
e-mail: paul.muschiol@uni-weimar.de
e-mail: reinhard.kunz@uni-weimar.de

Abstract— **This study examines how varying levels of human agency in generative artificial intelligence (GenAI) collaboration influence employees' perceived vulnerability and professional identity in creative work. It further investigates the moderating role of management support in shaping these effects. Grounded in Transformative Service Research (TSR), the study conceptualizes GenAI as a systemic shift that may disrupt autonomy and role identity. A two-study experimental design in the media industry provides empirical insight into the tensions between automation and human agency.**

Keywords-generative artificial intelligence; creative industry; perceived vulnerability.

I. Introduction

The rapid integration of generative artificial intelligence (GenAI) systems into organizational contexts – particularly within creative and knowledge-intensive industries – has introduced a renewed and multifaceted tension between automation and human agency [1]. This tension operates not only at the strategic level, where managers must weigh anticipated benefits such as efficiency gains, cost reduction, and competitiveness [2] against ethical considerations of transparency, fairness, and accountability [3]. It also extends into the lived experience of individual employees who must navigate the evolving transformation of their professional roles [4]. For many, particularly in the creative industry, this is not simply a technical or operational choice, it is a question that touches on professional identity, authority, autonomy, and consequently the future role of human agency in knowledge-based and creative labor [5]. In this study, GenAI is approached as a subset of artificial intelligence technologies that autonomously produce content such as text, images, and designs based on learned patterns [1].

The remainder of this paper is structured as follows. In Section 2, we outline the research goals that guide our investigation. Section 3 presents the theoretical background, drawing on Transformative Service Research (TSR) and the concept of identity threat. Section 4 describes the proposed methodological approach and data collection strategy. In Section 5, we discuss anticipated contribution. Finally, Section 6 concludes with a summary of suggestions for future research.

II. Research Goals

Despite growing academic interest in the implications of implementing GenAI within work environments, so far existing research has focused on outcomes such as task restructuring, job displacement, and evolving skill demands [4]. However, less attention has been paid to how GenAI affects the lived experience of employees, particularly in creative roles where GenAI extends into tasks traditionally tied to human judgment, authorship, and originality. Building on research on Human–AI collaboration [6] and algorithmic management [2], this study

(1) examines how different levels of human agency in human-GenAI collaboration affect employees' perceived vulnerability, particularly in creative work contexts; and

(2) investigates the moderating role of management support in shaping this relationship by exploring how different forms and levels of management support may mitigate the impact of GenAI integration on employees' perceived vulnerability.

III. Theoretical Background

Drawing on a TSR perspective [7], we conceptualize GenAI integration as a fundamental shift in creative service systems, with direct implications for employees' role identity and vulnerability. We build on this perspective to conceptualize vulnerability as a condition in which employees experience a reduced capacity to maintain well-being, dignity and agency in their roles, particularly when technological shifts like GenAI challenge their sense of professional identity. In the media industry, where creative and knowledge-intensive output is central to professional identity, GenAI is not only a tool for innovation, but also a potential disruptor of professional roles and expertise [5]. We extend the concept of identity threat [8] to argue that vulnerability may emerge when GenAI takes over tasks that employees perceive as central to their creative expertise. Importantly, the extent to which this vulnerability is experienced may depend on the presence and quality of managerial support, which can serve as crucial buffer shaping how employees experience these technological changes [9]. Thus, our conceptual framework positions vulnerability not as an incidental by-product of automation, but as a foreseeable outcome of organizational decisions. Particularly, regarding how GenAI is implemented, how human agency is structured, and how managerial support is communicated and enacted.

IV. Method and Data

We employ a two-study experimental research design to examine how varying levels of human–GenAI interaction affect employees´ perceived vulnerability in creative work contexts. The experimental conditions simulate three distinct modes of collaboration, each characterized by a different degree of co-authorship and content control: human-led scenarios in which GenAI acts as a supportive assistant, balanced co-authorship models where human and GenAI contributions are equally weighted, and GenAI-led conditions where the system autonomously generates content and the human's role is limited to approval. In this study, perceived vulnerability is conceptualized as a multidimensional construct and measured across technostress, job insecurity, and professional identity threat. All constructs are operationalized through validated instruments from organizational and service research and are currently undergoing pretesting for contextual alignment.

A. Study 1

Study 1 involves a field experiment, which will be conducted beginning of June 2025, with employees at a media organization in Germany that has integrated an in-house GenAI system into daily editorial workflows. Participants (N ~ 200) will be randomly assigned to one of four experimental conditions, varying the type of human–GenAI interaction: (1) a human-led condition (high human agency), where employees lead the content creation process and use GenAI as a support tool; (2) a GenAI-led condition (low agency), where GenAI generates the content and employees are limited to reviewing and approving it; (3) a balanced co-authorship condition, where control is shared between human and GenAI; and (4) a control condition that reflects a traditional workflow without any GenAI support. All participants will be randomly assigned to one of four conditions and complete the same type of content creation task to ensure comparability across conditions. The organization operates within a financially constrained media sector, where concerns over job security are salient, providing a meaningful context to investigate how different configurations of human–GenAI collaboration influence employees´ perceived vulnerability. The dependent variable, perceived vulnerability, is measured across three validated dimensions: professional identity threat, job insecurity, and technostress. Each construct will be assessed using established scales from organizational and service research.

B. Study 2

Study 2 employs a 2(management support: clear guidelines present vs. clear guidelines absent) x 2(human–GenAI interaction: human-led vs. GenAI-led) between-subject online experimental design. The online experiment (planned end of June 2025) is designed to test the role of management support in shaping employees' perceived vulnerability during collaboration with GenAI. Participants will be randomly assigned to conditions that manipulate the presence or absence of clear and supportive managerial guidance regarding the use of GenAI [9].

Together, both studies aim to provide insight into the human implications of GenAI integration in creative work and inform the development of supportive implementation strategies in organizations undergoing AI-driven transformation.

V. Contribution

Our findings contribute to research at the intersection of AI, work dynamics, and service systems. First, we advance research on human–GenAI collaboration in creative industries by examining how AI integration affects not just task outcomes but employees' professional identity and emotional vulnerability. By focusing on creative labor industry, we extend recent discussions around human-AI collaboration into domains where authorship and ownership are central to value creation. Second, we contribute to the TSR agenda by showing how service innovations like GenAI can unintentionally produce harmful or exclusionary conditions for employees. We argue that for GenAI to be truly transformative, implementation must prioritize not only efficiency and scalability but also psychological safety and equitable value co-creation. Third, we aim to offer new insight into the automation-agency tension, identifying the role of managerial support as key to shaping how employees experience GenAI collaboration not only in terms of performance, but also in relation to identity and well-being. Finally, we provide an industry-specific and methodological contribution through our field experiment in the media sector.

VI. Conclusion and Future Research

This research-in-progress proposes a conceptual and experimental framework to examine how varying degrees of human agency in GenAI collaboration influence employee vulnerability. Future steps will focus on implementing the proposed experiments to empirically test these relationships and generate insights for more inclusive GenAI implementation. Key challenges include isolating constructs like vulnerability in controlled settings, accounting for individual differences such as prior AI experience, ensuring validity, and securing access to relevant organizational contexts. Further research could expand this work by exploring additional moderating factors such as innovation culture or AI literacy and applying the framework across industries beyond the media sector.

References

[1] L. Bahn and G. Strobel, "Generative artificial intelligence," Electronic Markets, vol. 33, no. 1, pp. 33–63, 2023. https://doi.org/10.1007/s12525-023-00680-1

[2] S. Krakowski, J. Luger, and S. Raisch, "Artificial intelligence and the changing sources of competitive advantage," Strategic Management Journal, vol. 44, no. 6, pp. 1425–1452, 2023. https://doi.org/10.1002/smj.3387

[3] L. Alkrie et al., "RAISE: Leveraging responsible AI for service excellence," Journal of Service Management, vol. 35, no. 4, pp. 490–511, 2024.

[4] D. R. Lozie et al., "Examining the impact of generative artificial intelligence on work dynamics," Human Resources Management and Science, vol. 6, no. 2, 3420, 2024. https://doi.org/10.18282/hrms.v6i2.3420

[5] A. Autor, D. Mindell, and E. B. Reynolds, The work of the future: Building better jobs in an age of intelligent machines, MIT Press, 2023.

[6] M. Stelmaszak, M. Möhlmann, and C. Sørensen, "Algorithms delegate to humans: Exploring human–algorithm interaction at Uber," MIS Quarterly, vol. 49, no. 1, pp. 305–330, 2025.

[7] L. Anderson and A. L. Ostrom, "Transformative service research: Advancing our knowledge about service and well-being," Journal of Service Research, vol. 18, no. 3, pp. 243–249, 2015.

[8] H. Tajfel and J. C. Turner. An integrative theory of intergroup conflict. Brooks/Cole: Monterey, CA, 1979.

[9] L. Xiao and V. Kumar, "Robotics for customer service: A useful complement or an ultimate substitute?," Journal of Service Research, vol. 24, no. 1, pp. 9–29, 2021.

CineMods: Envisioning a Future of AI-Driven Film Personalization

Christoph Johannes Weber
University of Television and Film Munich
Munich, Germany
e-mail: c.weber@hff-muc.de

***Abstract*—Modding in the gaming industry has significantly expanded the longevity and value of digital games through user-driven creativity and customization. In contrast, the film industry has remained largely linear and non-interactive. With the emergence of generative Artificial Intelligence (AI) technologies, new opportunities arise for dynamic and personalized film experiences. This conceptual paper explores the concept of Cinematic Modifications (*CineMods*), AI-enabled, user- or provider-generated modifications to movies. We draw parallels to game modding culture, examine the technical, ethical, legal, and commercial implications, and propose a framework for user studies to investigate the desirability and potential adoption of this concept.**

Keywords-Generative Artificial Intelligence; Film Personalization; Ethics; User Modding.

I. Introduction

Digital media consumption is increasingly shaped by personalization. While video games have long embraced user-generated modifications, films remain largely fixed in form and narrative. Advances in generative AI may now open cinema to similar transformations. We introduce the concept of *CineMods*, AI-based modifications by users or providers that enable personalized reinterpretations of films. Inspired by game modding culture, *CineMods* allow viewers to alter visual style, tone, or narrative structure without interactivity. A single scene can be reimagined in distinctly different styles using generative AI, revealing the creative and emotional potential of customizable cinematic experiences. This paper outlines the conceptual foundation, technical feasibility, and ethical implications of *CineMods*, and proposes a research agenda to explore their desirability and impact. The anticipated contribution of this work is twofold: first, to establish a conceptual and technical framework for personalized cinematic modifications, and second, to initiate interdisciplinary dialogue around their cultural, ethical, and commercial implications. We expect that CineMods will prompt reconsideration of the role of authorship and participation in future media landscapes. This paper is structured as follows: Section II reviews related work. Section III outlines the CineMods concept and implementation strategies. Section IV describes a planned user study. Section V discusses ethical and legal aspects, and Section VI concludes the paper.

II. Background and Related Work

Game modding communities have long demonstrated the creative and commercial potential of user-generated content [1]. Titles like *Skyrim*, *Minecraft*, and *Half-Life* have fostered vibrant ecosystems in which players expand core experiences by introducing new mechanics, aesthetics, and narratives. Such mods can significantly increase a game's cultural relevance and commercial lifespan, and in some cases have led to independent commercial successes, such as *Counter-Strike*. In film and

Figure 1. A single film scene reimagined in five distinct styles using generative AI: from the original *Lord of the Rings* frame to reinterpretations in modern, Ghibli [2], Pixar, and sci-fi aesthetics. These illustrate how *CineMods* enable stylistic and narrative reconfiguration of cinematic content.

literature, participatory practices, such as fan fiction, unofficial recuts (for example, the "Topher Grace cut" of *Star Wars*), or independent remasters also reflect a strong desire to reinterpret narrative media. However, these practices typically remain outside formal distribution channels and often lack legal support or technical infrastructure. Interactive experiments like Netflix's *Bandersnatch* have explored branching narratives, though these rely on predefined choices and do not involve generative transformation. Recent advances in generative AI now enable dynamic, personalized media experiences. Tools, such as GPT [3], Stable Diffusion [4], and generative audio models [5][6] support the manipulation of visual, textual, and auditory elements in real time or through post-processing. These capabilities include natural language rewriting, visual style transfer, tone modulation, and audio synthesis, enabling rich and flexible cinematic transformations. Emerging text-to-video pipelines further demonstrate the potential for fully generative cinematic sequences [7]. These developments suggest that future media distribution could shift from full video files to compact prompts and latent codes, enabling the direct integration of *CineMods* into playback systems.

III. Vision and Implementation

We envision a future in which films become modifiable media artifacts, open to personalization and reinterpretation by viewers or content providers. Inspired by game modding culture, users could alter aesthetics, mechanics, or narratives to create new experiences. In a cinematic context, such modifications might include visual changes (for example, rendering a realistic film in anime or noir style), substitutions of characters, voices, or settings, or the application of emotional filters and cultural adaptations. Genre shifts, such as turning a drama into a comedy, represent the most comprehensive type of modification, as they typically require coordinated changes across multiple modalities.

The following algorithm illustrates a possible workflow for character-based style transformations within a film. For each scene, characters are identified and processed using a generative style transformer. To ensure consistency, once a transformation is generated, it is cached. This allows characters to retain a coherent visual identity throughout the entire film within the chosen mod style.

Algorithm 1 Character-Based Style Transformation in CineMods

Initialize empty style cache $\mathcal{M}$
for each frame $f \in F$ **do**
  for each character $c \in C(f)$ **do**
    if $c \notin \mathrm{dom}(\mathcal{M})$ **then**
      $s \leftarrow P(c)$ ▷ Generate style prompt
      $a \leftarrow A(c, s)$ ▷ Apply AI transformation
      $\mathcal{M}(c) \leftarrow a$ ▷ Cache result
    end if
    Apply $\mathcal{M}(c)$ to c in frame f
  end for
end for

Formally Defined Notation:

Let:

- $F = \{f_1, f_2, \ldots, f_n\}$ denote the ordered set of all frames in the film.
- $C(f) \subseteq C$ denote the set of all characters detected in frame f, where C is the set of all characters appearing throughout the film.
- $P : C \to S$ be a function generating a style prompt $s \in S$ based on a character $c \in C$.
- $A : C \times S \to T$ denote the transformation function applying an AI-based transformation using prompt $s \in S$ to character $c \in C$, resulting in a transformed representation $t \in T$.
- $\mathcal{M} : C \to T$ denote a cache mapping characters to their assigned transformations.

The algorithm thus ensures:

$$\forall f \in F, \forall c \in C(f) : \quad c \in \mathrm{dom}(\mathcal{M}) \Rightarrow \mathcal{M}(c) \text{ applied}$$

A familiar scene from The Lord of the Rings, for instance, could be rewatched in a distinct style (see Figure 1) such as anime, Pixar, or science fiction. While the core narrative remains, each version creates a different emotional experience, similar to how game mods offer aesthetic or tonal variation. In a sci-fi version, medieval weapons might be replaced with futuristic technology, and landscapes turned into alien worlds. Elements like costumes, lighting, and dialogue would adapt to preserve narrative coherence. These transformations show how *CineMods* can reshape film content while maintaining story engagement.

Technically, these modifications could be delivered in several ways. One approach involves real-time processing on smart TV devices, such as Android TV or Apple TV, where on-device AI modifies content during playback. Building on existing features like AI-based upscaling, this could be extended to support visual transformations, voice replacements, or tone adjustments. Alternatively, such functionality could be integrated directly into televisions. Studios might offer pre-rendered variants, while communities could contribute through officially supported remixing tools.

CineMods go beyond traditional style transfer by enabling deeper transformations across the full spectrum of cinematic expression. These include changes to genre, tone, pacing, characters, voices, language, plot, dialogue, and even the extension or rewriting of storylines, offering a fundamentally new form of personalized viewing. We propose a lightweight, interpretable structure, for example JSON-based, to define how and where modifications occur. These blueprints include time-stamped prompts, mod types (visual, audio, tone), and may reference specific models or presets to guide generative engines.

Effective personalization requires consistency across modalities. If a character's appearance changes, their voice and delivery should also adapt. A transformation cache can ensure coherence across scenes, episodes, or sequels. Genre shifts may involve coordinated changes in music, pacing, or lighting. A hybrid system of declarative manifests and adaptive engines could manage this complexity while preserving narrative integrity. In this vision, films become adaptable templates that respond to individual viewers. *CineMods* mark a step toward more participatory and emotionally responsive cinematic experiences.

While CineMods are conceptually rooted in fan culture and the creative remixing seen in game modding communities, their potential extends far beyond informal experimentation. If offered or supported by studios, broadcasters, or streaming platforms, such modifications could enable films to reach entirely new or previously underserved audiences. By adapting content for different age groups, cultural backgrounds, linguistic regions, or accessibility needs, CineMods can function as a powerful tool for inclusive storytelling and strategic audience expansion.

Modifications such as localized voice acting, culturally adapted references, or stylistic changes tailored to regional preferences may foster stronger identification and emotional resonance—particularly among audiences who are often underrepresented in mainstream media. As articulated in initiatives like I Want to See Me [8], personalized or culturally resonant media increases engagement by allowing viewers to see themselves reflected in the stories they consume. In this light, *CineMods* offer not only aesthetic variation, but also the potential to support diversity, representation, and emotional accessibility in cinematic experiences. In addition to supporting entertainment and personalization, CineMods hold significant potential in educational settings. They could allow educators to adapt documentary or narrative content to different learning levels, cultural backgrounds, or teaching goals. This opens possibilities for more engaging, age-appropriate, and context-sensitive learning materials that retain narrative richness while meeting diverse pedagogical needs.

IV. Planned User Study

To assess the feasibility and desirability of *CineMods*, we plan an exploratory user study targeting both general audiences and media professionals. The study will investigate user expectations around film personalization, preferred types of modifications (e.g., visual style, tone, character), and openness to AI-driven content transformations. We are particularly interested in differences between preferences for user-generated versus studio-provided mods, as well as how factors, such as control, authorship, and trust influence perceived value.

Participants will be presented with mock-ups and short video prototypes illustrating possible *CineMod* transformations. These include stylistic re-renderings (e.g., turning a realistic scene into animation), character substitutions, and tonal shifts. Surveys and focus groups will gather feedback on appeal, emotional impact, and ethical acceptability.

In addition to audience research, we also plan to engage with creators, including directors, screenwriters, actors, and producers. These interviews aim to understand professional attitudes toward modifiable cinematic content, concerns around artistic integrity and identity, and the potential role of creative control and consent mechanisms in future *CineMod* platforms. The study will also gauge willingness to pay for mod-enabled experiences and explore whether personalization enhances or undermines the perceived artistic value of films. Insights from this study will inform both technical implementation priorities and broader questions around content governance, audience agency, and monetization strategies. The user study is currently in preparation. We plan to conduct parts of it in a film school environment. While no empirical findings are included in this version, results may inform future work.

V. Ethical, Legal, and Economic Considerations

The concept of *CineMods* introduces significant ethical, legal, and economic dimensions that must be carefully navigated. From an ethical and legal standpoint, AI-generated film modifications raise critical questions about copyright, ownership, and the need for consent from filmmakers and actors, especially in cases of manipulations akin to deepfakes. Central to these concerns is the preservation of artistic integrity, as creators and performers may regard their original works as finalized and intentional expressions. Unintended consequences, such as distortions of cultural narratives or the dilution of intended messages, must also be proactively managed through robust platform governance and adaptive legal frameworks. In particular, adapting films to reflect the preferences or identities of specific ethnic or cultural groups introduces new layers of ethical complexity, including the risks of stereotyping, cultural appropriation, or misrepresentation, all of which must be addressed with cultural sensitivity and ethical rigor. Economically, *CineMods* present both promising opportunities and notable challenges. They have the potential to generate new revenue streams by offering personalized film experiences, thus extending the lifecycle and enhancing viewer engagement. Nevertheless, this emerging practice faces complex licensing issues, the risk of intellectual property fragmentation, and potential resistance from established filmmakers and studios. Successfully implementing *CineMods* will require interdisciplinary efforts to address intertwined ethical, legal, and commercial considerations responsibly.

VI. Conclusion and Future Work

CineMods represent a potential shift in how films are consumed, moving toward a more interactive and personalized media experience. As generative AI capabilities evolve, the boundaries between viewer, creator, and content may blur. Interdisciplinary research is essential to address technical, legal, and cultural aspects.

References

[1] D. Lee, D. Lin, C.-P. Bezemer, and A. E. Hassan, "Building the perfect game–an empirical study of game modifications," *Empirical Software Engineering*, vol. 25, pp. 2485–2518, 2020.

[2] PJaccetturo, *Lord of the rings trailer in ghibli style [ai-generated]*, https : / / x . com / PJaccetturo / status / 1905151190872309907/, Accessed: 2025-06-01, 2024.

[3] T. Brown *et al.*, "Language models are few-shot learners," *Advances in neural information processing systems*, vol. 33, pp. 1877–1901, 2020.

[4] R. Rombach, A. Blattmann, D. Lorenz, P. Esser, and B. Ommer, *High-resolution image synthesis with latent diffusion models*, 2022. arXiv: 2112.10752 [cs.CV]. [Online]. Available: https://arxiv.org/abs/2112.10752.

[5] J. Copet *et al.*, *Simple and controllable music generation*, 2024. arXiv: 2306.05284 [cs.SD]. [Online]. Available: https://arxiv.org/abs/2306.05284.

[6] F. Kreuk *et al.*, *Audiogen: Textually guided audio generation*, 2023. arXiv: 2209.15352 [cs.SD]. [Online]. Available: https://arxiv.org/abs/2209.15352.

[7] Y. Zhang *et al.*, *Generating animations from screenplays*, 2019. arXiv: 1904.05440 [cs.CL]. [Online]. Available: https://arxiv.org/abs/1904.05440.

[8] Vista Group International and Geena Davis Institute on Gender in Media, *I want to see me: Why diverse on-screen representation drives cinema audiences*, White Paper. https://vistagroup.co.nz/blog/i-want-to-see-me, Accessed: 2025-06-01.

Between Efficiency and Inspiration: Artificial Intelligence as a Creative Actor in the German Film Industry

Extended Abstract

Anna-Mishale Ilovar
Bauhaus-University Weimar
Weimar, Germany &
Macromedia University of Applied Sciences
Cologne, Germany
an.ilovar@macromedia.de

Castulus Kolo
Macromedia University of Applied Sciences
Munich, Germany
c.kolo@macromedia.de

Reinhard E. Kunz
Bauhaus University Weimar
Weimar, Germany
reinhard.kunz@uni-weimar.de

***Abstract*— The study analyses the role of artificial intelligence (AI) in the creative stages of film production in Germany. Based on 23 qualitative expert interviews, the study shows that AI is increasingly perceived as a supportive and inspiring tool that promotes and transforms creative processes. At the same time, challenges relating to copyright, responsibility and new skill requirements become apparent.**

Artificial intelligence, creativity, film production, value co-creation (key words).

I. Introduction

Artificial intelligence (AI) is fundamentally changing how value creation is organised, understood and experienced. While AI has long been viewed as a technical tool for process automation, AI is becoming an active co-creator, especially in areas traditionally considered typically human, such as creativity [4][13][14]. This raises the question of the role of AI in creative value creation processes: *What role does artificial intelligence play in the creative phases of film production in Germany?*

This extended abstract explores this question in the context of the German film industry, a sector characterised by its economic importance, international networking and high level of innovation. Germany is one of the largest film markets in the world: according to the British Film Institute [1], the country ranks fourth in terms of expected revenue from film productions by 2026. In terms of the total number of films produced, Germany ranks sixth internationally [6]. With a turnover of 2.691 million US dollars, the German market ranks fifth worldwide and second in Europe, just behind the United Kingdom [5]. At the same time, the industry is under pressure due to high production costs, a tense financing environment and a growing need for innovation, not least due to the upheavals caused by the pandemic, leading to increasing interest in strategic technology solutions such as AI [8]. This complex situation makes the German film industry a particularly insightful field of research.

We proceed as follows: First, the theoretical framework is presented, which is based on service-dominant logic and the concept of value co-creation [7]. This is followed by a methodological overview and the presentation of the results of a qualitative interview study with 23 industry experts. The results are then discussed with a focus on the role of AI in creative processes, its perceived opportunities and limitations, and the associated legal and ethical implications. Finally, implications for research and practice are derived and the central research question is answered.

II. Theoretical Framework

The theoretical framework of this study is based on the Service-Dominant Logic [10][11][12] and the concept of Value Co-Creation [7][12], which assumes that value is not created in isolation within companies, but through the interaction of multiple actors in dynamic exchange processes, increasingly also through non-human entities such as AI. From this perspective, AI is no longer seen as a passive tool, but as an operant resource within a service ecosystem that independently creates creative and strategic contributions [2][9]. In the sense of a relational understanding of agency, AI can thus be understood as a co-creator, especially in processes in which content is generated, decisions are made and narrative structures are formed.

III. Methodology

Empirically, the article is based on a qualitative interview study with 23 experts from various fields of the German film industry. The selection of interviewees covers the entire value creation process from content development and production to post-production, distribution, funding and technology development. The interviews were conducted using a guideline, transcribed and evaluated using qualitative content analysis according to Mayring [3].

IV. Findings

A. AI as a Creative Driving Force in the Film Industry

The findings show that AI is already used across all phases of the cinematic value chain. In pre-production, it is applied for idea generation, script development, visualisation, and planning. Experts described AI as an "inspiration tool" that provides impulses and helps structure creative processes. Six interviewees explicitly stated that AI can enhance human creativity, acting as a productive counterpart rather than a substitute.

In post-production, AI is also widely used. Applications include synchronisation, image correction, subtitling, and sound design. KI-generated voices and visual effects are being tested. The use of tools like DaVinci Resolve, Odio AI or Adobe Firefly indicates that generative AI is becoming part of everyday production workflows.

B. Tool Usage and Technological Diffusion

The study reveals broad and diverse tool usage. ChatGPT was the most frequently mentioned application, serving as a tool for research, creative development, and conceptual inspiration. Other tools include Midjourney, Stable Diffusion, Sono AI, Sora AI, and Adobe Firefly. While many respondents are still in a trial phase, the variety and regularity of usage reflect an increasing structural integration of AI into creative workflows.

C. Ambivalences and Critical Views

Despite overall positive evaluations, the perception of AI is not without reservations. Concerns include content homogenisation, loss of narrative originality, and the displacement of creative spontaneity through predictive systems. Some experts fear a broader unproductivity trend or job displacement, especially for roles involving standardised tasks such as voice acting.

D. Legal and Ethical Concerns

A major point of concern relates to legal uncertainty regarding AI-generated content. Several interviewees raised issues related to voice cloning and deepfake technologies. The imitation of real individuals without consent, combined with unclear authorship attributions, underscores the need for updated legal frameworks. The importance of personality rights and copyright protection was highlighted repeatedly.

V. Conclusion

The study reveals that the integration of AI into creative processes is not a future scenario, but a reality; albeit in different degrees, functions and interpretative frameworks. AI is increasingly understood as an independent actor within a cinematic service ecosystem that generates new patterns of interaction and creative role distributions. This not only opens up new perspectives on digital creativity in theory but also provides practical impulses for the further development of production models, education and training strategies, and technology policy measures in the film sector.

A. Limitations

This study is based on a qualitative sample of 23 experts. The findings are not statistically representative and reflect context-specific perspectives shaped by individual experiences and varying levels of technological engagement. Furthermore, the rapid pace of AI development may limit the long-term validity of specific assessments.

B. Implications for Research and Practice

The findings highlight several key implications.

For research, there is a need to further investigate human–AI co-creation in creative industries, particularly regarding authorship, narrative quality, and shifting professional roles. Legal and ethical frameworks for generative AI remain underdeveloped and require systematic exploration through interdisciplinary and longitudinal studies.

For practice, targeted training programmes should equip professionals with the skills to use AI responsibly and creatively. Clear legal guidelines on authorship and personality rights are essential, alongside the development of ethical standards. Media education institutions should integrate AI literacy into curricula to prepare practitioners for increasingly hybrid production environments.

Acknowledgment

The authors would like to thank the anonymous reviewers for their valuable and constructive feedback. This extended abstract presents preliminary findings and conceptual considerations that will be further developed following the conference. The contribution is intended as a foundation for a full-length research article, which will be revised and expanded based on scholarly feedback and subsequent analysis for future publication.

References

[1] British Film Institute, "The UK film market as a whole," BFI Statistical Yearbook 2022, pp. 3–9, 2022.

[2] P. Buxmann and H. Schmidt, "Grundlagen der Künstlichen Intelligenz und des Maschinellen Lernens," Künstliche Intelligenz, pp.3–22, 2021. doi:10.1007/978-3-662-61794-6_1.

[3] P. Mayring, and E. Brunner, "Qualitative content analysis," Qualitative market research, pp. 669–680.

Article in a journal:

[4] V. N. Antony and C.-M. Huang, "ID.8: Co-Creating Visual Stories with Generative AI," ACM Trans. Interact. Intell. Syst, vol. 14(3), pp. 1-29, Aug. 2024, doi:10.1145/3672277.

[5] British Film Institute. *Filmed entertainment revenue in selected countries worldwide in 2021 (in million U.S. dollars)* [Graph]. [Online]. Available from: https://www.statista.com/statistics/296431/filmed-entertainment-revenue-worldwide-by-country/

[6] Nash Information Services. *Movie production countries.* [Online]. Available from: https://www.the-numbers.com/movies/production-countries/#tab=territory

[7] C. K. Prahalad and V. Ramaswamy, "Co Creating Unique Vaule With Customers," Stretegy and Leadership, vol. 32(3), pp. 4–9. doi:10.1108/10878570410699249.

[8] Produzentenallianz. *Herbstumfrage 2024.* [Online]. Available from: https://produktionsallianz.de/wp-content/uploads/2024/11/2024-11-29-Herbstumfrage-2024.pdf.

[9] K. Totlani, "The Evolution of Generative AI: Implications for the Media and Film Industry," International Journal for Research in Applied Science and Engineering Technology, vol. 5(5), pp. 1-17. doi: 10.22214/ijraset.2023.56140.

[10] S. L. Vargo and R. Lusch, "Evolving to a New Dominant Logic," Journal of Marketing, vol. 68, pp. 1–17. doi:10.1509/jmkg.68.1.1.24036.

[11] S. L. Vargo and R. Lusch, "Institutions and axioms: An extension and update of service-dominant logic," Journal of the Academy of Marketing Science, vol. 44(1), pp. 5–23. doi:10.1007/s11747-015-0456-3.

[12] S. L. Vargo and R. Lusch, "Service Dominant Logic: Continuing the Evolution," Journal of the Academy of Marketing Science, vol. 36, pp. 1–10. doi:10.1007/s11747-007-0069-6.

[13] British Film Institute. *Filmed entertainment revenue in selected countries worldwide in 2021 (in million U.S. dollars)* [Graph]. [Online]. Available from: https://www.statista.com/statistics/296431/filmed-entertainment-revenue-worldwide-by-country/

Article in a conference proceedings:

[14] H. Singh, K. Kaur, and P. Singh, "Artificial Intelligence as a facilitator for Film Production Process," 2023 International Conference on Artificial Intelligence and Smart Communication (AISC), 2023, pp. 969-972, doi:10.1109/AISC56616.2023.10085082.

[15] S. Wang, S. Menon, T. Long, K. Henderson, D. Li, K. Crowston, M. Hansen, J. V. Nickerson and L. B. Chilton, "ReelFramer: Human-AI Co-Creation for News-to-Video Translation" Proceedings of the 2024 CHI Conference on Human Factors in Computing Systems, 2024, https://doi.org/10.1145/3613904.3642868.

Exploring Human-AI Collaboration in Creative Workflows: A Case Study on Acceptance and Efficiency in Brand Design

Katerina Vavatsi, Paul Heß, and Stephan Böhm,
CAEBUS Center for Advanced E-Business Studies
RheinMain University of Applied Sciences, Wiesbaden, Germany
e-mail: {katerina.vavatsi, paul.hess, stephan.boehm}@hs-rm.de

***Abstract*—Creative workflows are increasingly shaped by Generative AI (GenAI) tools supporting the ideation and design process. This is also relevant for brand design. Here, tools like DALL-E 3 (Deep Artificial Language Learning for Embedding - Version 3) enable designers to generate visual logo ideas from textual prompts, offering new levels of speed and inspiration. However, it is unclear to what extent such tools are accepted and perceived as efficient by designers. This study investigates Human-AI collaboration (HAIC) in the ideation phase of logo design by applying a research approach based on the Technology Acceptance Model (TAM) and the Task-Technology Fit model (TTF). A quantitative empirical study was conducted to analyze how perceived ease of use, usefulness, and task-technology fit influence the acceptance and efficiency of using the text-to-image GenAI tool DALL-E 3. The data of this study was collected through an online survey among students and professionals in the field of design in Germany. The results confirm that task fit and usability significantly impact the acceptance of the GenAI tool DALL-E 3, while task alignment contributes to increased efficiency in creative workflows.**

Keywords*-Human-AI Collaboration (HAIC); Creative Workflows, Logo Design; Generative Artificial Intelligence (GenAI); Technology Acceptance Model (TAM); Task-Technology Fit (TTF).

I. INTRODUCTION

GenAI tools are transforming creative workflows by enabling the automated generation of visual content based on text prompts. Within the design field, particularly in logo development, these tools offer new ways to explore ideas quickly and efficiently [1]. Unlike traditional software, text-to-image GenAI tools, such as DALL-E 3, combine machine learning with large-scale image data sets to help designers in the early ideation phase of the design process [2]. DALL·E 3 is a GenAI model developed by OpenAI that transforms natural language prompts into images by leveraging a multimodal architecture combining text and image embeddings, enabling users to generate detailed visuals from textual descriptions [3].

In the context of Human-AI Collaboration (HAIC), this development represents a shift from automation, where tasks are entirely delegated to machines, to augmentation, where Artificial Intelligence (AI) enhances human creativity without replacing it [4]. In creative design, a shift from linear AI tools toward nonlinear Human-AI collaboration, aligning better with designers' iterative and exploratory workflows, is seen. AI agents are increasingly perceived not just as tools but as opinionated collaborators who support creative reflection and remixing [5]. Studies have shown that such collaboration can improve creative output by combining human intuition with AI's generative capabilities [6]. However, the technology acceptance of these technologies is shaped mainly by designers' perceptions, particularly regarding the capabilities of AI and its integration into existing creative workflows [7].

Our empirical study investigates technology acceptance and efficacy using the GenAI tool DALL-E 3 in the ideation phase of logo design. We apply the xTAM-TTF model as proposed by [8], combining the TAM by [9] and the TTF model by [10]. We adopted the research model to the creative domain in early-stage design workflows, particularly logo design ideation, to analyze acceptance and perception on efficiency, regarding AI Tools in logo design. Against this background, we address the following research questions:

- **RQ1:** How do perceived ease of use and usefulness of DALL-E 3 influence its acceptance in the ideation phase of logo design?
- **RQ2:** To what extent does the task-technology fit of DALL-E 3 contribute to efficiency gains in creative workflows?

This article is structured as follows: Section II introduces the theoretical background on the TAM and the TTF, followed by a Section III on related work on HAIC in creative workflows. Section IV describes the methodology and approach of our study. The results are presented in Section V. Finally, a conclusion is given in Section VI, including a discussion, limitations, and outlook.

II. THEORETICAL FOUNDATION

In this section, we provide the theoretical background concerning this study by introducing the creative design process and HAIC (II-A and II-B). Moreover, we explain the TAM (II-C), followed by the TTF model (II-D).

A. Creative Workflows in the Design Process

Creative workflows describe a structured and dynamic process to generate, develop, and refine ideas. Especially in design, these workflows are essential for translating abstract concepts into concrete outcomes. Creative workflows typically consist of iterative phases supported by collaboration and feedback loops [11].

A fundamental characteristic of creative workflows is their non-linear nature. They adapt flexibly to evolving project goals, integrating new insights or shifts in direction. This dynamic balances structure and creative freedom, fostering innovation through exploration [12]. To support this, various methods and frameworks are often applied to clarify objectives and guide problem-solving activities [13].

An early model on creative workflows by [14] distinguishes four stages: ***(1) preparation*, *(2) incubation*, *(3) illumination***, and ***(4) verification*** [14]. These stages describe the path from initial problem definition and subconscious idea development to moments of insight and final evaluation. Additional research has identified an intermediary "intimation" phase, which bridges unconscious processing and conscious realization [15].

Modern approaches emphasize the relevance of social and contextual factors that shape creativity throughout the workflow. For example, studies have shown that factors, such as team dynamics, cultural background, and motivational drivers significantly influence the creative process, particularly in collaborative environments on design tasks [16]–[18].

For logo design, this creative process is described as ideation. Ideation is a central step in brand design and forms the bridge between the initial research and the final realization of the logo. In this phase, designers devote themselves intensively to the systematic exploration and development of concepts and sketches that are intended to express the identity and core values of the brand. This step in the creative workflow of brand designers follows a structured framework that includes the definition of brand values, the brainstorming of visual elements and the iterative refinement of ideas through feedback loops. Without AI support, brainstorming sessions are often held at the beginning to encourage creativity and collaboration between the designers. This open environment enables the development of different concept ideas. Visual elements, typography and symbols that specifically harmonize with the brand's mission and target group are analyzed [19]. Using GenAI tools as support of design activities can be classified to HAIC described in the following.

B. Human-AI Collaboration (HAIC)

HAIC describes a dynamic, interactive process in which humans and AI systems jointly contribute to task completion by combining their respective strengths [4]. Unlike fully automated systems, the HAIC model emphasizes augmentation, enhancing human capabilities through AI support [20].

Users rely on AI for data-driven input but retain control over decisions, ensuring that human expertise remains central [21]. In practice, this is reflected in forms such as task delegation, where AI takes over specific routine components, allowing users to focus on higher-level creative work [22].

AI can also support decision-making by offering context-relevant recommendations. The extent to which users accept these suggestions depends on the system's transparency and its ability to inspire trust [23] [24]. In creative fields, such as design, HAIC enables faster idea generation without replacing human judgment. This illustrates the difference between using AI for automation, which aims to replace human labor, and augmentation by AI according to the HAIC model [25].

C. Technology Acceptance Model (TAM)

The TAM by [9] is a foundational framework for analyzing user acceptance of new technologies. It builds on the Theory of Reasoned Action (TRA) and focuses on two key constructs: *Perceived Usefulness (PU)* and *Perceived Ease of Use (PEOU)*. PU refers to the degree to which a person believes that using technology enhances their job performance, while PEOU describes how effortless the technology appears to be in use [9]. The TAM is illustrated in Figure 1.

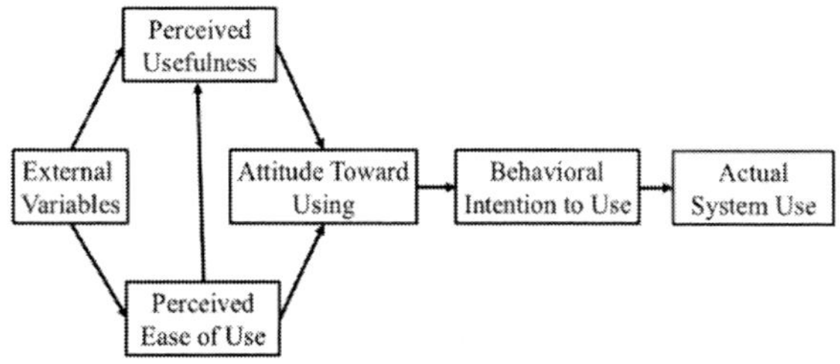

Figure 1. Technology Acceptance Model (TAM) by [9]

TAM suggests that both constructs influence the user's attitude toward using a system (AT), which in turn predicts behavioral intention. Moreover, PEOU indirectly impacts PU, as systems perceived as easy to use are often judged more useful. These interrelations have been confirmed across multiple domains, including mobile apps, online banking, and e-learning environments [26][27] [28].

Despite its wide application, TAM has been criticized for oversimplifying acceptance processes by excluding emotional, contextual, or experiential factors [29] [30]. In response, later extensions, such as the TAM3 incorporated constructs like Social Influence (SI) and facilitating conditions to enhance explanatory power [30]. Recent studies have also explored, for example, how individual differences and motivational factors affect acceptance across diverse cultural and technological contexts [31], [32]. In this study, we additionally included SI and Social Recognition (SR) as external variables to TAM. These factors are often examined in extended models to capture social dynamics that may shape users' attitudes towards technology adoption [30].

The continued evolution of the TAM results from the need for adaptive models that reflect the complexity and the context of user-technology interaction and motivational dimensions.. The TTF model, which describes such a context for the task environment, is described in the following.

D. Task-Technology Fit (TTF)

The TTF model developed by [10] provides a framework to assess how well a technology supports the tasks it is intended to facilitate. The core assumption is that a good match between task requirements and technological capabilities leads to higher performance and user satisfaction [10].

TTF distinguishes between the *Task Characteristics*, such as complexity and cognitive demand, and *Technology Characteristics*, like functionality and usability, illustrated in Figure

2. The better these two dimensions align, the more likely it is that users can accomplish their goals efficiently [33].

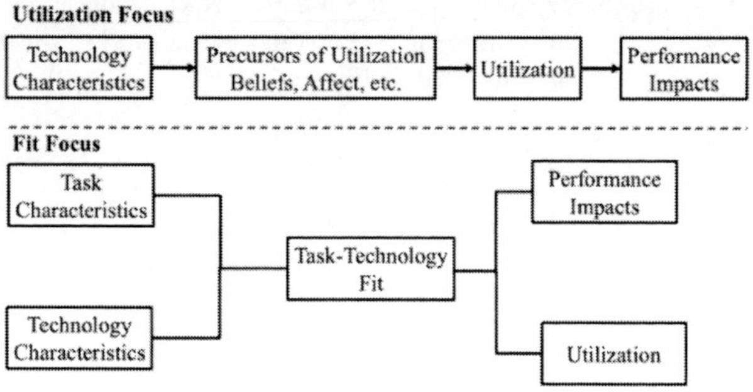

Figure 2. Task-Technology-Fit Frameworks by [10]

Although initially part of the broader Technology-to-Performance Chain (TPC), TTF has been widely adopted as a standalone approach due to its practical applicability. Empirical studies have confirmed its relevance across domains—for example, in healthcare systems where alignment between tools and clinical workflows improved user satisfaction, and in education where matched learning technologies enhanced engagement and outcomes [34][35].

In the context of creative work, TTF can be applied to evaluate whether generative AI tools meaningfully support design-specific tasks. The TTF can also be combined with the TAM, resulting in the xTam-TTF Model, later utilized for the research model. This enables the assessment of the perceived efficiency of AI on the process of logo design.

III. Related Work on HAIC in Creative Workflows

Research on generative AI in creative workflows is still in its early stages, particularly regarding domain-specific applications such as logo design.. While the number of studies is growing, most focus on technical capabilities or general user perceptions rather than domain-specific applications such as logo design. For example, the study conducted by [36] discusses ethical concerns and opportunities associated with DALL-E yet provides limited insight into workflow integration [36]. Similarly, [37] highlights the relevance of AI-generated content in creative industries but does not explore concrete use cases in branding [37]. To date, few empirical studies have examined how generative AI tools are integrated into the specific tasks and decision points of visual identity design, such as logo ideation.

Recent research on HAIC emphasizes the potential of AI to augment creative thinking and enhance task performance. However, it also stresses the importance of trust, transparency, and user-centered design in determining actual adoption [4][21]. These insights underline that beyond technical quality, the perceived integration into existing workflows plays a decisive role in acceptance.

Despite these contributions, a research gap remains regarding the evaluation of generative AI in specific phases of the creative process, especially early-stage ideation in visual design. This study aims to address this gap by analyzing the use of DALL-E 3 in the ideation phase of logo creation.

IV. Methodological Approach

We conducted a comprehensive study examining the technology acceptance, and efficiency using the GenAI tool **DALL-E 3** for supporting designers in the idea generation phase and logo design. DALLE-E 3 is the image generation tool from the company Open-AI [38]. It can be used to generate images based on textual prompts. The technology is included in the flagship product of Open-AI, ChatGPT. Here, DALL-E 3 can be accessed with a text request. DALL-E 3 is chosen as a research object based on the relevance of Chat-GPT, in which it is integrated. In 2024, 48% of German respondents stated to have used the tool within the last year.

For the analysis, we applied the *xTAM-TTF* model by [8], measuring its core constructs based on 21 validated items. It is chosen because the expansion on external factors enables a more differentiated analysis of user acceptance and ensures the fit between the tasks and the characteristics of the technology, making it eligible for acceptance and perceived efficiency increase in the design phases.

Here the TTF is applied. Within this model efficiency is assessed via the areas of speed, time-save, resources, quality, productivity, results and human factor. The research model and its respective hypotheses and constructs are explained in IV-A and IV-B. The study procedure is described in IV-C.

A. Research Model

The *xTAM-TTF* Model integrates the Technology Acceptance Model (TAM) proposed by [9] with the Task-Technology Fit (TTF) model developed by [10]. The xTAM-TTF model was developed to better explain user acceptance and effective use of gamified, technology-enabled training by integrating motivational, task-related, and technological factors [8].

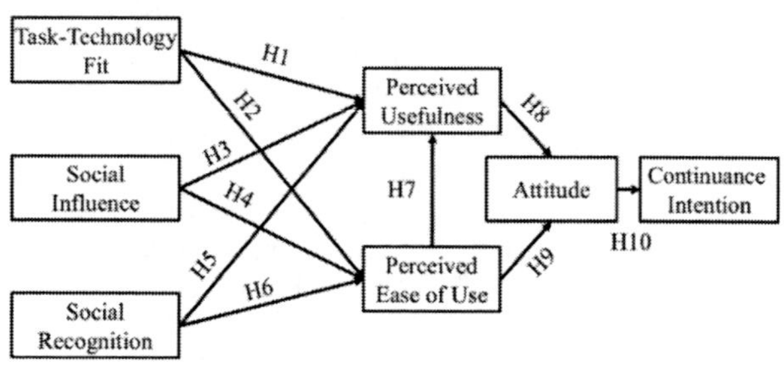

Figure 3. xTAM-TTF Model by [8]

The *xTAM-TTF* Model is illustrated in Figure 3. It further incorporates the factors of SI and SR contributing to social motivation. In particular, SI describes the influence of the social environment, such as colleagues or friends, on the acceptance and continuance intention (CI) to use a technology. It analyzes the extent to which the behavior or recommendations of others influence the decision-making processes of users. SR measures the importance of recognition users receive through the use of a technology. This includes aspects such as increased self-perception, social affirmation, and the feeling of being valued by the environment. By integrating these factors with the core constructs of the TAM and the TTF, the research model enables a comprehensive analysis of both individual and social acceptance. Based on the proposed model, we provide the respective hypotheses in the following.

B. Model Constructs and Hypotheses

The xTAM-TTF model applied in our study comprises the following seven constructs and their corresponding measurement items as defined by [8]:

- **TTF**: Perceived alignment between technology features and task requirements
- **SI**: Influence of the social environment on tool adoption
- **SR**: Visibility and perceived ease of tool
- **PEOU**: Perceived effort required to use the tool
- **PU**: Perceived value in improving productivity or creativity
- **AT**: Users' general stance toward using the tool
- **CI**: Intention to keep using the tool over time

Based on these constructs, ten hypotheses were formulated, indicating the causal relationship between the constructs in the research model (See Table I). In addition, the hypotheses were adapted to the object of the study–logo design ideation.

TABLE I: OVERVIEW OF MODEL HYPOTHESES

Nr.	Hypothesis	Variables
H1	TTF positively affects the perceived usefulness of DALL-E 3 in logo design ideation.	TTF → PU
H2	TTF positively affects the perceived ease of use of DALL-E 3 in logo design ideation.	TTF → PEOU
H3	SI positively affects the perceived usefulness of DALL-E 3 in logo design ideation.	SI → PU
H4	SI positively affects the perceived ease of use of DALL-E 3 in logo design ideation.	SI → PEOU
H5	SR positively affects the perceived usefulness of DALL-E 3 in logo design ideation.	SR → PU
H6	SR positively affects the perceived ease of use of DALL-E 3 in logo design ideation.	SR → PEOU
H7	PEOU positively affects the perceived usefulness of DALL-E 3 in logo design ideation.	PEOU → PU
H8	PU positively affects the attitude toward using DALL-E 3 in logo design ideation.	PU → A
H9	PEOU positively affects the attitude toward using DALL-E 3 in logo design ideation.	PEOU → A
H10	Attitude toward using DALL-E 3 in logo design ideation positively affects continued use intention.	A → CI

C. Study Approach

We conducted a quantitative study using an online survey based on a convenience sample regarding individuals with experience in brand and visual design. The survey was deployed digitally using the platform *Unipark* [39] and remained accessible from *December 16, 2024* until *January 10, 2025*. Participants were recruited as a convenience sample from various channels, including social media, academic networks, mailing lists, academic networks, and professional communities.

Participants were selected based on predefined criteria to ensure domain relevance regarding logo design: Only individuals with either academic or professional experience in design-related fields or specific expertise in branding were included. Respondents who did not meet these qualifications were excluded from the analysis to ensure the validity of the results.

To standardize participants' understanding of the study context, a design scenario involving using DALL-E 3 for a fictional brand was presented. Participants were introduced to the tool via a short explanation and a demonstration video, followed by a detailed use case description. This was done to align their responses with a consistent frame of reference. The use case is described in the following:

> A brand designer has been tasked with creating a logo for a new client. The client is the brand "BubbleBloom", which stands for refreshing, botanical-inspired craft soft drinks made from natural ingredients. The brand is aimed at a young, creative audience that values aesthetics, sustainability, and enjoyment. The logo should appear playful, modern, and authentic. The designer would like to develop initial visual concepts for the logo during the brainstorming phase. To support his creative approach, he decides to use Dall-E

Examples of possible logo designs created for this use case with DALL-E, were shown to respondents of the survey to assess to potential of the tool. One example is shown in Figure 4.

Figure 4. Exemplary AI-generated Logo-Design

Based on the contextualization of the application area of DALL-E in the logo design process, the supplementary description of the use case on the use case of logo design ideation to be evaluated, and the exemplary results of the DALL-E tool, the participants were asked to complete a questionnaire. This online questionnaire contained the following sections:

- Demographic questions, prior experience with brand design, perception of and collaboration with GenAI tools.
- Validated items adopted from the xTAM-TTF model by [8] to evaluate factors for HAIC acceptance of DALL-E as presented in Section IV-A.
- Additional questions to access the expected efficiency of using DALL-E in the design process based on [16].

To assess efficiency, respective aspects concerning the logo design process (see Section II-A) are conceptualized based on relevant criteria from different research articles. In particular, the five aspects simplicity [40], memorability [41], relevance [42], versatility [43] and uniqueness [44] were applied. All items are based on a five-point Likert scale ranging from "strongly disagree" (1) to "strongly agree" (5).

V. Results

This section summarizes the empirical evaluation results of this study. In V-A, demographic information regarding the convenience sample and general insights into the perception and usage of GenAI tools are provided. Concerning the research model, we applied a Partial Least Squares Structural Equation Modeling (PLS-SEM) approach following the standard procedure by [45] using SmartPLS4 software [46] for the statistical evaluation of both, the measurement and the structural model. Section V-B presents the empirical findings.

A. Descriptive Evaluation Results

1) Sample Demographics: A total of 135 responses were collected, with 109 completed questionnaires. The final sample of 83 valid cases was determined by filtering based on the proposed eligibility criteria. Concerning their background, most identified as either students in design-related programs or professionals in the creative industry. Participants were well-distributed across age groups, with the highest representation in the 25–34 age range. Nearly half of the respondents were actively employed in design-related fields, while around a third were current students. The sample demographic is shown in Table II.

TABLE II: DEMOGRAPHIC OVERVIEW OF THE SAMPLE

Category	Attribute	Count
Gender	Female	46
	Male	37
	Diverse	0
Age Group	18–24 years	26
	25–34 years	29
	35–44 years	15
	45–54 years	6
	55+ years	7
Occupational Status	Working in design-related field	40
	Studying design-related subject	29
	Neither	14
Study Field	Media Management	13
	Media Design	9
	UX/UI Design	2
	Other / No response	5
Job Field	Graphic Design	10
	UX/UI Design	9
	Illustration	7
	Branding / Corporate Design	4
	Product Design	4
	Fashion / Textile Design	3
	Other Design-Related	3

Moreover, we examined the participants' experience in brand design, aiming to contextualize their familiarity with the tasks relevant to the study. Over three-quarters (64 out of 83) reported direct experience with branding processes, including logo creation, concept development, and brand communication. Regular involvement in brand-related tasks (23 out of 32) and over five years of experience were common among professionals (10 out of 23).

2) Perception and Usage of GenAI Tools in Brand Design: We further explored the use and perception of AI tools in design contexts, particularly on generative image models such as DALL-E 3. Results revealed that nearly half of the participants had already used DALL-E 3 (43%), primarily for ideation and concept development, followed by Adobe Firefly (40%). The most common use cases for GenAI tools among respondents included idea generation and concept development (63%), creating visual drafts (36%), and modifying designs (36%).

Participants expressed their attitude on a scale of 1 (strongly disagree) to 5 (strongly agree), shown in Table III. Overall, participants expressed a positive attitude toward the tool's usefulness and ease of integration (3,9) while remaining cautious about issues such as output quality (3,0) and legal implications (3,5). Nevertheless, the participants acknowledged the tool's capacity to enhance efficiency in the initial creative phases (3,8). However, they also emphasized the necessity of human judgment in refining and evaluating design outcomes (4,1).

TABLE III: PARTICIPANTS' PERCEPTION OF EFFICIENCY GAINS THROUGH AI TOOLS

No.	Statement	M
1	AI tools can accelerate ideation and lead to quicker first concepts.	4.0
2	Using AI tools can save time and resources during creative work.	3.7
3	AI tools improve the quality of generated designs.	2.9
4	I believe AI tools can boost my personal productivity during ideation.	3.7
5	While AI makes brand design more efficient, the results become more interchangeable.	3.6
6	Despite AI, humans remain essential for efficient brand design.	4.1

Approximately half of the participants emphasized data privacy as a significant concern for the effective use of AI in design (49%). Additionally, ease of use (41%), along with the transparency and explainability of AI systems (40%) were regarded as important factors. In contrast, the availability of training offers or the exclusive use of ethically sourced data for AI training was not considered essential (31%).

TABLE IV: RELIABILITY AND VALIDITY EVALUATION RESULTS

Construct	Item	Loading	Cronbach's α	rho_A	rho_C	VIF	AVE
TTF	TTF1	0.860	0.809	0.821	0.875	2.029	0.637
	TTF2	0.772				1.695	
	TTF3	0.709				1.360	
	TTF4	0.844				1.949	
SI	SI1	0.816	0.883	0.916	0.927	1.870	0.810
	SI2	0.948				4.072	
	SI3	0.931				3.596	
SR	SR1	0.887	0.878	0.893	0.925	2.407	0.804
	SR2	0.887				2.756	
	SR3	0.877				2.231	
PU	PU1	0.903	0.868	0.870	0.919	2.461	0.791
	PU2	0.872				2.104	
	PU3	0.894				2.327	
PEOU	PEOU1	0.869	0.851	0.878	0.908	2.233	0.767
	PEOU2	0.886				1.845	
	PEOU3	0.873				2.356	
A	A1	0.874	0.858	0.858	0.913	2.057	0.778
	A2	0.865				2.063	
	A3	0.907				2.584	
CI	CI1	0.929	0.848	0.848	0.929	2.178	0.868
	CI2	0.934				2.178	

B. *Empirical xTAM-TTF Model Evaluation*

1) Measurement Model: The evaluation of the measurement model included the analysis of indicator reliability, internal consistency, convergent validity, and discriminant validity following the standard procedure as defined by [45].

First, indicator reliability was evaluated based on the standardized outer loadings, all exceeding the recommended threshold of 0.708. Internal consistency was validated by Cronbach's Alpha, composite reliability (rho_c), and reliability coefficient (rho_a), all of which were within the acceptable range of 0.60 to 0.90. Table IV shows the evaluation results regarding the quality criteria.

Convergent validity was assessed using the average variance extracted (AVE), with all constructs exceeding the minimum requirement of 0.50. Although the Heterotrait-Monotrait (HTMT) ratio exceeded the critical value of 0.90 (illustrated in *cursive*) in two cases (see Table V), the Fornell-Larcker criterion and cross-loading analysis indicated sufficient discriminant validity. Consequently, no changes to the measurement model were required.

TABLE V: HTMT EVALUATION RESULTS

	A	CI	PEOU	PU	SI	SR	TTF
A	1						
CI	*0.949*	1					
PEOU	0.561	0.519	1				
PU	0.885	0.840	0.769	1			
SI	0.569	0.697	0.327	0.408	1		
SR	0.734	0.681	0.369	0.572	0.651	1	
TTF	0.894	0.771	0.838	*1.037*	0.340	0.588	1

2) Structural Model: The structural model was analyzed to examine the relationships between the latent variables. All variance inflation factor (VIF) values were below the critical threshold of 5, indicating no serious multicollinearity issues.

Path coefficients, t-values, and p-values were calculated using bootstrapping with 5,000 iterations and a significance level of 5%. A visual representation of the structural model and its path coefficients is shown in Figure 2.

TABLE VI: STRUCTURAL MODEL EVALUATION RESULTS

H.	Relationship	VIF	Coeff.	t-Val.	p-Val.	Sig.
H1	TTF → PU	1.000	0.758	10.025	0.000	Yes
H2	TTF → PEOU	1.855	0.716	8.654	0.000	Yes
H3	SI → PU	2.078	0.086	1.594	0.111	No
H4	SI → PEOU	1.855	0.111	1.207	0.227	No
H5	SR → PU	1.487	0.047	0.631	0.528	No
H6	SR → PEOU	1.512	-0.071	0.572	0.567	No
H7	PEOU → PU	1.787	0.097	1.900	0.058	No
H8	PU → A	1.797	0.794	10.341	0.000	Yes
H9	PEOU → A	1.323	-0.042	0.453	0.651	No
H10	A → CI	2.388	0.809	15.990	0.000	Yes

TTF showed significant positive effects on both PU and PEOU, supporting hypotheses H1 and H2. This indicates that a higher alignment between the tool's features and the requirements of the ideation task is associated with more positive evaluations regarding usefulness and usability.

PU also had a significant effect on AT, confirming H8. Additionally, ATshowed a strong and significant effect on CI, confirming H10. These two relationships complete the model's output side, connecting perceptions of usefulness to long-term use intentions via user attitude.

No significant relationships were observed for SI or SR on PU or PEOU (H3 to H6). Similarly, PEOU did not significantly affect PU or A (H7, H9), and those hypotheses were rejected.

In total, four out of ten hypotheses (H1, H2, H8, and H10) can be confirmed by the statistical analysis.

VI. Conclusion

A. *Discussion and Implications*

This study examined the acceptance and perceived efficiency of the AI-based image generator DALL-E 3 in the ideation phase of logo design. The perception of efficiency gains through AI tools shows the potential for AI-Tools in ideation, saving resources and increasing productivity. However, since quality of output of AI tools is not seen as beneficial. Human impact on the design process is still needed to benefit from efficiency gains. By applying the extended xTAM-TTF model, key factors influencing user perception and tool adoption were identified. In particular, **TTF** positively influences both Perceived Usefulness and Perceived Ease of Use. Moreover, Perceived Usefulness has a positive influence on Attitude, which in turn positively influences CI, thus confirming the core constructs of the TAM. To conclude, using DALL-E 3 in the ideation phase of logo design is generally accepted positively. Moreover, the findings show that the alignment between the tool's functionalities and task requirements plays a central role in shaping perceived usefulness and ease of use. Regarding practical implications, designers are likelier to adopt and use GenAI tools like DALL-E 3 when tailored to specific design tasks and seamlessly integrate into creative workflows.

In contrast, social factors such as SI and SR did not show significant effects. This result suggests that individual and task-related assessments are more relevant for tool adoption in creative workflows than external opinions. Overall, the results underline that functional value and task relevance are more decisive for designers than social dynamics when considering the use of generative AI tools.

B. Limitations

However, several limitations must be drawn. Although the study targeted participants with relevant design experience, the sample size was relatively small (n = 83), limiting the statistical power and generalizability of the findings. Moreover, the convenience sampling approach merges two distinct user groups—students and professionals—who may differ significantly in design experience, technological familiarity, and attitudes toward GenAI tools. This may affect the generalizability of the results. Using a hypothetical case study ("BubbleBloom") and a predefined DALL-E 3 interaction provided a controlled basis for evaluation. Still, it may not fully capture the complexity and variability of real-world design processes. Participants did not actively use the tool themselves, which may have influenced their evaluation of efficiency and creative potential. By focusing solely on DALL-E 3, the findings are limited in scope and may not be directly transferable to other generative AI tools or domains beyond logo design. Differences in capabilities, UI, and output quality across different tools were not explored.The study relies on established acceptance models (TAM and TTF) and did not include qualitative methods such as interviews or diary studies. While effective for quantifying relationships, this reduces the methodological novelty and limits the depth of contextual understanding. Although ethical concerns such as copyright and data privacy were briefly addressed in the survey, these aspects were not explored in detail.

C. Outlook & Future Research

The study results provide valuable insights into the factors influencing the acceptance and perceived efficiency of AI-based tools, such as DALL-E 3, in creative workflows for practitioners and researchers. However, GenAI evolves rapidly, as recent ChatGPT 4o Image Generation developments show [38]. Thus, further research is needed to deepen our understanding of its role in design practice. Future research could also examine how the rise of autonomous AI agents may affect established HAIC models, particularly in terms of user trust, role delegation, and co-creative dynamics in complex design processes.

The study should be replicated with a broader and more diverse sample. In addition, different creative domains, such as advertising, product design, or illustration, can be targeted. Furthermore, combining quantitative results with qualitative methods, such as interviews or observational studies, could deepen the understanding of how designers interact with AI tools in practice.

REFERENCES

[1] J.-F. Chen, C.-C. Ni, P.-H. Lin, and R. Lin, "Designing the future: A case study on human-ai co-innovation", *Creative Education*, vol. 15, no. 3, pp. 474–494, 2024. DOI: 10.4236/ce.2024.153031.

[2] M.-H. Temsah *et al.*, "Art or artifact: Evaluating the accuracy, appeal, and educational value of ai-generated imagery in dall·e 3 for illustrating congenital heart diseases", *Journal of Medical Systems*, vol. 48, no. 1, p. 54, 2024. DOI: 10.1007/s10916-024-02083-9.

[3] OpenAI, *Dall·e 3*, https://openai.com/dall-e-3, Accessed: 2025-05-27.

[4] J. Rezwana and M. L. Maher, "Designing creative ai partners with cofi: A framework for modeling interaction in human-ai co-creative systems", *ACM Transactions on Computer-Human Interaction*, vol. 30, no. 5, pp. 1–28, 2023. DOI: 10.1145/3519026.

[5] J. Zhou *et al.*, "Understanding nonlinear collaboration between human and ai agents: A co-design framework for creative design", in *Proceedings of the 2024 CHI Conference on Human Factors in Computing Systems (CHI '24)*, ACM, 2024, pp. 1–16. DOI: 10.1145/3613904.3642812.

[6] M. Guzdial and M. Riedl, "An interaction framework for studying co-creative ai", *arXiv*, 2019. DOI: 10.48550/arXiv.1903.09709. eprint: 1903.09709.

[7] R. A. Bertão and J. Joo, "Artificial intelligence in ux/ui design: A survey on current adoption and [future] practices", *Blucher Design Proceedings*, pp. 404–413, 2021. DOI: 10.5151/ead2021-123.

[8] V. Z. Vanduhe, M. Nat, and H. Hasan, "Continuance intentions to use gamification for training in higher education: Integrating the technology acceptance model (tam), social motivation, and task technology fit (ttf)", *IEEE Access*, vol. 8, pp. 21 473–21 484, 2020. DOI: 10.1109/ACCESS.2020.2966179.

[9] F. D. Davis, "User acceptance of information systems: The technology acceptance model (tam)", Ph.D. dissertation, University of Michigan, 1987.

[10] D. L. Goodhue and R. L. Thompson, "Task-technology fit and individual performance", *MIS Quarterly*, vol. 19, no. 2, pp. 213–236, 1995. DOI: 10.2307/249689.

[11] A. Arias-Rosales, "The perceived value of human-ai collaboration in early shape exploration: An exploratory assessment", *PLOS ONE*, vol. 17, no. 9, e0274496, 2022. DOI: 10.1371/journal.pone.0274496.

[12] L. Antonczak and T. Burger-Helmchen, "Creativity on the move: Nexus of technology, slack and social complexities", *Journal of Open Innovation: Technology, Market, and Complexity*, vol. 8, no. 2, p. 64, 2022. DOI: 10.3390/joitmc8020064.

[13] E. A. López Jiménez and T. Ouariachi, "An exploration of the impact of artificial intelligence (ai) and automation for communication professionals", *Journal of Information, Communication and Ethics in Society*, vol. 19, no. 2, pp. 249–267, 2021. DOI: 10.1108/JICES-03-2020-0034.

[14] G. Wallas, *The Art of Thought*. Harcourt, Brace and Company, 1926.

[15] E. Sadler-Smith, "Wallas' four-stage model of the creative process: More than meets the eye?", *Creativity Research Journal*, vol. 27, no. 4, pp. 342–352, 2015. DOI: 10.1080/10400419.2015.1087277.

[16] M. C. Caniëls, K. De Stobbeleir, and I. De Clippeleer, "The antecedents of creativity revisited: A process perspective", *Creativity and Innovation Management*, vol. 23, no. 2, pp. 96–110, 2014. DOI: 10.1111/caim.12051.

[17] Y. Shao, C. Zhang, J. Zhou, T. Gu, and Y. Yuan, "How does culture shape creativity? a mini-review", *Frontiers in*

Psychology, vol. 10, p. 1219, 2019. DOI: 10.3389/fpsyg.2019.01219.
[18] M. A. R. Malik, J. N. Choi, and A. N. Butt, "Distinct effects of intrinsic motivation and extrinsic rewards on radical and incremental creativity: The moderating role of goal orientations", *Journal of Organizational Behavior*, vol. 40, no. 9-10, pp. 1013–1026, 2019. DOI: 10.1002/job.2415.
[19] M. N. A. Aziz, A. K. A. Ahmad, M. K. Ramlie, I. N. F. M. Fuad, and A. A. Rahaman, "Exploring the five-i logo process: A case study of ifix brand", *International Journal of Academic Research in Business and Social Sciences*, vol. 13, no. 5, pp. 2545–2555, 2023. DOI: 10.6007/IJARBSS/v13-i5/17146.
[20] Y. Lai, A. Kankanhalli, and D. Ong, 2021.
[21] G. C. Saha *et al.*, "Human-ai collaboration: Exploring interfaces for interactive machine learning", *Tuijin Jishu/Journal of Propulsion Technology*, vol. 44, no. 2, pp. –, 2023, Article ID or additional identifier may be needed.
[22] P. Hemmer *et al.*, "Human-ai collaboration: The effect of ai delegation on human task performance and task satisfaction", pp. 453–463, Mar. 2023. DOI: 10.1145/3581641.3584054.
[23] H. Tejeda Lemus, A. Kumar, and M. Steyvers, "An empirical investigation of reliance on ai-assistance in a noisy-image classification task", in *HHAI2022: Augmenting Human Intellect*, IOS Press, 2022, pp. 225–237. DOI: 10.3233/FAIA220125.
[24] H. Tejeda Lemus, A. Kumar, and M. Steyvers, "How displaying ai confidence affects reliance and hybrid human-ai performance", in *HHAI 2023: Augmenting Human Intellect*, IOS Press, 2023, pp. 234–242. DOI: 10.3233/FAIA230130.
[25] C. J. Cai, J. Jongejan, and J. Holbrook, ""Hello AI": Uncovering the onboarding needs of medical practitioners for human-ai collaborative decision-making", *Proceedings of the ACM on Human-Computer Interaction*, vol. 3, no. CSCW, pp. 1–24, 2019. DOI: 10.1145/3359206.
[26] F. E. Saputra, A. Makhrian, and B. S. Grahatama, "Online learning acceptance model of indonesian students during the covid-19 pandemic", pp. 196–210, 2023. DOI: 10.18502/kss.v8i5.12974.
[27] F. Muñoz-Leiva, S. Climent-Climent, and F. Liébana-Cabanillas, "Determinants of intention to use the mobile banking apps: An extension of the classic tam model", *Spanish Journal of Marketing-ESIC*, vol. 21, no. 1, pp. 25–38, 2017. DOI: 10.1016/j.sjme.2017.01.001.
[28] T. Pikkarainen, K. Pikkarainen, H. Karjaluoto, and S. Pahnila, "Consumer acceptance of online banking: An extension of the technology acceptance model", *Internet Research*, vol. 14, no. 3, pp. 224–235, 2004. DOI: 10.1108/10662240410542652.
[29] J. W. Moon and Y. G. Kim, "Extending the tam for a world-wide-web context", *Information Management*, vol. 38, no. 4, pp. 217–230, 2001. DOI: 10.1016/S0378-7206(00)00061-6.
[30] V. Venkatesh and H. Bala, "Technology acceptance model 3 and a research agenda on interventions", *Decision Sciences*, vol. 39, no. 2, pp. 273–315, 2008. DOI: 10.1111/j.1540-5915.2008.00192.x.
[31] F. An, L. Xi, and J. Yu, "The relationship between technology acceptance and self-regulated learning: The mediation roles of intrinsic motivation and learning engagement", *Education and Information Technologies*, vol. 29, no. 3, pp. 2605–2623, 2024. DOI: 10.1007/s10639-023-11927-6.
[32] J. Dalle, H. Aydin, and C. X. Wang, "Cultural dimensions of technology acceptance and adaptation in learning environments", *Journal of Formative Design in Learning*, pp. 1–14, 2024. DOI: 10.1007/s41686-024-00147-9.
[33] A. Ahmed, "Role of gis, rfid and handheld computers in emergency management: An exploratory case study analysis", *Journal of Information Systems and Technology Management*, vol. 12, no. 1, pp. 03–28, 2015. DOI: 10.4301/S1807-17752015000100001.
[34] E. Ammenwerth, C. Iller, and C. Mahler, "It-adoption and the interaction of task, technology and individuals: A fit framework and a case study", *BMC Medical Informatics and Decision Making*, vol. 6, no. 1, pp. 1–13, 2006. DOI: 10.1186/1472-6947-6-3.
[35] T. J. McGill and V. J. Hobbs, "How students and instructors using a virtual learning environment perceive the fit between technology and task", *Journal of Computer Assisted Learning*, vol. 24, no. 3, pp. 191–202, 2008. DOI: 10.1111/j.1365-2729.2007.00253.x.
[36] K. Q. Zhou and H. Nabus, "The ethical implications of dall-e: Opportunities and challenges", *Mesopotamian Journal of Computer Science*, pp. 17–23, 2023. DOI: 10.58496/MJCSC/2023/003.
[37] A. Tuomi, "Ai-generated content, creative freelance work and hospitality and tourism marketing", in *Information and Communication Technologies in Tourism 2023*, B. Ferrer-Rosell, D. Massimo, and K. Berezina, Eds., Springer Nature Switzerland, 2023, pp. 323–328. DOI: 10.1007/978-3-031-25752-0_35.
[38] OpenAI, *Introducing 4o image generation*, Accessed: 2025-04-15, Mar. 2025.
[39] Tivian, *Unipark Academic Edition*, https://www.tivian.com/de/feedback-software/marktforschung-software/academic-edition/, Acessed: 16/04/2025, 2025.
[40] J. Luffarelli, M. Mukesh, and A. Mahmood, "Let the logo do the talking: The influence of logo descriptiveness on brand equity", *Journal of Marketing Research*, vol. 56, no. 5, pp. 862–878, 2019, Original work published 2019. DOI: 10.1177/0022243719845000.
[41] Y. Liang, S.-H. Lee, and J. E. Workman, "Implementation of artificial intelligence in fashion: Are consumers ready?", *Clothing and Textiles Research Journal*, vol. 38, no. 1, pp. 3–18, 2020, Original work published 2020. DOI: 10.1177/0887302X19873437.
[42] A. Salgado-Montejo, C. Velasco, J. S. Olier, J. Alvarado, and C. Spence, "Love for logos: Evaluating the congruency between brand symbols and typefaces and their relation to emotional words", *Journal of Brand Management*, vol. 21, pp. 635–649, 2014. DOI: 10.1057/bm.2014.10.
[43] A. S. Williams and S. Son, "Sport rebranding: The effect of different degrees of sport logo redesign on brand attitude and purchase intention", *International Journal of Sports Marketing and Sponsorship*, vol. 23, no. 1, pp. 155–172, Jun. 2021. DOI: 10.1108/IJSMS-01-2021-0016.
[44] R. Xiong, "Application of brand visual design in e-commerce", pp. 86–92, 2023, ISSN: 2352-5398. DOI: 10.2991/978-2-38476-122-7_14.
[45] J. F. Hair, G. T. M. Hult, C. M. Ringle, and M. Sarstedt, *A primer on partial least squares structural equation modeling (PLS-SEM)*, Third edition. SAGE Publications, Incorporated, 2022.
[46] SmartPLS GmbH, *SmartPLS – Software für Strukturgleichungsmodelle (SEM)*, https://www.smartpls.com/, Acessed: 16/04/2025, 2025.

From Metadata to Meaning: GPT-4 Reveals Bias Trends in YouTube

Nitin Agarwal
COSMOS Research Center, University of Arkansas, Little Rock, USA
International Computer Science Institute, University of California, Berkeley, USA
e-mail: nxagarwal@ualr.edu

Abstract—**YouTube's recommendation system significantly shapes user experiences but has raised concerns over potential bias and the formation of filter bubbles. Traditional studies have primarily relied on metadata, such as video titles, which often fail to capture the full context or nuance of video content. This study harnesses recent advancements in Artificial Intelligence (AI)—specifically the capabilities of Generative Pre-trained Transformer 4 (GPT-4)—to conduct a deep comparative analysis of sentiment, emotion, and toxicity across multiple layers of YouTube video content. By leveraging AI to extract and interpret narrative elements beyond superficial metadata, the research uncovers key patterns: a shift from neutral to positive sentiment and emotion (especially joy) with increased content depth, a consistent decrease in anger, and divergent toxicity trends—rising in titles but decreasing in deeper narrative analysis. These findings underscore AI's transformative role in enhancing content understanding and addressing long-standing challenges in recommendation system bias.**

Keywords-YouTube recommendation system; artificial intelligence (AI); GPT-4; sentiment analysis; emotion analysis; toxicity analysis; bias; narrative analysis; recommender systems; social media algorithms; human-centered AI component; Open AI Whisper model.

I. Introduction

YouTube reports that 70% of user watch time is spent on recommended content. Powered by a multi-billion-dollar recommendation system, the platform drives average mobile viewing sessions beyond 40 minutes. This system forms a feedback loop: after a user selects a recommended video, new suggestions are generated, continuing the cycle. With over 2.7 billion users globally [1], and one-quarter of Americans using it as a primary information source [2], YouTube holds significant influence. This raises a crucial question: how much does the platform shape users' narratives?

Initially a video-sharing site, YouTube has evolved to maximize engagement, leveraging AI—particularly Google Brain—to personalize content delivery. This shift introduced algorithmic biases, such as selection bias [3], position bias [4][5], and popularity bias [6][7]. These biases contribute to "filter bubbles" and "echo chambers," where users are exposed to homogenous content, reinforcing existing views and limiting exposure to diverse perspectives.

Previous studies on YouTube's recommendation system have mostly relied on metadata like titles and descriptions. While useful, this approach often fails to capture the full context or narrative of the videos. Titles, crafted for brevity or clickbait, may not reflect the depth or tone of the actual content. This gap complicates content analysis and risks misrepresenting the emotional or toxic elements embedded within videos.

Our study addresses this gap by analyzing deeper content layers, focusing on sentiment, emotion, and toxicity. We use Generative Pre-trained Transformer 4 (GPT-4) to generate abstractive narrative summaries from video content, moving beyond surface-level metadata. This allows us to explore complex topics, such as the South China Sea dispute, through the lens of embedded narratives, diasporic perspectives, foreign policy, and global economic dynamics.

The goal is to understand how content evolves in depth and how it may influence recommendation patterns. We investigate whether deeper content carries different emotional or toxic tones compared to titles and descriptions. This approach helps reveal underlying shifts in content nature and user experience as influenced by AI-driven recommendations.

The remainder of the paper is structured as follows: Section II reviews related literature, Section III outlines our methodology, and the subsequent sections present the results and conclusions.

II. Literature Review

This section reviews relevant literature on morality assessment, emotion detection, and bias in recommendation systems. Substantial research has addressed recommendation bias, particularly in areas, such as radicalization and the spread of misinformation and disinformation [8]. Studies have examined the emergence of homophilic communities within recommended video content and the factors driving their formation. Some have also identified coordinated behavior among YouTube commenters, potentially shaping user engagement and content visibility [9][10][11]. These findings reveal patterns of homogeneity, networked communities, and systemic bias within recommendation algorithms.

A key method for studying content evolution is "drift" analysis. O'Hare et al. [12] used a sentiment-tagged corpus to detect topic drift in texts, while Liu et al. [13] applied Latent Dirichlet Allocation (LDA) to monitor topic drift in micro-blogs. Venigalla et al. [14] examined emotional trends in India during COVID-19 using real-time Twitter data, presenting mood shifts through line graphs and radar maps over a defined period. In this study, we apply drift analysis to assess shifts in emotion and morality, aiming to uncover latent biases in YouTube's recommendation algorithm. This dual analysis provides a comprehensive view of how emotional and moral tones evolve within recommended content.

Prior research has also focused on how biases in algorithmic suggestions foster ideological clustering and the spread of uniform viewpoints [15]. These studies highlight the formation of like-minded groups and user-driven amplification of content through coordinated interactions in comment sections [16]. Understanding these behaviors is critical to identifying how bias reinforces content homogeneity and the influence of algorithmic curation.

To examine narratives within content, researchers have drawn on the field of Computational Narratology, which explores narrative structures from an algorithmic and information-processing perspective. This involves steps, such as preprocessing, parsing, identifying and linking narrative components, representing narratives, and evaluating them [17]. The rise of large pre-trained language models, like GPT-3, has revolutionized narrative extraction, enabling models to identify key features and execute varied tasks with minimal training—often requiring only a well-crafted prompt. Advancements like trainable continuous prompt embeddings have improved model performance, enhancing GPT and Bidirectional Encoder Representations from Transformers (BERT) accuracy by up to 80% [18].

Recent work has also advanced the understanding of figurative language across both discriminative and generative tasks, narrowing the gap between model output and human interpretation [19]. These developments are central to our study, which uses GPT-4 to analyze YouTube narratives beyond surface-level metadata, enabling deeper insights into the emotional and moral dimensions embedded in recommended content.

III. Methodology

Next, we describe the research methodology, including data collection, transcript generation, narrative extraction, sentiment, emotion, and toxicity analysis.

A. Data Collection

YouTube's recommendation algorithm is heavily influenced by a user's viewing history, resulting in highly personalized suggestions. To minimize personalization bias and maintain experimental control, we applied the following precautions during data collection:

1. All watch sessions were conducted without logging into a YouTube account.
2. A fresh browser instance was launched for each new recommendation depth.
3. Cookies were cleared between depths to avoid cross-session influence and ensure unbiased retrieval.

We collected data from YouTube's "watch-next" panel using this setup. To define our video corpus, we collaborated with subject matter experts in structured workshops to develop a targeted list of keywords related to the South China Sea Dispute. Table 1 provides these keywords. These keywords were then used to generate search queries, producing an initial set of seed videos.

TABLE I. South China Sea Dispute Keywords.

South China Sea, SCS dispute, SCS conflict, Nine-dash line, Maritime sovereignty, Territorial waters, EEZ, Exclusive Economic Zone, Freedom of navigation, UNCLOS, United Nations Convention on the Law of the Sea, China South China Sea, Philippines South China Sea, Vietnam South China Sea, Malaysia South China Sea, Indonesia Natuna Sea, Taiwan South China Sea, US Navy South China Sea, PLA Navy, People's Liberation Army Navy, South China Sea military drills, Naval exercises SCS, Militarization of islands, Artificial islands South China Sea, Spratly Islands conflict, Paracel Islands tension, Freedom of navigation operations, FONOP, Aircraft carrier SCS, Strategic waterway Asia-Pacific, Hague tribunal South China Sea, PCA ruling 2016, South China Sea arbitration, Maritime law dispute, Sovereignty claims Asia, ASEAN South China Sea, South China Sea diplomacy, Regional security Indo-Pacific, #SouthChinaSea, #SCSdispute, #MaritimeTensions, #FreedomOfNavigation, #StopAggression, #DefendSovereignty, #AsiaSecurity, #GeopoliticsAsia

From these seeds, we extracted recommendations across three recursive depths, with each video in one tier serving as the basis for collecting recommendations in the next. This iterative process produced a dataset of 9,372 videos. The initial tier included the top 75 most viewed seed videos, and each successive depth expanded by a factor of five to capture a broader and more representative sample with varying video quality.

B. Transcript Generation

1) Collecting Transcripts from YouTube

Efficient caption collection from YouTube requires extracting available manual or automatic transcripts, excluding videos with mixed-language dialogue. However, the YouTube Data API v3 [20], while rich in video metadata, restricts caption access due to copyright and privacy concerns. Even with policy changes, issues like rate limits and API key requirements would remain.

To address this, the study employed the YouTube Transcript API by Jonas Depoix [21], which bypasses official restrictions by simulating YouTube's client-side HTTP requests, accessing captions without authentication. The retrieval strategy prioritized human-generated English captions, followed by auto-generated English, then non-English captions—favoring human-created and English-language transcripts for greater accuracy.

To improve processing efficiency, the Python ThreadPoolExecutor [22] from the concurrent.futures module was used. This allowed concurrent caption retrieval across multiple videos, significantly reducing time delays from network calls.

Despite this streamlined approach, limitations persisted. Some videos lacked captions due to creator choices, legal constraints, or difficulties in transcribing multilingual content. As a result, the study underscores the need for alternative transcription methods, such as audio-based transcription for videos with no available captions, ensuring comprehensive dataset coverage.

2) Generating Transcripts Unavailable from YouTube

To transcribe YouTube videos without captions, we utilized the OpenAI Whisper model [23], which is trained on 680,000 hours of diverse, multilingual data. Whisper uses an encoder-decoder Transformer architecture [24] to convert audio into text, excelling in recognizing varied accents and background noise. Although it doesn't always outperform task-specific models, Whisper's broad training makes it ideal for general transcription.

Due to Whisper's processing latency, we adopted faster-whisper [25], a high-performance CTranslate2-based reimplementation. To boost efficiency, we customized several parameters. Disabling word-level timestamps reduced unnecessary computation, and enabling the vad filter removed non-speech audio, shortening transcription time. We also turned off condition on previous text to treat audio chunks independently, enabling parallelization with minimal quality loss.

Key decoding parameters were adjusted: temperature was set to 0 for deterministic outputs, while beam size was reduced from 5 to 3 to explore fewer yet high-quality paths, balancing speed and accuracy. Additionally, we lowered the patience parameter from 1.0 to 0.9, slightly shortening the beam search duration.

To further enhance throughput, we used Python's ProcessPoolExecutor [26] for parallel processing across multiple GPUs. This approach allowed us to simultaneously download audio and generate transcriptions, maximizing computational efficiency.

In sum, our optimized pipeline—built on Whisper and faster-whisper, combined with parallel execution—achieved high transcription accuracy and speed, enabling scalable caption generation for large video datasets.

3) Translating Transcripts to English

To standardize transcriptions in non-English or mixed languages, we translated them into English to enhance usability. Although the YouTube Transcript API and Whisper offer translation features, we opted for tools specifically optimized for speed and quality. First, we used fasttext-langdetect by Facebook AI Research [27] to detect the language of each transcription. This model uses word embeddings and n-gram analysis for high-accuracy detection across numerous languages, allowing us to bypass translations for transcriptions already in English.

For non-English content, we employed the M2M100 model [28], a multilingual encoder-decoder developed by Facebook AI. M2M100 supports direct translation between 100 languages without requiring English as an intermediary. It is particularly effective at preserving meaning, even for less common language pairs, and can be run locally without the constraints of commercial APIs. Despite its slower CPU performance, M2M100's translation quality made it the preferred choice.

To address performance limitations, we leveraged Python's ProcessPoolExecutor and multi-GPU batch processing. This setup allowed us to divide workloads across GPUs efficiently, significantly accelerating the translation process while preserving high accuracy. These strategies enabled us to streamline transcription and translation workflows for multi-language video datasets effectively and reliably. A detailed performance analysis of this approach is presented in [29].

C. Narrative Extraction

While much of the existing research focuses on analyzing YouTube's metadata to uncover user opinions, our approach advances this by extracting deeper narratives directly from YouTube video transcripts. Given that video lengths vary widely—from a few minutes to several hours—it poses a significant challenge to derive meaningful emotional content from such extensive transcripts. To address this, we utilized large language models like GPT-4 ("gpt-4-0125-preview"), which support up to 128,000 tokens, enabling us to process lengthy transcripts effectively.

To extract coherent and structured narratives from these transcripts, we designed specific prompts tailored for GPT-4. During generation, we configured the temperature parameter to 0, ensuring deterministic outputs—this means the model consistently generates the same result given the same input. Additionally, we set both the frequency penalty and presence penalty to 0, which helps avoid the inclusion of repetitive phrases in the generated narratives.

For brevity and focus, we limited the model's output using a max_tokens value of 25, enabling us to generate concise yet informative narrative summaries. This methodological setup allowed us to capture the embedded storytelling within the transcripts efficiently while maintaining consistency and clarity in the outputs generated by the language model.

D. Sentiment Analysis

RoBERTa-based sentiment analysis leverages the RoBERTa architecture, an enhanced version of BERT designed for improved accuracy and efficiency. Trained on extensive datasets with labeled text, RoBERTa excels at identifying sentiment by capturing nuanced contextual cues within the input. This allows it to classify text into sentiment categories, such as positive, negative, or neutral, with high precision (94.2%). Its strong performance in understanding context has made it a popular choice for tasks like social media sentiment tracking and opinion analysis.

E. Emotion Analysis

We analyzed the emotional content embedded in video-related text, including titles and extracted narratives, with a focus on seven key emotions: anger, disgust, fear, joy, neutral, sadness, and surprise. To identify emotional bias across various levels of video recommendations, we applied the concept of emotion drift. This drift was visualized using a line graph, where each point along the depth axis represented a different layer of the recommendation pathway. For improved accuracy in emotion classification, we employed a fine-tuned transfer learning model—

Emotion-English-DistilRoBERTa-base—tailored for Natural Language Processing (NLP) tasks.

F. Toxicity Analysis

Detoxify, an open-source tool developed by Unitary AI [30], uses a Convolutional Neural Network (CNN) trained on word vector inputs to evaluate whether a given piece of text could be perceived as "toxic" within a conversational context. Upon receiving a text input, the Detoxify API generates a probability score between 0 and 1, with higher values indicating an increased likelihood of toxicity.

Detoxify provides toxicity scores across seven dimensions: overall toxicity (1), severe toxicity (2), obscenity (3), threats (4), insults (5), identity attacks (6), and sexually explicit content (7). The tool is particularly valuable due to its specialization in detecting harmful or inappropriate language online, making it a useful resource for analyzing user-generated content. Its accessibility as a Python library enhances its utility in research and application development aimed at moderating or understanding toxic discourse in digital environments.

IV. FINDINGS AND ANALYSIS

This section discusses our findings and their implications.

A. Sentiment Analysis

Sentiment analysis of YouTube video content reveals a stark contrast between the emotional tone of titles and that of full narratives. Video titles generally exhibit a neutral sentiment, occasionally leaning positive as more descriptive language is used (see Figure 1). This neutral framing may be intentional—crafted to appeal broadly while concealing the more emotionally resonant elements of the content itself.

In contrast, the narratives embedded within video transcripts demonstrate a clear and consistent emotional progression, shifting from neutrality to distinctly positive sentiments over time (see Figure 2). This evolution suggests that the deeper emotional context and storytelling are largely reserved for the video's main content, rather than being reflected in the title. The result is a layered communication strategy in which the title functions as a broad hook, while the narrative delivers greater emotional nuance and engagement.

B. Emotion Analysis

Figures 3 and 4 illustrate a clear emotional progression within YouTube video content, showing that as narrative depth increases, the expression of joy becomes more pronounced. This upward trend in positive emotion suggests a deliberate content strategy aimed at gradually eliciting stronger positive emotional responses from viewers. Simultaneously, there is a noticeable decline in negative emotions, such as anger, disgust, and sadness, indicating a possible intent to maintain viewer engagement through a more uplifting emotional arc.

When comparing emotional patterns between video titles and narratives, a distinct difference emerges. Titles tend to feature higher levels of negative emotions—especially disgust—at the outset. This may be a calculated use of emotional provocation or sensationalism to capture initial attention. However, as the content unfolds and narrative complexity increases, both titles and narratives begin to converge in emotional tone, trending more positively.

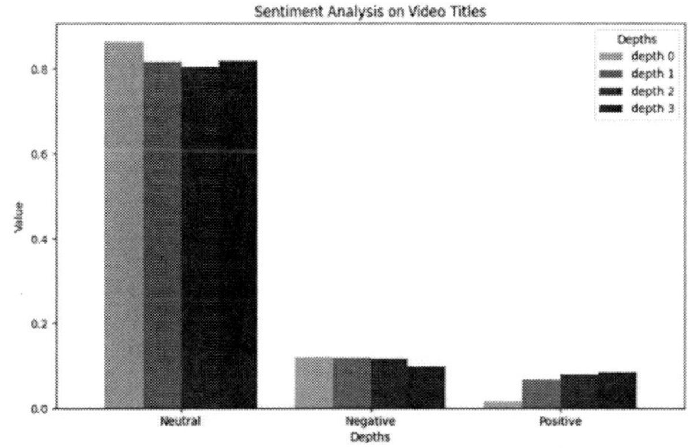

Figure 1. Sentiment trends for YouTube's video titles in different recommendation depths.

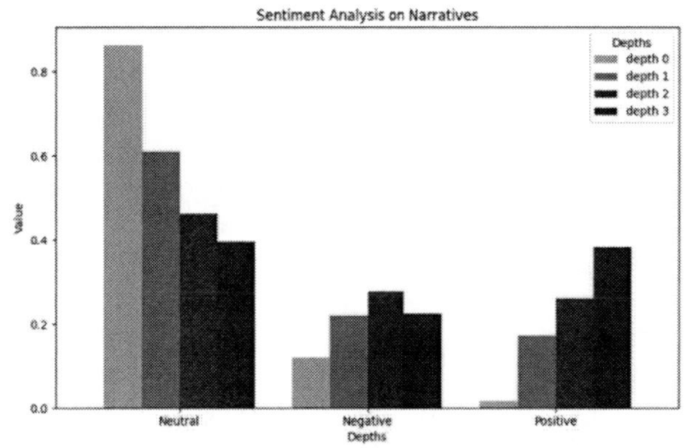

Figure 2. Sentiment trends for YouTube's video narratives in different recommendation depths.

This transition reflects a purposeful emotional modulation embedded in the content design. By initiating with emotionally charged titles and gradually shifting toward more positive sentiments in the narrative body, content creators appear to be leveraging emotion as a tool to sustain viewer interest while guiding the audience toward a more favorable emotional experience.

C. Toxicity Analysis

As we explore successive layers of YouTube's recommendation system, the data reveals fluctuating yet overall increasing patterns in toxicity expressed in the video titles. Notably, an analysis of the corresponding video narratives shows a consistent decline in toxicity levels with each deeper level of recommendation. This downward trend in toxic content suggests that YouTube's algorithm may be effectively optimizing for more constructive or less harmful content over time. Figure 5 illustrates this progression, emphasizing how content becomes increasingly less toxic as users are guided further into the recommendation chain. This pattern points to a potential refinement in the platform's content curation strategy, aimed at fostering a healthier viewing environment.

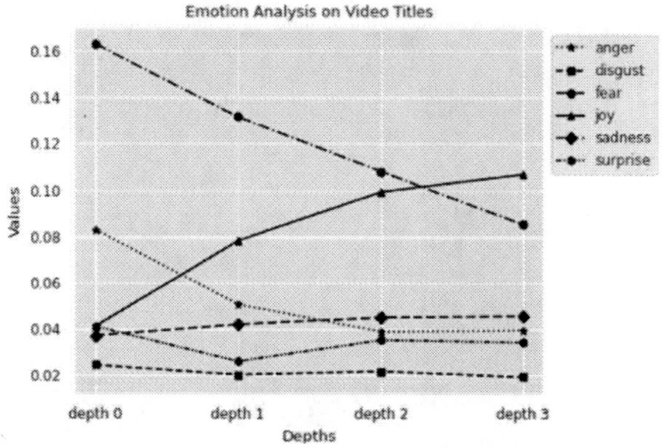

Figure 3. Emotion trends for YouTube's video titles in different recommendation depths.

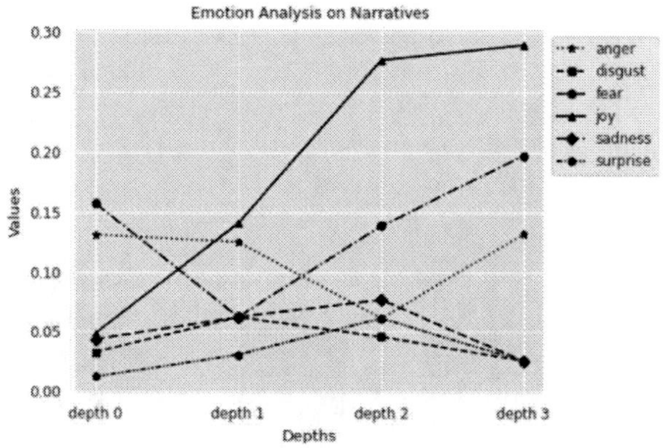

Figure 4. Emotion trends for YouTube's video narratives in different recommendation depths.

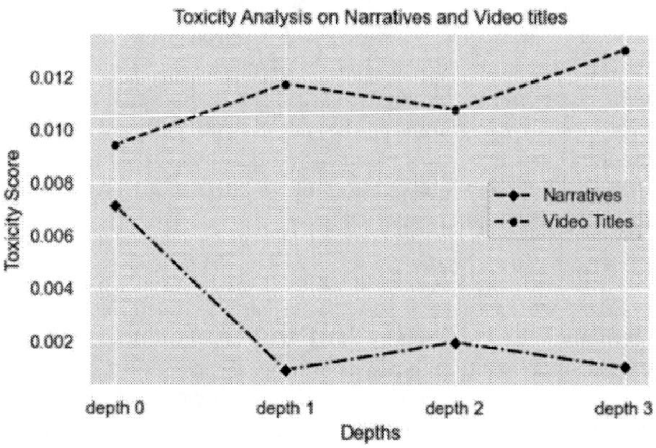

Figure 5. Toxicity trends for YouTube's video titles and narratives in different recommendation depths.

V. Conclusion and Future Work

This study underscores the transformative role of AI in advancing the analysis of online video content. Traditional approaches that rely primarily on metadata, such as video titles, for sentiment and toxicity assessment are increasingly insufficient for capturing the nuanced emotional and behavioral dynamics present in digital media. Leveraging recent breakthroughs in AI, this research moves beyond surface-level indicators to extract, process, and interpret the rich narrative content found within YouTube videos.

By employing cutting-edge AI tools, such as large language models (e.g., GPT-4 for narrative extraction), fine-tuned transformer-based emotion classifiers (Emotion-English-DistilRoBERTa), and toxicity detection systems (Detoxify), this study taps into the full potential of modern NLP. These models enable the automated processing of large-scale video transcript data, allowing for the detection of subtle emotional patterns and toxic content that would be otherwise missed by metadata analysis alone.

The findings reveal that narratives contain more consistent and revealing emotional trajectories, particularly a notable increase in joy correlating with reduced toxicity, unlike the more volatile and superficial signals found in titles. These insights, powered by AI, advocate for a paradigm shift in content analysis methodologies. This research has several implications for media managers, strategic communications, content strategy, audience retention, ethical curation, competitive intelligence, and brand monitoring. Recommendations include moving beyond superficial engagement metrics, designing emotionally intelligent content strategies, ethically curating media to foster trust and long-term loyalty, and gaining a competitive edge by understanding how joy, coherence, and emotional authenticity drive success.

In essence, this research demonstrates how AI is not merely a tool but a driving force enabling deeper, more accurate, and scalable investigations into online media content. It highlights the need to embed AI-driven narrative analysis into future content moderation strategies and recommendation systems, setting a new standard for understanding the sentiment and toxicity landscape of platforms like YouTube.

Acknowledgment

This research is funded in part by the U.S. National Science Foundation (OIA-1946391, OIA-1920920), U.S. Office of the Under Secretary of Defense for Research and Engineering (FA9550-22-1-0332), U.S. Army Research Office (W911NF-23-1-0011, W911NF-24-1-0078), U.S. Office of Naval Research (N00014-21-1-2121, N00014-21-1-2765, N00014-22-1-2318), U.S. Air Force Research Laboratory, U.S. Defense Advanced Research Projects Agency, the Australian Department of Defense Strategic Policy Grants Program, Arkansas Research Alliance, the Jerry L. Maulden/Entergy Endowment, and the Donaghey Foundation at the University of Arkansas at Little Rock. Any opinions, findings, and conclusions or recommendations expressed in this material are those of the authors and do not necessarily reflect the views of the funding organizations. The researchers gratefully acknowledge the support.

References

[1] Statista Research Department, "YouTube users worldwide 2020-2029," Statista, March 2025. [Online]. Available from: https://www.statista.com/forecasts/1144088/youtube-users-in-the-world [Last accessed: May 27, 2025].

[2] G. Stocking, P. Kessel, M. Barthel, K. Matsa, and M. Khuzam, "Many Americans Get News on YouTube, Where News Organizations and Independent Producers Thrive Side by Side," Pew Research Center, September 2020. [Online]. Available from: https://www.pewresearch.org/journalism/2020/09/28/many-americans-get-news-on-youtube-where-news-organizations-and-independent-producers-thrive-side-by-side/ [Last accessed: May 27, 2025].

[3] Z. Ovaisi, R. Ahsan, Y. Zhang, K. Vasilaky, and E. Zheleva, "Correcting for selection bias in learning-to-rank systems," In Proceedings of The Web Conference 2020, pp. 1863-1873, 2020.

[4] A. Agarwal, I. Zaitsev, X. Wang, C. Li, M. Najork, and T. Joachims, "Estimating position bias without intrusive interventions," In Proceedings of the twelfth ACM international conference on web search and data mining, pp. 474-482, 2019.

[5] X. Wang, N. Golbandi, M. Bendersky, D. Metzler, and M. Najork, "Position bias estimation for unbiased learning to rank in personal search," In Proceedings of the eleventh ACM international conference on web search and data mining, pp. 610-618, 2018.

[6] R. Cañamares and P. Castells, "Should I follow the crowd? A probabilistic analysis of the effectiveness of popularity in recommender systems," In The 41st International ACM SIGIR Conference on Research & Development in Information Retrieval, pp. 415-424, 2018.

[7] H. Abdollahpouri, R. Burke, and B. Mobasher, "Controlling popularity bias in learning-to-rank recommendation," In Proceedings of the eleventh ACM conference on recommender systems, pp. 42-46, 2017.

[8] M. Faddoul, G. Chaslot, and H. Farid, "A longitudinal analysis of YouTube's promotion of conspiracy videos," arXiv preprint arXiv:2003.03318, 2020.

[9] S. Shajari and N. Agarwal, "Safeguarding YouTube Discussions: A Framework for Detecting Anomalous Commenter and Engagement Behaviors," Journal of Social Network Analysis and Mining (SNAM), vol. 15, no. 54, pp. 1-24, Springer, 2025, DOI: 10.1007/s13278-025-01470-7.

[10] S. Shajari and N. Agarwal, "Developing a Network-Centric Approach for Anomalous Behavior Detection on YouTube," Journal of Social Network Analysis and Mining (SNAM), vol. 15, no. 3, pp. 1-16, Springer, 2025, DOI: 10.1007/s13278-025-01417-y.

[11] S. Shajari, M. Alassad, and N. Agarwal, "Commenter Behavior Characterization on YouTube Channels," In Proceedings of the Fifteenth International Conference on Information, Process, and Knowledge Management (eKNOW 2023), pp. 59-64, Venice, Italy, April 24 – 28, 2023.

[12] N. O'Hare, M. Davy, A. Bermingham, P. Ferguson, P. Sheridan, C. Gurrin, and A. Smeaton, "Topic-dependent sentiment analysis of financial blogs," In Proceedings of the 1st international CIKM workshop on Topic-sentiment analysis for mass opinion, pp. 9-16, 2009.

[13] Q. Liu, H. Huang, and C. Feng, "Micro-blog post topic drift detection based on LDA model," In International Workshop on Behavior and Social Informatics and Computing, pp. 106-118, Cham: Springer International Publishing, 2013.

[14] A. Venigalla, S. Chimalakonda, and D. Vagavolu, "Mood of India during Covid-19-An interactive web portal based on emotion analysis of Twitter data," In Companion Publication of the 2020 Conference on Computer Supported Cooperative Work and Social Computing, pp. 65-68, 2020.

[15] A. Chaney, B. Stewart, and B. Engelhardt, "How algorithmic confounding in recommendation systems increases homogeneity and decreases utility," In Proceedings of the 12th ACM conference on recommender systems, pp. 224-232, 2018.

[16] K. Hosanagar, D. Fleder, D. Lee, and A. Buja, "Will the global village fracture into tribes? Recommender systems and their effects on consumer fragmentation," Management Science, vol. 60, no. 4, pp. 805-823, 2014.

[17] B. Santana et al., "A survey on narrative extraction from textual data," Artificial Intelligence Review, vol. 56, no. 8, pp. 8393-8435, 2023.

[18] D. Stammbach, M. Antoniak, and E. Ash, "Heroes, villains, and victims, and GPT-3: Automated extraction of character roles without training data," arXiv preprint arXiv:2205.07557, 2022.

[19] X. Liu et al., "GPT understands, too," AI Open, vol. 5, pp. 208-215, 2024.

[20] Google Developers, "YouTube Data API,". Google, n.d. [Online]. Available from: https://developers.google.com/youtube/v3 [Last accessed: May 27, 2025].

[21] J. Depoix, "youtube-transcript-api," GitHub. [Online]. Available from: https://github.com/jdepoix/youtube-transcript-api [Last accessed: May 27, 2025].

[22] Python Software Foundation, "ThreadPoolExecutor," in concurrent.futures — Launching parallel tasks, Python 3 documentation. [Online]. Available from: https://docs.python.org/3/library/concurrent.futures.html [Last accessed: May 27, 2025].

[23] A. Radford et al., "Robust Speech Recognition via Large-Scale Weak Supervision," in Proceedings of the 40th International Conference on Machine Learning, vol. 202, pp. 28492-28518, July 2023.

[24] A. Vaswani et al., "Attention is all you need," Advances in Neural Information Processing Systems, vol. 30, 2017.

[25] SYSTRAN, "faster-whisper," GitHub. [Online]. Available from: https://github.com/SYSTRAN/faster-whisper [Last accessed: May 27, 2025].

[26] Python Software Foundation, "ProcessPoolExecutor," in concurrent.futures — Launching parallel tasks, Python 3 documentation. [Online]. Available from: https://docs.python.org/3/library/concurrent.futures.html [Last accessed: May 27, 2025].

[27] A. Joulin, E. Grave, P. Bojanowski, and T. Mikolov, "Bag of Tricks for Efficient Text Classification," arXiv preprint arXiv:1607.01759, 2016.

[28] A. Fan et al., "Beyond English-centric multilingual machine translation," Journal of Machine Learning Research, vol. 22, no. 107, pp. 1-48, 2021.

[29] M. Cakmak and N. Agarwal, "High-speed transcript collection on multimedia platforms: Advancing social media research through parallel processing," In 2024 IEEE International Parallel and Distributed Processing Symposium Workshops (IPDPSW), pp. 857-860, IEEE, 2024.

[30] Unitary AI, "Unitary Virtual Agents: Effortless Automation with Human-level Precision," [Online]. Available from: https://github.com/unitaryai/detoxify [Last accessed: June 14, 2025].

Human-AI Collaboration and Creative Skills: A Panel-based Industry Study from the Germany Media Sector

Paul Heß and Stephan Böhm
Center for Advanced E-Business Studies
RheinMain University of Applied Sciences, Wiesbaden, Germany
e-mail: {paul.hess, stephan.boehm}@hs-rm.de

Abstract—**The growing development of Artificial Intelligence (AI) tools such as ChatGPT and Midjourney is transforming creative processes in the media industry. This transformation shows itself not only through full automation, but also through Human-AI Collaboration (HAIC), in which AI systems support rather than replace creative professionals. However, there is a lack of empirical studies that systematically capture media professionals' perspectives on creative competencies in the context of AI. Addressing this research gap, this study aims to investigate how media professionals in Germany perceive and use AI related to creative tasks and skills. Based on a quantitative panel survey of 128 respondents, the study analyzes both, current practices and future expectations regarding AI's role in creative work. The findings reveal that AI tools are already widely integrated into creative workflows. At the same time, respondents with a strong creative self-concept tend to view AI as both a supportive tool and a potential threat to creative roles. The study contributes to the ongoing discourse on the AI-based transformation of creative labor and the future of skills in AI-augmented work environments.**

Keywords-Artificial Intelligence (AI); Human-AI Collaboration (HAIC); Creativity, Creative skills; Media industry, Workforce transformation; Generative Artificial Intelligence (GenAI).

I. Introduction

The adoption of Generative Artificial Intelligence (GenAI) tools with potential for creative work, such as ChatGPT, Midjourney, or Adobe Firefly, has fundamentally reshaped workflows in the media industry. While earlier waves of automation primarily targeted routine or physical tasks [1] [2], the latest developments increasingly touch upon creative domains long considered resistant to automation. These tools now support ideation, content generation, and even strategic planning, raising the question of how creative work is changing and which creative skills remain essential in a media environment disrupted by AI. Yet, despite this growing influence, it remains unclear how professionals themselves perceive this transformation. In particular, there is limited understanding of how generative AI is reshaping the skill requirements and self-conception of creative workers in practice.

In light of these developments, the concept of creativity itself is being reexamined not only as a cultural ideal, but as a productive skill relevant to future work scenarios across industries. Creativity is gaining prominence as a core, future professional competency. Reports, such as the World Economic Forum's Future of Jobs [3] emphasize creative thinking as one of the most in-demand skills in the coming years. However, creativity is not a static trait, it is embedded in specific roles, tasks, and work contexts. This is true especially in the media industry, where creative output coexists with structured workflows and increasing AI integration. The media sector, in particular, stands at the intersection of automation and creativity. It is both early adopter of GenAI tools but still heavily reliant on human-centered creative judgment [4]. These developments align with the concept of HAIC, which emphasizes joint decision-making, complementary strengths, and a redefinition of task distribution between humans and AI [5][6].

While the capabilities of GenAI are transforming creative processes, empirical studies that capture the experiences and expectations of creative professionals remain scarce. As [7] notes in a recent systematic review, the field remains at an early stage, with a lack of quantitative studies examining how practitioners evaluate the role of GenAI in creative work.

To address this gap, the study takes a practitioner-centered perspective to examine how media professionals assess the role of AI in creative workflows and skill demands. In particular, this paper investigates how creative work and creative skills are shaped by the integration of AI in the German media sector. For this purpose, we explore how media professionals position themselves in relation to AI, both in terms of current work practices and future expectations, as well as the question of AI for augmentation vs. automation. Against this background, we address the following research questions:

RQ1: Which professional characteristics are associated with the use of creative skills and AI in current media work?

RQ2: How does the perception of one's own creative work relate to expectations about AI's role in supporting or replacing creative skills in the future?

To explore these questions, we conducted a panel-based quantitative survey among 128 media professionals in Germany. Building on the previously outlined research gap, the goal of this study is to generate empirical insight into how creative professionals perceive and integrate artificial intelligence into their workflows. Rather than focusing on the technical capabilities of GenAI, the study centers on the human perspective. It seeks to understand how individuals experience the transformation of creative tasks, how they evaluate the role of AI in augmenting or substituting creativity, and what expectations they hold for the future. Here, we designed a structured questionnaire based on the literature on HAIC and creative skills in digital work.

The survey captures both current practices and attitudes, as well as respondents' expectations regarding the evolving role of AI in their professional environment.

The paper is structured as follows: Section 2 provides the theoretical foundation, covering HAIC, definitions of creativity, and the role of AI in the media industry. Section 3 reviews related empirical work on AI, creativity, and skills. Section 4 outlines the survey design and methodological approach. Section 5 presents the empirical results, including descriptive statistics and correlation analyses. Section 6 discusses the implications of the findings, followed by a conclusion summarizing key insights and future research directions.

II. Theoretical Foundation

In this section, we describe the concept of Human-AI Collaboration and the media industry. Also, definitions for creativity and creative work are described.

A. Media and AI

The media industry represents a particularly relevant context for studying the integration of AI, given its dual nature. It combines structured information processing with human-centered creative production [4]. Understanding how AI affects this sector requires conceptual clarity regarding both AI and media as domains of work and technology.

In this study, we refer to AI as "a machine-based system that can, for a given set of human-defined objectives, make predictions, recommendations, or decisions influencing real or virtual environments" [8, p. 2]. This definition highlights AI not merely as a technical tool, but as a system capable of taking on decision-relevant roles in complex environments—an important distinction when evaluating its influence on creative tasks.

Similarly, media companies are understood as "companies that deal with the procurement, selection, processing, utilization, bundling, and distribution of information or entertainment" [9, p. 5]. This broad scope reflects the increasingly hybrid nature of media work, which spans data-driven processes and expressive, aesthetic production. In such environments, AI adoption does not simply automate workflows, but alters the structure of creative roles and task delegation [9].

This lays the groundwork for analyzing how AI is reconfiguring the media industry's creative capacities—especially in relation to HAIC, where AI does not replace, but cooperates with, human expertise.

B. Human-AI Collaboration

HAIC refers to a collaborative process in which human users and AI systems work together by leveraging their complementary abilities to accomplish tasks [10]. Unlike approaches focused on full automation, the HAIC framework centers on augmentation, with AI technologies enhancing rather than replacing human performance [5]. Central to this partnership is the establishment of trust: while users benefit from AI-generated input, they remain the primary decision-makers, preserving the centrality of human judgment [6].

This collaborative dynamic can be seen in situations where AI handles repetitive or routine elements of a task, enabling humans to concentrate on more complex or creative dimensions [11]. Furthermore, AI may provide context-sensitive suggestions to aid decision-making [12]. This highlights the distinction between AI used for automation—aimed at substitution and AI employed for augmentation in line with HAIC principles [13].

C. Creativity and Creative Work

Regarding creativity, [14] provides a definition within their theoretical framework, stating that both originality and effectiveness are necessary for creativity. This is then further developed into a more dynamic definition, which also encompasses relevant areas of creativity, such as focus areas, creativity goals, the creative potential of an agent and their environment, and other detailed examinations of creativity [14]. This definition is important to narrow down on what qualifies as creative. In their theoretical examination of the creative economy, [15] distinguishes between two types of conceptualizing creative work. The first area of includes workers employed in cultural industries, while the second includes workers engaged in cultural occupations. The distinction lies in the fact that one group produces creative products (i.e., graphic designers, art directors, writers, or animators), whereas the other experiences a creative work environment, while not necessarily having a creative job themselves (i.e., film industry, radio, or publishing). In this model, cultural and creative work are treated the same [15]. The conceptual distinction between products and work helps clarify the relationship between creative occupations and creative tasks. Importantly, however, creativity is not bound to a specific industry, but can emerge across sectors, depending on how individuals define and experience their work. Therefore, creativity can be empirically examined not only by industry classification, but also through self-assessment, task characteristics, and the use of specific skills. This perspective informs the design of the present study, which explores how media professionals perceive and engage with creative work in relation to AI integration.

III. Related Work

A comprehensive literature review was conducted in two stages to identify relevant work on AI and skills, with a particular focus on creative tasks in media-related occupations. Relevant literature was identified through a search of scholarly databases, with Google Scholar, Web of Science, ResearchGate. The research was carried out in two stages. In the first step, research papers on AI skills were searched (keywords: {"AI" OR "Artificial Intelligence" } AND "Skills"). These search results were then screened for relevance based on an analysis of title, abstract, and number of citations. Furthermore, the literature was categorized in general work and more specific research on the AI-impact on creative work in media-related occupations. Table I summarizes the selected literature, structured into general work on AI and skills, and specific studies on AI's role in creative media work.

As Table I shows, the research findings are diverse and relate to different aspects of the impact of AI on skills. Independent from the skill-impact, some research shows that AI can enhance creative task and may result in a productivity increase for creative work [16]. Other research highlights that results generated with support of AI may lack originality, narrative intent and inspiration [7], [17]–[19]. From a task-impact perspective, [20] predicts that AI might lead to a new way of creative work, with some activities automated and more time for the human to focus on creative tasks.

TABLE I
AI IMPACT ON CREATIVITY AND FUTURE SKILLS

	AI and skills	
Ref.	**Key Findings**	**Cit.**
[21]	Automation mainly affects predictable physical tasks; creativity noted, not analyzed.	1257
[22]	Technical and collaborative skills needed for AI use.	897
[23]	ChatGPT impacts 32.8% of jobs fully, esp. high-skilled.	219
[24]	Digital/social-emotional skills rise; creativity is augmented.	90
[25]	AI hurts skilled cognitive labor, helps unskilled labor.	26
[26]	AI demands both technical and soft (incl. creative) skills.	14
	AI and creative media skills	
Ref.	**Key Findings**	**Cit.**
[18]	AI augments creativity but can't replace human originality.	718
[17]	AI stimulates but limits originality; risks creative labor devaluation.	155
[20]	Journalists shift to creative/strategic tasks via automation.	77
[27]	AI recombines existing ideas; acts as creative catalyst.	41
[16]	AI boosts efficiency, not originality or narrative control.	7
[28]	AI users produce more art, gain popularity, but less novelty.	4
[7]	AI is changing but not replacing creative work. Focus on co-creation and prompt literacy.	2
[19]	AI raises productivity in media; humans remain essential.	0

In the following, we distinguish between general literature on AI-related skill shifts and studies specifically focused on creative tasks in media professions. In the broader discourse on AI and workforce skills, early studies such as [21] emphasize that automation primarily affects predictable physical and routine cognitive tasks, while creativity is mentioned as less vulnerable but remains under-examined in detail. More recent analyses extend this view. Enholm et al. [22] and Babashahi et al.[26] stress the increasing importance of technical and collaborative skills, with the latter explicitly including soft and creative skills in future competence profiles. Ellingrud et al. [24] add that digital and emotional-social skills are gaining relevance, and views creativity as a skill to be augmented, not replaced, by AI. However, not all perspectives are optimistic [25], for instance, argues that AI tends to harm skilled cognitive labor, while supporting lower-skilled tasks. Similarly, [23] identifies a high degree of exposure to AI substitution, especially among high-skilled professions. Regarding creative work in media-related occupations, research is both more focused. Anantrasirichai and Bull [18], as well as Kirkpatrick [27] argue that AI can effectively augment creative processes, for instance by recombining existing ideas or increasing productivity, yet without replacing human originality or intentionality. Simon [20] and Lee[17] highlight a functional shift: Media workers, especially journalists, are moving toward strategic and creative roles, even as AI introduces risks of deskilling or devaluing creative labor. Zhou and Lee [28] find that AI-supported creators produce more and gain visibility, but often at the cost of novelty and originality, echoing concerns raised by [16] about narrative flattening. Doyle and Baumann [19] conclude that while AI tools enhance productivity in media contexts, human input remains essential, particularly for original ideation and contextual interpretation. While these studies offer important conceptual and technological insights, they rarely include the perspectives of creative professionals themselves. This highlights the need for empirical research that captures how practitioners experience and assess the role of AI in their actual workflows, particularly in terms of task structures and perceived creative competencies. Taken together, these findings suggest a growing consensus. These existing studies also inform key dimensions of the present study's survey design, such as the focus on creative tasks, skill profiles, and the perceived trade-off between augmentation and substitution. While AI is unlikely to fully replace creative professionals, it is actively reshaping the meaning, value, and required competencies of creative work. Creativity is increasingly framed not as a static trait but as a dynamic skill, one that co-evolves with AI capabilities, sometimes enhanced, sometimes challenged.

IV. STUDY APPROACH

This study builds on a broader research project investigating how AI is reshaping labor in the German media industry, with a specific focus on creative tasks. The aim of this sub-study is to empirically analyze how media professionals perceive and apply AI in their creative work, how they assess their own creative competencies, and how they evaluate the potential of AI to support or replace creative skills.

A. Survey Design and Conceptual Foundations

To explore these dimensions, a quantitative panel survey was conducted via the Unipark platform [29] between December 17, 2024, and January 06, 2025. Respondents were first screened to ensure they (1) work in the media sector and (2) have experience using AI technologies in a professional context. This resulted in a sample of 128 valid responses.

The questionnaire was theory-driven and built upon the concepts outlined in Section II. In particular, it was structured in three major areas:

1) **Skills and workflows:** Respondents were asked to indicate which professional competencies (e.g., creative, technical, interpersonal), based on the top skills, defined by [3] they regularly use, and to characterize their daily workflows in terms of routine, structure, and cognitive/social complexity. The level of routine in this section were inspired by the

relevance for level of routine in AI substitution stated by [30].

2) **AI use and practices:** Participants reported how frequently they use selected Generative AI (GenAI) tools (e.g., ChatGPT, Midjourney, Copilot, based on [31] and for which types of tasks (ideation, writing, planning, etc.). This section also included questions about whether AI is already being used in creative work and how respondents perceive its current and future relevance.
3) **Creative self-assessment and AI expectations:** To explore the relationship between perceived creativity and attitudes toward AI, participants provided a personal judgment about their work in terms of creativity and evaluated whether AI could support or replace such creative processes in the future. Respondents were also asked to estimate how much of their current work could, in principle, be replaced by AI technologies.

The overall goal was to connect individual-level assessments of creative skills with perceived opportunities and risks of AI integration, thus linking subjective experience with broader theories of skill transformation in AI-mediated environments.

B. Data Analysis

The collected data were analyzed descriptively and for item correlations. Descriptive statistics provided insight into the distribution of skills, workflow characteristics, and the use of AI among media professionals. To examine relationships between creative self-perception and attitudes toward AI, Pearson correlation coefficients (r) were calculated.

The correlation analysis aimed to test whether the self-assessment on the level of personal creativity is related to openness to using AI or an increased concern about potential substitution. It also explored how perceptions of AI creativity or relevance correlate with expectations about the future of creative work.

This analytic approach addresses two research questions. First, which professional profiles and tasks are associated with creativity and AI use (RQ1). Second, how creative self-perception shapes the anticipation of AI's role in future work (RQ2).

V. Results

This pre-study among media workers in Germany was conducted to gain initial quantitative insights into the impact of AI on the media workforce.

A. Demographic Data

From a total sample of 723 study participants, 21% worked in the media industry, from which 83% had experience with artificial intelligence, resulting in a sample of 128 participants. Most of the study participants are male (60%) young professionals with master's or bachelor's degrees (66%) and belong to the age group of 25-34 years. As shown in Table II, most study participants are employed in larger media companies, and since worked 4-6 years in the media industry.

TABLE II
DEMOGRAPHICS OF PANEL STUDY RESPONDENTS

Question	%
Company size	
Up to 499 employees	52
500 to 2,999 employees	37
From 3,000 employees	10
Media industry experience	
3 years and under	26
4–6 years	36
7–10 years	16
Over 10 years	22
Professional status	
Employed in a company	92
Self-employed entrepreneur	5
Freelance for companies	2
Other	1

Most respondents classify their own knowledge of AI solutions as very or rather comprehensive (57%), while 30% classify it as medium and only 14% as low or very low, indicating a broad arrival of AI solutions in media work. Regarding the professional use of popular AI tools, ChatGPT is the most utilized tool, with 51% reporting that they use it regularly or very frequently. This is followed by Meta AI (34%), Microsoft Copilot (33%), and Google Gemini (32%). The least used tools, with under 30% indicating regular or very frequent use, are DeepL (29%), Microsoft Bing AI (27%), Adobe Firefly (27%), and Snapchat MyAI (25%). This still demonstrates the dominance of OpenAI and ChatGPT within the GenAI tools.

B. Descriptive Results

In terms of competencies applied in daily work (Figure 1), communication skills ranked highest, used by 57% of respondents. Leadership and management skills followed closely (54%), as did technical skills (51%). Creative skills were also named by nearly half of the participants (49%), confirming the central role of creativity in many professional roles. Analytical skills (45%) and interpersonal skills (40%) were used less frequently, while only 28% reported using organisational skills regularly. This distribution reflects a broad mix of cognitive, interpersonal, and technical demands, with creativity positioned alongside other high-order skills.

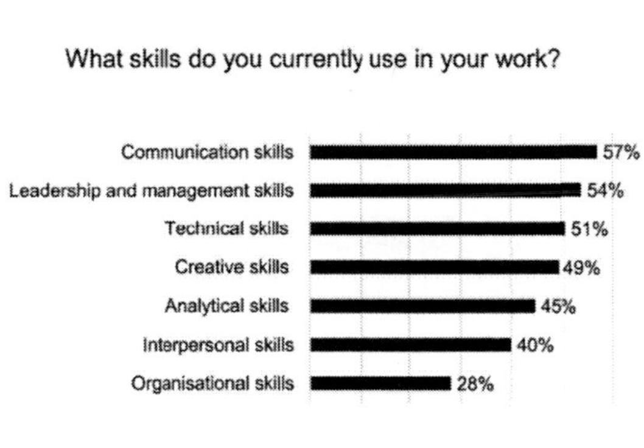

Figure 1. Skills used by media workers (n=128).

As shown in Figure 2, the majority of respondents (70%) stated that their work is predominantly creative. However, the majority of the participants also perceives their work as data-driven and repetitive: 54% reported that their work depends heavily on structured data, and 53% indicated that decisions are based on clear rules or algorithms. More than half (52%) described their workflows as having a high degree of routine. Interestingly, 50% said their work requires little complex thinking and simple problem-solving, and 48% reported that their work involves little social or emotional interaction. These results indicate a prominent role of creativity in media workflows, next to more structuring aspects.

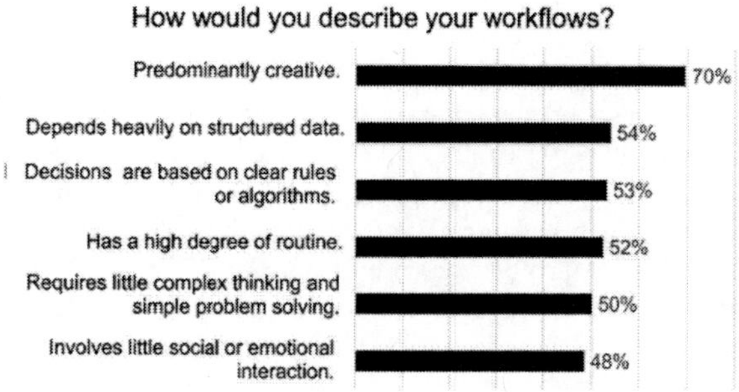

Figure 2. Perceived workflow characteristics (n=128).

According to the study results, AI is already widely used in creative professional contexts. 76% of the respondents stated that they use AI for creative tasks in their work. This widespread adoption indicates that AI has become a tool not just for repetitive tasks, but also for creative work.

When asked whether cooperation with or substitution by AI is expected, the responses were relatively balanced. 38% of participants tended toward (rather) substitution, while 34% expected (rather) collaboration, as shown in Figure 3. A further 27% remained undecided. These results reflect a notable degree of uncertainty and ambivalence regarding the future role of AI in individual workflows, with a slight tendency toward perceiving AI as a substitutive rather than a collaborative force.

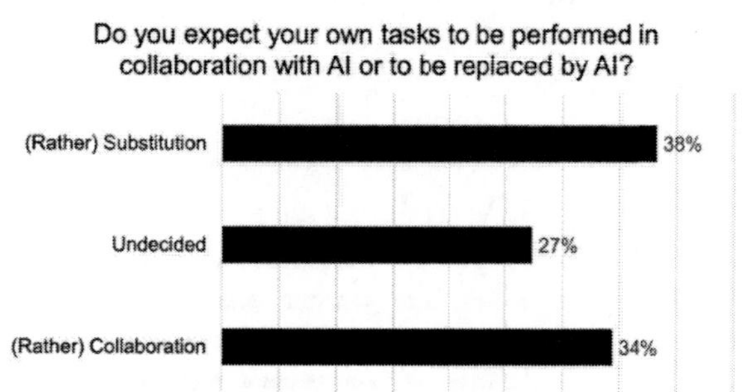

Figure 3. Perspective on AI collaboration or substitution (n=128).

The descriptive results paint a nuanced picture of creative professional work within the media industry, shaped by both human and technological capabilities. Creativity is shown as a central characteristic of work, described by media workers, next to structured, data-driven, and even routinized settings. AI is also, already widely integrated into creative workflows. Regarding HAIC a balanced view is presented, with media workers divided between collaboration with- or substitution due to AI. Together, these findings provide a foundation for the following correlation analysis exploring how creative workers perceive the creative use of AI.

C. Correlations Analysis

To further explore the relationship between individual perceptions and the role of AI in creative work, we conducted bivariate correlation analyses. The aim was to identify statistical associations between key variables such as creative self-assessment, frequency and type of AI use, and expectations regarding AI's role in supporting or substituting creative tasks. These correlations provide insight into how media professionals' subjective views on their creativity relate to their engagement with AI tools and their attitudes toward future work developments. The following section presents selected significant results from this analysis, highlighting how perceived creativity correlates with beliefs about the relevance, usefulness, and substitutive potential of AI in creative contexts.

Several significant but rather weak ($0.20 \leq r \leq 0.39$) or very weak ($r \leq 0.19$) correlations highlight how media professionals perceive the role of AI in creative contexts, as shown in Table III. The self-assessment of one's work as predominantly creative correlates positively with the belief that AI is becoming increasingly important for creative tasks ($r = .343, p < .001$) and with the perception that AI supports creative processes in the workplace ($r = .361, p < .001$). A similarly weak correlation is found with the frequency of AI use in creative tasks ($r = .363, p < .001$), suggesting that individuals who describe their work as creative are also more likely to integrate AI tools into their workflows. Additionally, the belief that AI can be creative is significantly, though more weakly, associated with creative self-assessment ($r = .221, p = .012$). The notion that AI may even replace creative skills shows a weak positive correlation as well ($r = .284, p = .001$). An even weaker but still significant correlation also emerges with the belief that creative thinking as a skill is gaining relevance ($r = .192, p = .030$), suggesting that those engaged in creative work are expecting a change of relevance for human creativity in the age of AI. Together, these results suggest that creative professionals not only recognize the growing relevance of AI for their work but also engage with its potential benefits and risks. This ranges from support and enhancement to possible substitution of human creativity.

Table IV presents the results of the correlation analysis for the self-perception as creative worker related to current and future AI job replacement potential (measured in percent). The perceived present-day potential of AI to replace one's own tasks correlates weakly with the creative self-assessment ($r = .325, p < .001$). Similarly, it correlates with the long-term expectation of AI substituting one's own tasks. The results revealed a significant positive correlation ($r = .227, p = .010$),

TABLE III
PEARSON CORRELATIONS WITH THE STATEMENT
"MY WORK IS PREDOMINANTLY CREATIVE." (N=128)

Correlated statement	r	p-value
The use of AI is becoming increasingly important for creative tasks	0.343	< 0.001
Artificial intelligence can be creative	0.221	0.012
I frequently use artificial intelligence in creative tasks	0.363	< 0.001
The use of AI supports creative processes in my work	0.361	< 0.001
The use of AI replaces creative skills in my field	0.284	0.001
Creative thinking (will increase in relevance)	0.192	0.030

indicating that individuals who expect a higher percentage of their tasks to be potentially replaced by AI in the future are more likely to describe their work as creative. These findings suggest that individuals working in creative roles may be particularly aware of, or engaged with, the capabilities of AI technologies, both now and in the future.

TABLE IV
PEARSON CORRELATIONS WITH THE STATEMENT
"MY WORK IS PREDOMINANTLY CREATIVE."

Correlated statement	r	p-value
I already see a high potential for AI to replace parts of my current work	0.325	< 0.001
I expect AI to replace a larger share of my tasks in the long-term	0.227	0.010

The results of this exploratory panel study provide a view of how media workers in Germany perceive and integrate artificial intelligence into their creative work. The demographic profile shows a sample of predominantly young, well-educated professionals working in larger media organizations, with most having several years of experience in the industry. A significant majority reports substantial familiarity with AI solutions and regular use of tools, such as ChatGPT, highlighting the growing penetration of generative AI in everyday media work. The descriptive findings further underscore the central role of creativity in these professionals' self-descriptions and workflows. While 70% describe their work as predominantly creative, many also report operating within structured, routinized, and data-driven environments.

Creative skills are widely used but coexist with strong demands for communication, leadership, and technical competencies. The use of AI for creative tasks is also, already widespread, within media workers. Furthermore, HAIC is seen ambivalent, with a balanced division between substitution or collaboration. The correlational analysis reinforces these patterns: Those who describe their work as creative are significantly more likely to perceive AI as relevant, supportive, and even creative in itself. Positive attitudes toward AI's role in creative processes correlate with both frequent use and a sense of increasing importance. Creative professionals also assess substitutions due to AI, which may shift or redefine their roles. This is seen in current, as well as future, substitution potential.

All in all, the findings suggest that creativity is a relevant part of media workflows and skills. Most media workers use AI already and see potential for AI for creative taskswith the possibility of replacing skills, leading to a possible reshaping of creative work.

VI. DISCUSSION

This study explored how media professionals in the Germany perceive and engage with AI in relation to creative work. The results provide a differentiated view of the role of creativity in media professions and how AI integration is shaping both current practices and future expectations.

The study's results indicate that creativity is a key aspect of media work. Most respondents describe their daily work as predominantly creative, yet this creative activity occurs alongside structured, routinized, and rule-based elements. This confirms the hybrid character of contemporary media work, as described in prior literature on creative occupations [15] [20]. The frequent and purposeful use of AI tools like ChatGPT within these settings suggests that creative work is already undergoing transformation through AI augmentation, especially in contexts aligned with HAIC, where AI tools assist human workers but do not replace their creative judgment or authorship.

At the same time, the study reveals a found ambivalence. Correlational analyses show that those who describe their work as creative are not only more likely to adopt AI tools, but also slightly more aware of AI's potential to replace certain creative tasks. This perception highlights the tensions in HAIC: While professionals appreciate AI's supportive capabilities, they remain aware of the risk of creative deskilling or decreased autonomy [12][17] . Importantly, the perception of AI as a supportive tool and the anticipation of its potential to substitute are not mutually exclusive, but are both found in professionals' perception. Future studies should also further differentiate between collaborative and substitutive AI implementations to better understand how HAIC models are perceived and enacted in practice.

These results suggest that creativity is increasingly considered a dynamic, adaptable skill, one that is both enhanced and challenged by AI technologies. From a practical standpoint, this raises questions for skill development and workforce planning. Media organizations may need to re-evaluate how they support creative roles, not only through technical upskilling but also by fostering critical, reflective capacities in dealing with AI systems.

Despite these insights, several limitations must be acknowledged. The study is based on self-reported data and captures only a snapshot in time, and the sample was conducted through a panel provider who has monetarily incentivized participation. It also focuses on a specific national context and industry.

VII. CONCLUSION AND FUTURE WORK

This paper examined the role of AI in creative work within the German media industry. Based on a panel survey of 128 media professionals, two research questions guided the analysis.

Regarding RQ1, the findings indicate that creative skills are widely used and required in media work today, with 70% of respondents describing their tasks as predominantly creative. AI tools, especially ChatGPT, are already integrated into creative workflows by a majority of professionals. Moreover, the use of AI positively correlates with higher self-assessed creative engagement. This could be because GenAI tools are becoming available in an increasing number of areas for content creation and editing, opening up new possibilities in creative work and thus driving GenAI adoption.

In relation to RQ2, the results indicate that media professionals with a strong creative self-concept are also more likely to view AI as relevant, helpful, and even creative. At the same time, they are more likely to anticipate that AI could possibly substitute aspects of their work. These professionals recognize both the substitutive and augmentative potentials of AI the later a pattern that closely aligns with emerging visions of future HAIC models, where human labor is interacting with AI.

In sum, the study suggests that the use of AI is not perceived by media professionals as incompatible with creative work. Corresponding GenAI tools are being used and tested, even if people are still unsure about the impact on their own working environment. One explanation could be that although the use of GenAI offers potential for automation, much of its use still involves massive human involvement for exploring the new possibilities of the tools (e.g., extensive prompting). The required curiosity, openness, and the joy of creating and exploring new frontiers is closely linked to creative mindsets. In the long term, however, GenAI solutions can be expected to be more closed and integrated solutions, which could, in some cases, lead to a reassessment of the corresponding effects and also to new resistance to the use of AI in the creative sector, especially for those who could then be affected by substitution effects and excluded from previously creative work steps. For the media industry, this implies a strategic need to support AI-related future skills to make use of AI as an enabler and not a substitute for creative work in ways that reflect an evolving collaboration with AI, beyond replacement logics and toward co-creation.

Future research could explore the ethical implications of professional exclusion due to automation or extend the anaylsis to other cultural contexts. Also, the view of media experts could be explored qualitatively, to gain further insight into the creative processes with AI. Also, it could adopt mixed-method designs. In particular, qualitative studies could offer more profound insight into how creative media work is influenced by AI.

REFERENCES

[1] M. Arntz, T. Gregory, and U. Zierahn, "The risk of automation for jobs in oecd countries: A comparative analysis", OECD Social, Employment and Migration Working Papers 189, 2016. DOI: 10.1787/5jlz9h56dvq7-en.

[2] J. Badet, "AI, automation and new jobs", *Open Journal of Business and Management*, vol. 9, no. 5, pp. 2452–2463, 2021. DOI: 10.4236/ojbm.2021.95132.

[3] World Economic Forum, "Future of jobs report 2023", World Economic Forum, Tech. Rep., 2023.

[4] A. L. Guzman and S. C. Lewis, "What generative AI means for the media industries, and why it matters to study the collective consequences for advertising, journalism, and public relations", *Emerging Media*, vol. 2, no. 3, pp. 347–355, Sep. 2024. DOI: 10.1177/27523543241289239.

[5] Y. Lai, A. Kankanhalli, and D. Ong, "Human-ai collaboration in healthcare: A review and research agenda", *Hawaii International Conference on System Sciences (HICSS)*, pp. 660–669, 2021. DOI: 10.24251/HICSS.2021.083.

[6] G. C. Saha *et al.*, "Human-ai collaboration: Exploring interfaces for interactive machine learning", *Tuijin Jishu / Journal of Propulsion Technology*, vol. 44, no. 2, 2023. DOI: 10.52783/tjjpt.v44.i2.148.

[7] R. Heigl, "Generative artificial intelligence in creative contexts: A systematic review and future research agenda", *Management Review Quarterly*, pp. 1–38, 2025, Online First. DOI: 10.1007/s11301-025-00494-9.

[8] A. Khan, *Artificial Intelligence: A Guide for Everyone*, English. Springer Cham, 2024, ISBN: 978-3-031-56712-4. DOI: 10.1007/978-3-031-56713-1.

[9] K. Beck, Ed., *In die Zukunft publizieren (Publish into the future)*, German. Springer Fachmedien Wiesbaden, 2023, ISBN: 978-3-658-36533-2. DOI: 10.1007/978-3-658-36533-2.

[10] J. Rezwana and M. L. Maher, "Designing creative AI partners with cofi: A framework for modeling interaction in human-AI co-creative systems", *ACM Transactions on Computer-Human Interaction*, vol. 30, no. 5, pp. 1–28, 2023. DOI: 10.1145/3519026.

[11] P. Hemmer *et al.*, "Human-ai collaboration: The effect of ai delegation on human task performance and task satisfaction", pp. 453–463, Mar. 2023. DOI: 10.1145/3581641.3584052.

[12] H. T. Lemus, A. Kumar, and M. Steyvers, "An empirical investigation of reliance on ai-assistance in a noisy-image classification task", in *Proceedings of the 1st International Conference on Hybrid Human-Artificial Intelligence (HHAI 2022)*, S. Schlobach, M. Pérez-Ortiz, and M. Tielman, Eds., ser. Frontiers in Artificial Intelligence and Applications, vol. 352, IOS Press, Jun. 2022, pp. 225–237. DOI: 10.3233/FAIA220201.

[13] C. J. Cai, S. Winter, D. Steiner, L. Wilcox, and M. Terry, "Hello ai: Uncovering the onboarding needs of medical practitioners for human-ai collaborative decision-making", *Proceedings of the ACM on Human-Computer Interaction*, vol. 3, no. CSCW, pp. 1–24, 2019. DOI: 10.1145/3359206.

[14] G. E. Corazza, "Potential originality and effectiveness: The dynamic definition of creativity", *Creativity Research Journal*, vol. 28, no. 3, pp. 258–267, 2016. DOI: 10.1080/10400419.2016.1195627.

[15] A. Markusen, G. H. Wassall, D. DeNatale, and R. Cohen, "Defining the creative economy: Industry and occupational approaches", *Economic Development Quarterly*, vol. 22, no. 1, pp. 24–45, 2008. DOI: 10.1177/0891242407311862.

[16] K. Horska, "A new test of artificial intelligence: Should the media industry be afraid?", *Science and Education a New Dimension*, vol. VIII, no. 231(39), pp. 26–29, 2020. DOI: 10.31174/SEND-HS2020-231VIII39-06.

[17] H.-K. Lee, "Rethinking creativity: Creative industries, AI and everyday creativity", *Media, Culture & Society*, vol. 44, no. 3, pp. 601–612, 2022. DOI: 10.1177/01634437221077009.

[18] N. Anantrasirichai and D. Bull, "Artificial intelligence in the creative industries: A review", *Artificial Intelligence Review*, vol. 55, no. 1, pp. 589–656, 2022. DOI: 10.1007/s10462-021-10039-7.

[19] G. Doyle and S. Baumann, *AI: A cure for baumol's disease?*, Dataset on Zenodo, Working paper, Aug. 2024. DOI: 10.5281/zenodo.13167298.

[20] F. M. Simon, "Artificial intelligence in the news: How AI retools, rationalizes, and reshapes journalism and the public arena", Tow Center for Digital Journalism, Columbia University, Tech. Rep., 2024.

[21] J. Manyika *et al.*, "A future that works: AI, automation, employment, and productivity", McKinsey Global Institute, Research Report 60, 2017.

[22] I. M. Enholm, E. Papagiannidis, P. Mikalef, and J. Krogstie, "Artificial intelligence and business value: A literature review", *Information Systems Frontiers*, vol. 24, no. 5, pp. 1709–1734, 2022. DOI: 10.1007/s10796-021-10186-w.

[23] A. Zarifhonarvar, "Economics of chatgpt: A labor market view on the occupational impact of artificial intelligence", *Journal of Electronic Business & Digital Economics*, vol. 3, no. 2, pp. 100–116, 2024. DOI: 10.1108/JEBDE-10-2023-0021.

[24] K. Ellingrud *et al.*, "Generative AI and the future of work in america", McKinsey Global Institute, Tech. Rep., 2023.

[25] C.-H. Lu, "Artificial intelligence and human jobs", *Macroeconomic Dynamics*, vol. 26, no. 5, pp. 1162–1201, 2022. DOI: 10.1017/S1365100520000528.

[26] L. Babashahi *et al.*, "Ai in the workplace: A systematic review of skill transformation in the industry", *Administrative Sciences*, vol. 14, no. 6, p. 127, 2024. DOI: 10.3390/admsci14060127.

[27] K. Kirkpatrick, "Can AI demonstrate creativity?", *Communications of the ACM*, vol. 66, no. 2, pp. 21–23, 2023. DOI: 10.1145/3575665.

[28] E. Zhou and D. Lee, "Generative artificial intelligence, human creativity, and art", *PNAS Nexus*, vol. 3, no. 3, pgae052, 2024. DOI: 10.1093/pnasnexus/pgae052.

[29] Tivian, *Unipark Academic Edition*, https://www.tivian.com/de/feedback-software/marktforschung-software/academic-edition/, Acessed: 16/04/2025, 2025.

[30] F. Montobbio, J. Staccioli, M. E. Virgillito, and M. Vivarelli, "The empirics of technology, employment and occupations: Lessons learned and challenges ahead", IZA – Institute of Labor Economics, Tech. Rep. IZA Discussion Paper No. 15731, 2022.

[31] Statista, *Nutzung von ki-tools in deutschland (usage of ai tools in germany)*, https://de.statista.com/infografik/33526/nutzung-von-ki-tools-in-deutschland/, Acessed May, 14th 2025, 2024.

International Academy, Research, and Industry Association (IARIA)
412 Derby Way
Wilmington, DE 19810

ISBN 979-8-3313-2335-6

CURRAN ASSOCIATES INC.
proceedings.com

Fourteenth International Conference on Advances in System Simulation (SIMUL 2022)

Held at SoftNet 2022

Lisbon, Portugal
16-20 October 2022